CERVANTES
IN RUSSIA

CERVANTES IN RUSSIA

BY

LUDMILLA BUKETOFF

TURKEVICH

GORDIAN PRESS
NEW YORK
1975

Originally Published 1950
Reprinted 1975

Copyright © 1950
By Princeton University Press
Published by Gordian Press, Inc.
By Arrangement

179007

Library of Congress Cataloging in Publication Data

Turkevich, Ludmilla Buketoff.
    Cervantes in Russia.

    Reprint of the 1950 ed. published by Princeton
University Press, Princeton, N. J., which was issued as
no. 8 of Princeton publications in modern languages.
    "A bibliography of the Russian translations of
Cervantes' works": p.
    Includes index.
    1. Cervantes Saavedra, Miguel de, 1547-1616--
Appreciation--Russia. 2. Literature Comparative--
Spanish and Russian. 3. Literature, Comparative--
Russian and Spanish. I. Title. II. Series: Prince-
ton University. Princeton publications in modern
languages ; no. 8.
PQ6349.R9T8 1975   863'.3 [B]   75-31685
ISBN 0-87752-175-1

TO MY HUSBAND

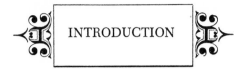

INTRODUCTION

FOREIGN penetration has always been for Russia a matter of vital importance and great controversy. Lying as it does between Asia and Europe, Russia has ever been faced with the question of whether the East, the West, or its own national heritage is to determine its life and destiny. At times, Russia had no choice in the matter. When Asia heaved its barbaric hordes into the Steppe for the destruction of Kiev, Russia had to accept the East. Then, after it had recovered from the numbness of the Mongolian paralysis, the problem reappeared. The West began to filter in, sporadically during the reigns of Ivan the Terrible and Peter the Great, and continually after that of Catherine the Great. This flow was frequently impeded by hostile currents and the resulting turmoil was often violent, as in the struggle of the Westernists with the Slavophils. Today the stream of Western culture is still striving to penetrate into Russia. It is resisted by a strong nationalism which in the nineteenth century found expression in the philosophical concepts of Slavophilism, and now in the twentieth serves as the basis of Soviet diplomacy.

The question naturally arises whether this barrier is the same for all cultural elements. An examination of Russia's history reveals that for truly great literary masterpieces barriers do not exist. Characters like Don Quixote, Hamlet, Faust and Don Juan, the Western world's exponents of man's varying attitudes towards himself and society, by their very universality extended their appeal beyond national frontiers. Their contours are evident in some of the important works of the greatest Russian authors. It is not surprising that Ivan Turgenev, the leader of Westernism, should have been influenced by Cervantes. It is, however, curious that a writer like Dostoyevski, leader of Slavophilism, should have been deeply affected by the same exponent of Western culture.

It is the purpose of this work to discover and analyze the penetration of Cervantes into Russia. However, before that is undertaken, criteria must be established by which to evaluate the effect of that penetration.

A given literary work may produce two effects: provoke imitation, or exert a more diffused influence. Of the two, direct imitation is more superficial and less important. It takes on a variety of forms. It may produce, as in the case of *Don Quixote*, a novel like the spurious *Quixote* of Avellaneda. It may consist of the use of the characters or an episode of the original work, presented in a different technical form, such as a poem, a ballet, a play, a short story or a fable, like I. Dmitryev's adaptation of Florian's *Don Quichotte*. It may make use of parts of the original to propound a completely new idea, as in Lunacharski's *The Liberated Don Quixote*.

Influence, the profound and elusive effect of one work on another, is far more important. Whereas a mediocre author will produce only an imitation, a man of talent will create an original work, bearing within it the influence of one or many authors. Often the work thus affected is as great as the one influencing it, or it may surpass it. The later work may, for example, stress some particular point of the earlier one so effectively that the influence will be transmitted to others. The more talented the author affected, the greater is the importance of the influence and the more potent its effect.

The first step in investigating an influence is to ascertain an author's acquaintance with the work in question. Second, it must be discovered, if possible, what particular aspect of the work the author admired or condemned. Then one must determine the author's receptivity—aesthetic, emotional and intellectual—to the earlier work. Similarity in temperament or outlook may lead to heightened receptivity, and thus enhance its influence.

Another important clue is whether the book under discussion, or any other material written during its genesis,
betrays the writer's awareness of the earlier work. However, not every book containing references to a given
work is necessarily influenced by it. The next step is to
relive with sympathy and understanding the entire creation of the influenced work, disentangle in so far as possible the elements that went into its composition, label
them and set them up. Finally, a comparative study of
the two works can be made, showing how material drawn
from the earlier work has been transfigured by the creative genius of the later writer.

Forms of influence are numerous. Anything from the
general tone or spirit of the earlier work to the smallest
detail contained therein may constitute an influence,
which, in turn, may extend over the entire work affected,
or may limit itself to an episode or even a phrase. An influence may be technical, affecting vocabulary, style,
composition, choice of literary device or mechanical
scheme. It may be aesthetic, determining genre, characters or setting. It may be ideological, involving the main
problem of the work, its theme (main or secondary), or
some idea which it expresses or implies. For instance, a
writer may pause on a problem presented by another
author, consider it and proceed to his own interpretation.
Or the earlier work may contain the germ of an idea
which, as it is developed, leads to a result remote from
the original suggestion. In this form, as well as in others,
the theme may be transmitted from one work to another,
assuming diverse guises, being projected from different
angles, in varied intensities or on different planes. It may
be simplified or complicated, blended with other ideas,
stressed in points different from the original. In spite of
all the metamorphoses that an idea may undergo at the
hands of other artists, its origin remains the same, and
must not be rejected because of the apparent remoteness
of the final concept from the *idée génétrice*.

An influence may come as an afterthought. A writer
may derive the original idea for his work from his own

experience, for example, but, as he considers it from ethical, social or other points of view, literary reminiscences, images, moods, ideas, mental or emotional experiences induced by another work may intrude. They may thus determine the nature of the expansion and development of the original theme.

An influence may be positive or negative, and may act directly or inversely. The positive effect is far more usual. It occurs when an author, favorably impressed by some feature of an earlier work, uses it consciously or subconsciously in his own. Negative influence takes place when the author disapproves of something in an earlier work and gives expression to this attitude in an original creation. The relationship between *Don Quixote* and the chivalric novels,[1] between Dostoyevski's *The Double* and Gogol's *The Cloak*, are examples of negative influence. This influence may be active directly; that is, the idea expressed in the earlier work is recast along similar lines in the later one, as, for instance, the character of Don Quixote is reworked by Dostoyevski in Prince Myshkin. An inversion of an influence may take the form of Chichikov in Gogol's *Dead Souls*, where the noblest of heroes, Don Quixote, is inverted into the basest of men.

Lastly, transmission of influences may be direct, or may occur through intermediaries—followers, or even imitators, of the earlier work. And the same author may manifest both direct and indirect influences simultaneously.

It is with such concepts and analytical technique that the influence of Cervantes upon Russian writers is approached in this study. The nature of the material, involving overlapping literary movements and writers who pursued their careers in the midst of political and social fluctuations, has made chronological classification arbitrary. However, to give some organization to the study, the following divisions have been selected as best suited for the presentation of the material: The Pre-Pushkin and

---

[1] In the conception of the *Quixote* the influence of the novels of chivalry was negative; in the execution of the work it was positive.

Pushkin Eras, the Age of Realism, the Passing of the Empire, and the Marxists and the Soviet.

In each of these sections, attention is first directed to the cultural intercourse between Russia and Spain during the period in question. Included in this background material is a survey of current translations of Cervantes' works into Russian, and information on outstanding ballets and plays with Cervantian themes. These theater productions, incidentally, should be considered as imitations, rather than manifestations of Cervantes' influence. Allusions to Cervantes in Russian literature are copious; a selection has been made for the first three periods to give some indication of the Russians' growing familiarity with the Spaniard and his works.

Following this general background material, more detailed consideration is given to Cervantes criticism. Some passages are quoted at length for the benefit of scholars who do not read Russian freely. Finally, separate chapters are devoted to the major figures in Russian literature who are demonstrably influenced by Cervantes. When possible, any pertinent comments by Russian critics regarding this influence have been introduced into the discussion. Certain generalizations about the effect of Cervantes on Russian literature have been gathered together as a conclusion to the book.

It gives me great pleasure to thank Professor Américo Castro and Ira O. Wade of Princeton University for active encouragement in the work, to Professor Federico de Onís of Columbia University under whose direction the subject was initially investigated and to Miss Jean MacLachlan for editorial assistance. I also wish to thank the Princeton University research fund for the grant which made the publication of this book possible.

L. B. T.

CONTENTS

CONTENTS

TRANSLITERATION

The transliteration scheme used in this work follows somewhat that of the New York Public Library.

а	a	о	o
б	b	п	p
в	v	р	r
г	g	с	s
д	d	т	t
е	e	у	u
э	e	ф	f
ж	zh	х	kh
з	z	ц	ts
и	i	ч	ch
і	i	ш	sh
й	i	щ	sch
к	k	ы	y
л	l	ю	yu
м	m	я	ya
н	n		

At the beginning of a word or a syllable *e* is rendered by *ye*.

The soft sign accompanying a vowel is usually indicated by an inserted *y*. Otherwise it is omitted. The hard sign is also omitted.

The group кий is rendered as кі, ия, ыя as ia to avoid confusion with я, ые, ие, as ie, ий as i and ый as y.

This system has been used consistently in the transliteration of Russian words, titles of books and names of persons. Exceptions to it are names of those persons who either through fame or previous publications spell their names differently, as for example Tchaikovsky.

PART I

THE PRE-PUSHKIN
AND PUSHKIN ERAS

1763-1850

1 · BACKGROUND

THE first recorded official contact between Spain and Russia was made in 1524. "A Russian embassy was sent to Emperor Charles V by the Grand Duke of Moscow, Vasili Ivanovich.[1] Duke Ivan Yaroslavski Zaseikin arrived in Madrid and carried out the mission. During the reign of Ivan Vasilyevich IV[2] there was among the number of foreign merchants residing in Russia the Spaniard Ivan Devaja Beloborod,[3] a trader in precious stones who enjoyed royal favor. Spanish and Dutch merchants were at the time permitted to carry on their business in the Pudozherski Pust."[4] At the beginning of the seventeenth century, the number of these Spaniards was augmented by some Jesuit, Augustine and Carmelite monks.[5] These groups were for Russia an important source of information about Spain.

Another contemporary channel of news was correspondence; for example, John Merrick's letters to Boris Godunov (reigned 1598-1605)[6] and A. Vlasyev,[7] and Possevin's letters to the Duke of Tuscany.[8]

---

[1] Reigned 1505-1534.

[2] Ivan IV, the Terrible or the Dread, reigned 1534-1584.

[3] This name is a curious mixture of Russian and Spanish. Rendered all in Spanish, it would read "Juan Devaja Barbablanca."

[4] V. I. Lamanski, "Istoricheskia zamechania k sochineniyu 'O slavyanakh v Maloi Azii, v Afrike i v Ispanii'" [Historical comments on the work 'Slavs in Asia Minor, Africa and Spain'], *Uchenia Zapiski vtorogo otdelenia Imperatorskoi Akademii Nauk*, v (St. Petersburg, 1859), 185.

[5] Emile Gigas, "Etudes sur quelques comedias de Lope de Vega, IV," *Révue Hispanique*, LXXXI, part II (1933). 177-88; cf. pp. 186-87.

[6] V. N. Aleksandrenko, "Materialy po smutnomu vremeni na Rusi XVII veka" [Material on the turbulent period in Russia of the

3

A half-century later, in 1667, Tsar Aleksei Mikhailovich (reigned 1645-1676) sent Petr Ivanovich Potemkin as ambassador to Spain. He was accompanied by Semeon Rumyantsev. They left Moscow early in July, landed in Cadiz on December 4, and arrived in Madrid February 27, 1668. On March 7 the ambassador and his suite were received by the young King Carlos II, and on March 15 by the widowed queen and regent Mariana of Austria. Having fulfilled their mission and exchanged royal gifts, they left Madrid on June 7. Potemkin's report[9] contains a detailed account of the journey. It includes a brief chapter on such features of the Spanish government as the royal councils, juntas, tribunals; another devoted to a discussion of the losses of the Spanish dominions in the seventeenth century, titles of the sovereigns, and a description of the ceremonial reception of the ambassadors. He then speaks of the military orders of the Golden Fleece, Calatrava, Alcántara and Santiago, of the Inquisition, Spanish agriculture, industry, and the customs, manners and character of the people. It is interesting to note the attention Potemkin pays to the two Madrid theaters. He describes with care their construction, performances, and particularly the actors' costumes.

In 1680 another order was issued sending Potemkin as ambassador to Western Europe. Leaving Russia at the

---

XVII century], *Starina i Novizna*, XIV (1911), 185-453, letter dated Oct. 7, 1602.

[7] *Ibid.*, letter dated July 5, 1604.

[8] *Ibid.*, p. 374. Russian events of the time were given wider publicity in Spain by Lope de Vega, who, drawing probably on *Relación de la señalada y como milagrosa conquista del paterno imperio, conseguido del Principe Juan Demetrio, Gran Duque de Moscovia, en el año de 1605 . . .* by Juan Mosquera, wrote *El Gran Duque de Moscovia*. Cf. Gertrud v. Poehl, "La Fuente de *El Gran Duque de Moscovia* de Lope de Vega," *Revista de Filología Española*, XIX (1932), 47-63.

[9] Prince Augustine Petrovich Golitzin, *La Russie au XVIIIe siècle: mémoires inédits sur les regnes de Pierre le Grand, Catherine I et Pierre II* (Paris, 1863), pp. 88-107. C. Derjavin has excerpts of the report in an appendix to his article "La primera embajada rusa en España," *Boletín de la Real Academia de la Historia*, XCVI (1930), 877-96.

end of October, he arrived in Madrid July 25, 1681, and had an audience with the king on August 2. He left for London on September 9, without having reached any agreement with regard to reciprocal freedom in trade relations.[10]

Peter the Great (reigned 1682-1721), the son of Aleksei Mikhailovich, shared the general European curiosity about the Spanish succession. Among Peter's papers[11] are numerous reports on this question from Izmailov, Matveyev and Vinius. He manifested a more active interest in Spain during the Russian war with Sweden, when he sought both military and matrimonial alliances with Spain. These never materialized.[12]

In 1727 it was Spain's turn to solicit Russian help. She was involved in the European struggle and needed Russian aid in the restoration of James to the English throne. In return for this assistance to the Pretender, she hoped to have Gibraltar. D. Jacobo Francisco Fitz-James Stuart, Duque de Liria, was therefore dispatched to the court of young Peter II (reigned 1727-1730). Stuart's account of this journey relates his own difficulties, aspirations and achievements, and gives detailed information concerning those phases of Russian life that he thought would be of interest to his country.[13]

Despite the existence of diplomatic and commercial relations between Spain and Russia, trade between them did not prosper, because of the lack of Russian export firms and dependence on foreign middlemen. The greater

[10] *Russki Biograficheski Slovar*, XIV (St. P., 1905), 682-85; cf. p. 685. During this visit Carreno painted a portrait of Potemkin.

[11] *Pisma i bumagi Imperatora Petra Velikago* [Letters and papers of the Emperor Peter the Great] I [1688-1701] (St. P., 1887), 284 and 772; IV [1706] (St. P., 1900), 911, 915, 1074, 1089, 1097.

[12] Cf. Peter's letters of Sept. 20, 1719, and of Sept. 27, 1718, to Prince Kurakin, reprinted in Lamanski's *Istoricheskia zamechania* . . . 188-89 and 192-93 respectively.

[13] D. Jacobo Francisco Fitz-James Stuart, Duque de Liria, "Diario del viaje a Moscovia," *Colección de documentos inéditos para la historia de España por el Marqués de la Fuensanta del Valle*, D. Jose Sancho Rayón and D. Francisco de Zabalburu (eds.), XCIII (Madrid, 1889).

part of the trade was carried on through foreign merchants who had obtained important concessions from the Russian monarchs. Peter I tried to ameliorate the situation through the establishment of consulates,[14] and for this purpose sent Prince Golitzin to Spain. This envoy supplied the first official information concerning Spanish trade in a letter of July 15/26, 1723. In a secret message of October 7/18, 1724, he amplified the data given in the earlier report.[15]

In accordance with Peter's instructions, Golitzin approached the Spanish government for the establishment of direct commerce with Russia. The Spanish king responded warmly to these overtures, and even considered extending to the Russians the same privileges heretofore enjoyed only by the English.[16] To this end, three ships with merchandise, traders and consuls[17] departed for the Spanish ports, but the consuls' incompetence ruined the project.

The question of renewing commerce with Spain was raised again in 1760 by Prince P. Repnin, minister to Madrid.[18] Plans were proposed, but the Russian merchants did not respond. The Russian government took the matter into its own hands and two companies were founded: the Volodimirov Company, in 1763, subsidized by Catherine, for trade in Spain and on the Mediterranean; and the Rogovikov, Gubkin and Schukin Company, exclusively for Spain.[19] Consuls were again sent to Spain. In Russia, on the other hand, Spanish trading firms like Shono y Soto and Domilan and Company were

[14] V. A. Ulianitski, "Istoricheski ocherk russkikh consulstv za granitsei" [A historical sketch of Russian consulates abroad], *Sbornik moskovskago glavnago arkhiva Ministerstva Inostrannykh Del*, VI (Moscow, 1899), 289.

[15] *Ibid.*, appendix 31, p. cvii and pp. cx-cxvii.

[16] *Ibid.*, appendix 31, pp. cxii, cxxiii.

[17] *Ibid.*, appendix 31, pp. cxii-cxv. The consuls were Prince Ivan Scherbatov, Aleksei Veshnyakov and Yakov Yefreinov.

[18] *Ibid.*, p. 296.

[19] For documents concerning these companies, see Lamanski, *op. cit.*, pp. 202-27.

founded.[20] After that time, commercial relations between the two nations progressed steadily.

Commercial relations were followed by social intercourse. In the beginning of the nineteenth century Russian soldiers and travelers appeared in Spain. Dimitri Petrovich Buterlin participated under the Duc d'Anguillême in the taking of Trocadero, and the journalist Faddei Bulgarin (1789-1859) went into Spain with Napoleon. Bestuzhev, Glinka and, if the reports may be trusted, Gogol came to the peninsula as travelers. Some of these Russians left interesting accounts of their visits.[21]

One of them, N. Bestuzhev (1797-1837), traveling on a British ship in 1825, came to Gibraltar, only to find the door into Spain closed and the fireworks of the Constitutionalist insurrection going off within. The situation was a tantalizing one. Though disappointed, Bestuzhev made the best of it by learning what he could about Spain and her people on her doorstep, and described his findings in his short essay "Gibraltar."[22]

Spain held a great attraction for the composer Mikhail Ivanovich Glinka (1804-1857), who is often considered the father of Russian music. In Spain he sensed a kinship to his native Russia, particularly as expressed in Spanish folk melodies, which he hoped some day to develop into a major work. Glinka's longing to visit Spain was, after much delay, gratified in 1845. He loved it, and found it

[20] Ulianitski, *op. cit.*, p. 337.

[21] "Perepiska kn. P. A. Vyazemskago s A. I. Turgenevym" [Prince P. A. Vyazemski's correspondence with A. I. Turgenev], *Ostafyevski Arkhiv Kn. Vyazemskikh*, published by Count C. D. Sheremetev, edited and annotated by V. I. Saitov, I (St. P., 1899), 540; N. Bestuzhev, "Vzglyad na russkuyu slovesnost v techenii 1823 goda" [A glance at Russian letters for 1823], *Polyarnaya Zvezda* (1824), pp. 1-14; N. Grech, "A Sketch of Russian Literature, 1822," *Foreign Review* (St. P., 1828), pp. 279-309. The latter article is in English. For information on the account by Solowieski, see J. Juderías, "D. Juan Valera, apuntes para su biografía," in *La Lectura* (Feb. 1914), p. 168; for Anatole de Demidoff, author of "Etapes maritimes sur les côtes d'Espagne, de la Catalogne à l'Andalousie," see R. Foulché-Delbosc, "Bibliographie des voyages en Espagne et Portugal," *Révue hispanique*, III (Paris, 1896), 426.

[22] Bestuzhev, "Gibraltar," *Polyarnaya Zvezda* (1825), 193-224.

more congenial than any country other than his homeland. Eagerly he immersed himself in Spanish mores, language, people, dances and music.[23] In 1847 he returned
to Russia, bringing with him a Spanish friend, Don
Pedro.[24] Glinka never did write the major work of Spanish inspiration he had planned, but he wove Spanish mo-
tifs into his *Spanish Overture, Jota Aragonese* and *Spanish Night.*

Prior to the reign of Catherine the Great, Spanish
books in Russia and books about Spain in Russian were
very scarce. From the fifteenth to the seventeenth centuries there were many editions of Raimundo Llulio's
Ars magna generalis et ultima in translation.[25] It is also
known that some of the apologues of Petrus Alfonsus'
Disciplina Clericalis came into Russia through Poland in
the translations of the *Gesta Romanorum* and the *Speculum Exemplorum.*[26] The Italian dramatic companies im-
ported by Peter the Great brought with them the *capa y
espada* type of play and in their repertoire is found a play
on the Don Juan theme entitled *Don Pedro i Don Yan,*
presented in 1659.[27] Bulgakov's list of foreign periodicals
subscribed to in Russia between the years 1631 and 1762
mentions that the *Gaceta de Madrid* was received in
1728.[28]

[23] Lamanski, *op. cit.*, pp. 105-6.
[24] L. I. Shestakova, "Byloye M. I. Glinki i yego roditelei, vospominania" [M. I. Glinka and his parents], *Yezhegodnik imperatorskikh teatrov*, season 1892-1893 (St. P., 1894), 427-58.
[25] A. I. Sobolevski, "Perevodnaya literatura moskovskoi Rusi xiv-
xvii vekov" [Translated literature in Moscovite Russia of the xiv-
xvii centuries], *Sbornik otdelenia russkago yazyka i slovesnosti
Imperatorskoi Akademii Nauk*, lxxiv, no. 1 (St. P., 1903), 158.
[26] A. N. Pypin, *Istoria russkoi literatury* [History of Russian lit-
erature], ii (St. P., 1911). *Gesta Romanorum* was translated from
Polish at the end of the 17th century and *Speculum Exemplorum*
was also translated from the Polish in 1677. Cf. pp. 510-15.
[27] P. O. Morozov, "Russki teatr pri Petre Velikom" [The Russian
theater during the time of Peter the Great], *Yezhegodnik imperatorskikh teatrov*, season 1893-1894, supplement i (St. P., 1894),
52-81; cf. p. 63.
[28] A. Bulgakov, "Otvet na bibliograficheski vopros" [An answer
to a bibliographical question], *Moskovski Telegraf*, xvi (Moscow,
1827), 5-33; cf. p. 25.

An awakening interest in Spain marks Catherine's
reign, as is indicated by translations of books and articles
such as *The Life of Velasco de Figueroa*,[29] Robertson's
History of the Reign of Charles V,[30] Mariana's *Universal
History of Spain*,[31] *An Answer to the Question—In What
Way Are We Indebted to Spain?* by Abbé Denina,[32] Au-
guste Toine's work on the battles of the French and Span-
ish kings,[33] *The History of the Spanish Prince Don Carlos,
Son of King Philip II*,[34] and later *The Losses of the
French in Spain*,[35] dealing with the Napoleonic invasion.[36]
There is also a Russian article by Lykoshin, "Don
Carlos."[37]

At the beginning of the nineteenth century Spain figures more and more frequently in Russian periodicals,
personal correspondence,[38] and in literature—e.g., Derz-

[29] *Ispanets (uyedinenny), ili zhizn dona Varaska Figaroaza*, translated from the French, St. P. 1767-1768.

[30] Wm. Robertson, *Istoria o gosudarstvovania Karla Pyatago*,
translated from the French by Smirnov, St. P. Akademia Nauk,
1775-1778.

[31] *Istoria (vseobschaya) Ispanii, s primechaniami i kartinami,
sochinenie Ioana Mariany*, translated from the French, St. P., 1779-
1782.

[32] *Otvet na vopros: chem my odolzheny Ishpanii; soch. Abbata
Denina*, translated from the French by M. Vysheslavtsov, Moscow,
1786.

[33] *Dostopamyatnosti frantsuzskikh i ispanskikh korolei, s opisan-
iem proizvedennykh imi udachnykh ili neudachnykh srazheni i
zavoyevani, soch. Avg. Tuana*; translated from the Latin, Moscow,
1789.

[34] *Istoria o gishpanskom printse Don Karlose, syn gishpanskago
korolya Filipa II*, translated from the French, St. P. 1760 or 1792.

[35] *Urony frantsuzov v Ispanii i vzglyad na vazhneishia istoricheskia proizshestvia dostopyametnoi voiny na sem poluostrove*,
translated from the French, St. P. 1812.

[36] *Frantsuzy v Gishpanii, ili opisanie sobyti, soprovozhdavshikh
pokhischenie Gishpanskoi korony i kovarnykh sredstv, upotreblen-
nykh Imperatorom frantsuzov dlya dostizhenia sei tseli*, translated
from the French, published by D. P. Kevallos, St. P., 1812.

[37] *Don Karlos, istoricheskoe proisshestvie XVI st.*, St. P., 1821.

[38] E.g., M. Pogodin, *N. M. Karamzin, po yego sochineniam, pis-
mam i otzyvam sovremennikov. Materialy dlya biografii* [N. M. K.,
according to his works, letters and opinions of his contemporaries.
Material for a biography, notes and comments by Pogodin], II
(Moscow, 1866), 47-48; "Perepiska kn. P. A. Vyazemskago s A. I.
Turgenevym," I (St. P., 1899), 540; II (St. P., 1899), 14, 32, 36,

havin's *On the Victory of the Spaniards over the French*,[39] Karamzin's *Sierra Morena, Letter of Don García, Caliph Abdul Rahman* and *Conde Guarinos*,[40] Delvig's "Sonnet to S. D. P-oi,"[41] Polevoi's *Mother, a Spanish Woman*,[42] Zagoskin's *Nostalgia*,[43] Lermontov's *Spaniards*[44] and the original plans for his poems *Demon* and *Mtsyri*.[45]

Just as early acquaintance with Spanish history came through French intermediaries, so did theatrical works dealing with Spanish themes. There is, for example, the ballet *Caliph from Cordova*,[46] presented in Russia sometime between 1762 and 1792; *The Two Rogues from Spain*,[47] a three-act play translated into Russian in 1787; another three-act play, *Pizarro*,[48] the operas *The Mute in the Mountains of Sierra Morena, or The Mysterious Beggar*[49] and *Ferdinand Cortez, or The Conquest of Mex-*

97, 98, 110, 114, 167, 184, 321, 324, 365, 519; *Moskovski Telegraf*, 1826, VII, 200-5.

[39] G. R. Derzhavin, "Na porazhenie gishpantsami frantsuzov," *Sochinenia* (St. P., 1870), III, 337.

[40] N. M. Karamzin, *Sochinenia*, I (Petrograd, 1917). In reference to *Conde Guarinos*, D. K. Petrov, the Russian Hispanist, correctly points to the accurate rendering of the thought of the original version. The intermediary source, French or German, used by Karamzin has not been determined. *Ibid.*, pp. 407-8 (notes).

[41] A. A. Delvig, "Sonet S. D. P.-oi," *Polyarnaya Zvezda* (1824), 25-26.

[42] *Mat ispanka*, a very mediocre play in three acts, first published in *Russki Vestnik*, 1842, IV, sect. I, 21.

[43] *Toska po rodine.*

[44] M. I. Lermontov, "Ispantsy," *Sochinenia* (St. P., 1903), IV, 7-122.

[45] Lermontov, "Demon," *Sochinenia*, I, 155 ff.; "Mtsyri," *ibid.*, 132 ff.

[46] *Kalif iz Kordovy*, ballet cited by A. Pleschev in *Nash Balet (1673-1899)* [Our ballet] (St. P., 1899), p. 47.

[47] *Dva pluta v Gishpanii*, three acts, translated from the French, Moscow, 1787.

[48] P. Arapov, *Letopis russkago teatra* [Chronicle of the Russian theater] (St. P., 1861), p. 172. The translator of the play was Lifanov. It was presented on Nov. 3, 1805.

[49] *Nemoi v gorakh Sierry Moreny, ili tainstvenny nischi*, opera in three acts, with choruses and dances, music by Franzel, translated from the German by Svechinski. Samoilov played the role of Don Juan at the performance of Jan. 29, 1820. Arapov, *op. cit.*, p. 294.

ico,[50] the tragic ballet and drama of *Inés de Castro*,[51] the comic vaudeville sketches *The Bachelor from Salamanca*,[52] *Ferdinand, the King of Aragon*,[53] *The Sevillian Pearl*[54] and *Philip II, Spanish King*,[55] and, of course, *The Barber of Seville*[56] and *Don Juan*.[57]

At first, the Russians were satisfied with secondhand acquaintance with Spanish literature—through translations made from the French—but in the nineteenth century a need for Spanish grammars became apparent. In 1811 Yakov Langen produced a Spanish grammar[58] ac-

[50] *Ferdinand Kortes, ili zavoyevanie Meksiki*, a lyrical opera in three acts, in verse, with choruses and dances, music by Spontini, translated by D. N. Barkov, presented on Jan. 9, 1820. Arapov, *op. cit.*, p. 292.

[51] *Inesa de Kastro*, tragic ballet, presented on May 24, 1820 (Arapov, *op. cit.*, p. 296). Performed again in 1828 ("Spisok baletov dannykh na imperatorskikh stsenakh Sanktpeterburgskikh teatrov s 1828 goda") [List of ballets performed on the Imperial stages of the St. Petersburg theaters after 1828]. *Yezhegodnik Imperatorskikh Teatrov*, season 1899-1900 (St. P., 1900), supplement III, p. 53. Another long tragic ballet, *Inesa de Kastro*, in 5 acts, revived by Auguste, dances by Didelot, music by Boaldier, was performed on Jan. 21, 1829 (*ibid.*).

[52] *Bakalavr salamankhski*, in one act, translated from the French by Prince Shakhovskoi, presented on July 4, 1820. Arapov, *op. cit.*, p. 305.

[53] *Ferdinand, korol arragonski, ili tainstvenny pokrovitel*, an opera in two acts with choruses and ballets, in imitation of the French, by A. P. Veshnyakov and A. I. Shiller, music by Keitser. Arapov, *op. cit.*, p. 368.

[54] *Sevilskaya zhemchuzhina*, cited in *Spisok baletov dannykh na imp. stsenakh . . .* , p. 53.

[55] *Filipp II, korol ispanski*, tragedy in three acts, by Alfieri, translated from the Italian by E. V., "Khronika Sanktpeterburgskikh teatrov ot 18 Yanvarya do 20 Fevralya 1840 goda" [Chronicle of St. P. theaters from Jan. 18 to Feb. 20, 1840], *Repertuar russkago teatra*, 1840, III, 30-34.

[56] *Sevilski tsirulnik* had several performances in the late seventies and eighties of the eighteenth century. N. Findeizin, *Ocherki po istorii muzyki v Rossii s drevnikh vremen do kontsa XVIII veka* [Sketches of the history of music in Russia, from ancient times to the end of the XVIII century] (Moscow-Leningrad, 1828), II, issue 5, pp. 99, 126 and 257.

[57] *Don Zhuan*, ballet, composed by Canobbo and Pashkevich, had three performances in 1781. *Ibid.*, p. 108.

[58] Yak. Langen, *Grammatika (kratkaya) ispanskaya, raspolozhennaya po pravilam Grammatiki Korolevskoi Ispanskoi Akademii*, Mitava, 1811. Reviewed in *Sanktpeterburgski Vestnik*, 1812, VI, 312.

11

cording to the rules of the Real Academia Española, and in 1840 appeared I. Rut's *Guide for the Study of Spanish.*[59]

TRANSLATIONS

NOTE. A more detailed analysis of the translations of Cervantes into Russian, with parallel texts, is to be found in the dissertation MS, "Cervantes in Russia" by L. B. Turkevich, in the Princeton University Library.

THE first Russian translation of the *Quixote, A History of the Famous Knight of La Mancha, Don Quixote,* made by N. Osipov (1751-1799), appeared in 1769. Unlike the French and German translators, Osipov did not work directly from the Spanish, but from the then popular French version of Filleau de Saint-Martin. The labored quality of the text leaves no doubt that the *History of the Famous Knight* belongs to Osipov's school years. In subsequent years, Osipov's government and military service left him little time for translation, but on retirement he sought to capitalize on his youthful training. He touched up his early rendition of the *Quixote* and published it in 1791 under an elaborate new title: *A Strange and Droll Figure, or The Amazing and Extraordinary Adventures of the Brave and Famous Knight Errant Don Quixote.* This version had a second edition in 1812.[1]

Osipov's selection of the text of Filleau de Saint-Martin was most unfortunate, for Filleau, in accommodating the original to the French spirit, destroyed much of the Spanish color, character and charm of the *Quixote.*[2] Osipov tried to be faithful to his model, but errors due to inexperience in translation abound. There are numerous mistranslations, omissions and insertions. Proverbs are rendered by Russian equivalents, but often with small success. Osipov's style is verbose, clumsy and occasion-

[59] I. Rut, *Rukovodstvo k izucheniyu ispanskago yazyka* (St. P., 1840). Reviewed in *Literaturnaya Gazeta* (1840), no. xxii, 516-17.

[1] The data on Osipov's translations are not clear-cut. Consult Appendix, nos. 1-3.

[2] Maurice Bardon, *Don Quichotte en France au XVIIe au XVIIIe siècle 1605-1815* (Paris, 1931), i, 327 ff., has a good analysis of this translation.

ally ungrammatical. However, despite these shortcomings, credit must be given to Osipov for introducing Cervantes' masterpiece to Russian readers. For thirty-five years his translation was the only Russian version available.

To the youthful poet Vasili Andreyevich Zhukovski (1783-1852), later so eminent a figure in Russian letters, belongs the second Russian translation, *Don Quixote of La Mancha*.[3] Early in his career Zhukovski made a good many translations, and those turned out in the years 1804-1806 show a particular fondness for Florian and La Fontaine. It is Florian's version of *Don Quixote* that the twenty-one-year-old Zhukovski translated into Russian. The value of this French text has been fully discussed by Bardon in *Don Quichotte en France*.[4]

Florian's influence on Zhukovski extended to principles of composition and translation. Florian, it will be recalled, believed that fidelity to the original should be sacrificed to the creation of a pleasing impression in the translation. He felt that a translator, if he retains the author's idea, has the right to weaken some expressions in the original, soften others, discard any portions of the original which he considers in bad taste, and that on the whole he should concentrate on smoothness and purity of language. These were the precepts followed by Florian himself in his own translation of the *Quixote*[5] and, of course, omissions, mistranslations and variations were inevitable. It is only to be expected that such inaccuracies would also be found in a translation taken from this version, but the unfortunate Cervantes was subjected to Florian's treatment a second time! Florian had already done more than his share of cutting and toning down the original, and Zhukovski in turn is guilty of more omissions, more subduing of expressions and more misinterpretations. Divergence from the original does not end here. In an unsuccessful attempt to give his Russian the

[3] *Don Kishot La Mankhski* (Moscow, 1804), cf. appendix, No. 4.
[4] Bardon, *op. cit.*, II, 692-716.
[5] J. P. Claris de Florian, *Oeuvres* (Paris, 1820).

13

smoothness recommended by Florian, Zhukovski falls into the error of substituting racy colloquialisms for the classic dignity of Cervantes' prose. Little of the Cervantes spirit is retained in the Florian translation; none remains in Zhukovski's work.

The result is so far removed from the original version of Cervantes that Zhukovski was ashamed of it. He wrote to A. I. Turgenev: "You want me to send you a *complete* list of my works in poetry and prose and translations for publication in your survey. Hélas! Pauvre Jacques! Je sens trop fort ma misère. Let them say: He translated *Don Quichotte*, but not a word about how it is translated, or else . . . this creation will soon be printed in a second edition—*somewhat* mended; all the rest of my works can be found in the 'Messenger.' "[6]

Poetically, those portions of the *Quixote* that are in verse may be said to be superior in the translation to the original. Zhukovski was a very gifted poet and his talent is evident in this work. However, excellent though his verses may be, their sentiment, ideas and tone have nothing in common with the original. They sound like an outpouring from the lovelorn heart of a twenty-one-year-old poet, who is seizing the opportunity to set down his own emotions, apprehensions and desires.

Zhukovski's translation went through two, and possibly three, editions. The first appeared in 1804-1806; the second, "revised," in 1815; and the third, according to Fitzmaurice-Kelly, in 1820.[7]

Another translation of the *Quixote* was published either in 1831[8] or 1837.[9] It was made from the French version of S. de Chaplet.

[6] "Pisma V. A. Zhukovskago k A. I. Turgenevu" [V. A. Zh.'s letters to A. I. T.], *Russki Arkhiv* (1895), I-III, 52.

[7] James Fitzmaurice-Kelly, *The Life of Miguel Cervantes Saavedra* (London, 1892), p. 351.

[8] *Sistematicheski i khronologicheski katalog biblioteki bibliofila i bibliografa Ya. F. Berezina-Shiryaeva* [Systematic and chronological catalogue of the library of the bibliophile and bibliographer Ya. F. B.-Sh.], I (St. P., 1900), 168.

[9] Rius says, "Traducción de Chaplet, tomada del francés, según cita de Masalski," L. Rius y de Llosellas, *Bibliografía crítica de las obras de Miguel de Cervantes Saavedra*, I (Madrid, 1895), No. 821.

14

In 1838 appeared the first Russian version made directly from the Spanish, by Konstantin P. Masalski. Masalski (1802-1861) was both a Hispanist and an author. He was popular in the thirties and forties for his entertaining plays, *povesti* and novels, among which is found *Don Quixote of the Nineteenth Century*. He also wrote an account of the Potemkin embassy to Spain and France, but his greatest claim to fame rests in his translation, *Don Quixote of La Mancha*.[10]

This translation has not been available to the present writer, but a very careful review by a competent critic sheds a good bit of light upon it.[11] The critic evidently knew both Spanish and Russian thoroughly, as well as the *Quixote*. His chief criticism of Masalski's work is that the translator sacrificed smoothness of style to excessive literalism. He finds some mistranslations, omissions and inconsistencies, but if these are indeed all of Masalski's serious transgressions, the work is really as good as its reputation. The reviewer says that with all its faults, it is the best translation offered to date. A whole half-century later, P. Vainberg writes: "Of the Russian translations of *Don Quixote*, the best belong to Masalski (St. Petersburg, 1848, incomplete) and V. Karelin (St. Petersburg, 1866)."[12] A second edition of Masalski's translation appeared in St. Petersburg in 1848.

Turning to Cervantes' *Novelas ejemplares, Las dos doncellas* was translated into Russian from the French in 1763,[13] which is even earlier than the date of Osipov's *Don Quixote*. This *novela* is probably the first Spanish

---

[10] *Novy entsiklopedicheski slovar Brockhaus i Efron*, xxv (St. P.-Moscow, n.d.), 847.

[11] *Otechestvennie Zapiski* (St. P.), 1839, ii-2, 67-68. The name of the reviewer is unknown. Other reviews appeared in *Syn Otechestva*, 1838, iv, pt. 4, 64 ff.; v, pt. 4, 149 ff.; *Severnaya Pchela*, 1838, No. 248, article by F. Bulgarin; *Moskovski Nablyudatel*, April 1838, ii, 650, 651, 654; and *Moskvityanin*, 1846, i, no. 2, 192-97.

[12] P. Vainberg, "Cervantes," *Entsiklopedicheski Slovar*, xxix (St. P., 1900), 623-26; cf. p. 626.

[13] *Dve lyubovnitsy, gishpanskaya povest Mikh. Tservantesa Saavedry, avtora Don Kishota* (Moscow, 1763), cited in *Redkie i tsennie russkie izdania, No. 70, Antikvarny katalog, No. 14* issued by Mezhdunarodnaya Kniga (Moscow, 1932), p. 24, no. 124.

work to be translated into Russian, and seems to have enjoyed considerable success. Another edition appeared in 1769.[14] Except for a difference in the size of the volumes, the bibliographical data for the two publications are practically identical, thereby suggesting a second edition rather than a new translation. *La Gitanilla*, also taken from the French, was published in 1795.[15] In 1805 Kabrit translated all of the *Novelas ejemplares* from French versions.[16] Other new translations of *La fuerza de la sangre*[17] and *La Gitanilla*[18] appeared in 1839 and 1842 respectively.

The appeal of *Galatea* to the sentimental Russian taste of the late eighteenth century is indicated by the fact that two translations were made within one decade—one by Aleksei Pechenegov in 1790[19] and another by A. Khanenko in 1799.[20] These were likewise made from French texts.

THEATER PRODUCTIONS

THE earliest imitations of *Don Quixote* in the Russian theater belong to the ballet, where the choreographers were foreigners. In 1785 *Sancho Panza*, by the Italian composer Filidar, was performed in Moscow.[1] One would think that the pot-bellied Sancho would offer a splendid

[14] V. S. Sopikov, *Opyt rossiiskoi bibliografii, redaktsia primechania, doplonenia i ukazatel V. N. Rogozhina* [An experiment in Russian bibliography, edited by V. N. R.] (St. P., 1904-1906), II, no. 3104, *Dve lyubovnitsky, gishpanskaya povest Mikh. Tservantesa Saavedry*, Moscow, 1769.

[15] *Ibid.*, V (St. P., 1906), no. 12546, *Tsyganka (prekrasnaya) Neotsena*, Smolensk, 1795.

[16] *Ibid.*, IV (St. P., 1905), no. 8359, *Povesti Mikhaila Servantesa*, Moscow, 1805.

[17] "Sila krovi," in *Otecheskie Zapiski* (1839), cited in *Entsiklopedicheski slovar Brockhaus i Efron*, XXIX, cf. "Cervantes."

[18] *Ibid.*, "Khitana," *Syn Otechestva*, 1842.

[19] Sopikov, *op. cit.*, V, 12405, *Galatea, pastusheskaya povest*, Moscow, 1790.

[20] *Ibid.*, V, 12404, *Galatea, pastusheskaya povest*, St. P., 1799.

[1] N. Findeizin, *Ocherki po istorii muzyki v Rossii, s drevnikh vremen do kontsa XVIII veka* (Moscow-Leningrad, 1928), II, issue 5, p. 110.

subject for theatrical treatment, but apparently such was not the case here, for this ballet was presented only three times, the last being in 1787.

Some twenty years later, in 1809, Didelot, the talented choreographer and ballet-master, brought the *Quixote* story to the Russian stage for good, with his five-act ballet, *Don Kishot*.[2] Its success may be judged from the fact that before the end of the year another ballet, called *Don Kikhot*, was presented.[3] In the list of ballets performed in St. Petersburg during and after 1828 *Don Kikhot* is mentioned.[4] Whether this refers to the ballet first presented in 1809 or a new version or versions cannot be determined. In 1834 appears the first production of a comic ballet based on what became a very popular choreographic theme—*Don Quixote and Sancho Panza, or The Wedding of Gamacho.*[5]

There are also two instances of other types of theatrical imitation, one a translation from the German, and the other a Russian work. The former is (*The New*) *Don Quixote, or The Marvelous Adventures of Don Silvio Razalva*, a German play translated by Sapozhnikov, in two parts, produced in Moscow in 1782;[6] and the latter, *Don Quixote of La Mancha, the Knight of the Sad Visage*, a one-act comedy based on the novel by Cervantes.[7]

ALLUSIONS

CATHERINE THE GREAT (1729-1796) introduced Spanish literature into Russia by translating from the French portions of Calderón's *El escondido y la tapada*, and it was during her reign (1762-1796) that the first translations of

[2] L. Grossman, *Pushkin v teatralnykh kreslakh, kartiny russkoi stseny, 1817-1820* [Pushkin in the audience, pictures of the Russian stage, 1817-1820] (Leningrad, 1926), p. 18.

[3] Arapov, *Letopis russkago teatra*, p. 196. This ballet in two acts was presented in Dec. 1809.

[4] *Spisok baletov dannykh na imp. stsenakh Sanktpeterburgskikh teatrov* . . . , p. 53.

[5] *Ibid.*, p. 66. It was in two acts, by Milon, produced by Blash on Jan. 22, 1834.

[6] V. S. Sopikov, *Opyt rossiiskoi bibliografii*, II, no. 2482.

[7] Arapov, *op. cit.*, p. 368.

the *Quixote, Galatea, Las dos doncellas* and *La Gitanilla* were made. Both the time of the appearance of these classics and their sponsor are significant.

In the second half of the eighteenth century Russian society was beginning to read secular literature. There was a demand for reading material, and since there was a dearth of native talent the classics of the West were at a premium. Catherine encouraged the importation of literature, and herself set an example as an author and translator. That Cervantes, Lope and Calderón took firm root in Russian soil is attested to by the ever-increasing number of translations and references to their works. When Russian literature finally came into its own during the Pushkin era, some of its exponents found inspiration and guidance in this illustrious trio.[1]

The earliest Russian literary allusion to Don Quixote was made by Catherine. In her correspondence with Gustave III, reference is made to the Swedish king's vow that he had drawn his sword and would not sheathe it until he had attained his objective. Catherine received this declaration with the challenging remark, "Ah! Don Quichotte a tiré son épée et refuse de la rengainer, eh bien, il la jettera après le fourreau!"[2]

A. P. Sumarokov (1717-1774), an early classical poet, dramatist and critic, had little use for the novel. He wrote:

"Novels have multiplied to such an extent that they constitute just about half of the entire world library. They do little good and great harm. It is said that they relieve tedium, shorten time—our life, which in itself is all too short. . . .

"Although good novels may contain some worthwhile

[1] L. B. Turkevich, "Calderón en Rusia," *Revista de Filología Hispánica*, I (1939), 139-58.

[2] O.-G. de Heidenstam, *La Fin d'une dynastie, d'après les mémoires et la correspondance d'une reine de Suède Hedvig-Elizabeth-Charlotte (1774-1818)* (Paris, 1911), p. 217. Catherine again calls Gustave a "Don Quixote" in a letter quoted in *Joseph et Catherine de Russie, Correspondance*, editée par le chevalier Alfred d'Arneth (Vienna, 1869), pp. 314, 315, 316.

material, yet from a hundredweight of them one cannot distill a pound of essence. Their reading involves a greater consumption of time on worthless content than on worthwhile. I exclude *Télémaque, Don Quixote,* and only a very few other worthwhile novels. *Don Quixote* is a satire on the novel."[3]

N. M. Karamzin (1766-1826), a prominent Russian writer and historian of the period, had a particular affection for *Don Quixote.* It was among his earliest childhood reading and left him with an impression that was at once decisive and lasting. He made a number of references in his works to the effect of Cervantes' masterpiece on his childish imagination, and took pleasure in self-comparisons with the Spanish knight.[4]

During the pre-Pushkin and Pushkin era, acquaintance with *Don Quixote* was by no means limited to men of letters. References to Cervantes' hero occur, for instance, in a recorded conversation at the court of Emperor Paul, and in the letters of a military figure, A. Chicherin.[5]

Romanticism contributed greatly to the diffusion of Cervantes' works in Russia. As Pypin says in his *History of Russian Literature,* the Romantic writers, with their interest in world literature, "brought into circulation numerous works of other literatures. They revived the memory of the famous old Italians: Dante, Boccaccio, Petrarch, Ariosto . . . ; they recalled Cervantes and the Span-

[3] A. P. Sumarokov, *Polnoye sobranie sochineni* [Complete works] (St. P., 1781), vi, 371.

[4] N. M. Karamzin, *Pisma russkago puteshestvennika* [Letters of a Russian traveler] (Moscow, 1900), pp. 37, 100, 204; *Sochinenia Karamzina* [Works] (Petrograd, 1917), i, 167-70, 427; *Starina i Novizna* (St. P., 1897), i, 99; "Rytsar nashego vremeni" [Knight of our times], *Sochinenia Karamzina* (Moscow, 1820) ix, 36. Cf. also M. Pogodin, *N. M. Karamzin, po yego sochineniam, pismam i otzyvam sovremennikov, materialy dlya biografii* [N. M. K. as seen through his works, letters, and comments of contemporaries] (Moscow, 1866), part i, p. 7.

[5] *Perepiska Kn. P. A. Vyazemskago s A. I. Turgenevym,* ii, 314. M. N. Tolstoi, "Pisma Grafini Stavroginoi i A. Chicherina" [Letters of Countess Stavrogin and A. Chicherin], in *Starina i Novizna,* xvii (Moscow, 1914), 361, 375; cf. p. 370, letter dated Dec. 6, 1812.

ish drama; they brought back the old novels of chivalry; they became interested in folk poetry and traditions. . . ."[6]

Pypin's remark that Romanticism "recalled Cervantes" is very apt, for hitherto Cervantes had been completely eclipsed by his famous characters. The Romantics, however, did not confine themselves to the plot of the *Quixote*, or to the knight and his squire. They went further. They studied the aesthetic aspects of the work and referred to it in literary polemics and in their correspondence. Furthermore, they acquainted themselves with Cervantes' eventful life. The allusions, for instance, of K. N. Batyushkov (1787-1855), one of the most gifted pre-Pushkin poets, indicate his familiarity with Cervantes the man as well as with his masterpiece.[7]

P. A. Vyazemski (1792-1878), the journalistic leader of Russian Romanticism, provides the first evaluation of Don Quixote as a character: "Originality, when it is not affected, studied, superimposed, adulterated, is always more or less a sign of independence of character. This independence is a form of manliness, a kind of virtue. Thus, although Don Quixote may be comical, he is first and foremost chivalrously noble."[8]

Several other references occur in his writings,[9] and then, at a time when he felt Romanticism had reached its decline, Vyazemski uses Don Quixote and Rosinante in an interesting metaphor. He compares the beauty of the poetry of former years—that is, of Romanticism—to Pegasus, who with a stamp of his hoof opened streams that quenched the noble and poetic thirst of generations and

[6] A. N. Pypin, *Istoria russkoi literatury* [History of Russian literature] (St. P., 1913), 208.

[7] K. N. Batyushkov, Sochinenia [Works], II (St. P., 1885), 160, 221, 362; III (St. P., 1886), 409.

[8] P. A. Vyazemski, "Staraya zapisnaya knizhka" [An old notebook], *Polnoye sobranie sochinenii kn. P. A. Vyazemskago*, VIII (St. P., 1883), 223.

[9] Cf. also *Perepiska kn. P. A. Vyazemskago s A. I. Turgenevym*, II, 120-21, letter to Turgenev of Dec. 18, 1820; Vyazemski, "Zhukovski-Pushkin, o novoi shitke basen" [Zhukovski-Pushkin, on the new tailoring of fables], *Polnoye sobranie sochineni*, I (St. P., 1878), 178-85.

generations. Now, he feels, industrialization has converted that fiery-winged steed into "Rosinante upon whom the Knight of the Sad Visage traveled. The age of poetry is in the past." Genuine poets seem to Vyazemski non-existent and, therefore, "a poet in our day would be a true Don Quixote."[10] He would be out of place and out of date. He would be attempting to restore the Age of Gold in an Age of Iron.

Other allusions to Cervantes by significant figures of this period are to be found in the works of the brilliant novelist A. Bestuzhev (1797-1837),[11] A. S. Griboyedov (1795-1828), who was the author of the great comedy *Woe from Wit*,[12] and N. I. Grech (1787-1867), who has left a record of a conversation of his with Ludwig Tieck in which Tieck's new translation of the *Quixote* was discussed.[13]

N. I. Turgenev (1789-1871), a prominent economic reformer and intellectual, is perhaps the only Russian writer of the time to comment unfavorably on Cervantes. When one considers his profuse commentaries on other books, and the speed with which he read them, reading the *Quixote* seems to have been a chore to Turgenev. It took him at least two and a half months to finish, and there are only three entries in his diary about the work. The earliest one reads: "Well, it is time to get to *Don Quixote*, whom the author presents excessively mad. To

[10] P. A. Vyazemski, "Vzglyad na literaturu nashu posle Pushkina" [A glance at our literature after Pushkin], *Pol. sob. soch.*, II (St. P., 1879), 348-79.

[11] A. Marlinski, "O romane N. Poleyogo: Klyatva pri grobe Gospodnem" [About Polevoi's novel: The Oath at the Lord's Sepulchre], *Polnoye sobranie sochineni* (St. P., 1847), part XI, IV, 159-224; A. Bestuzhev, "Vecher na bivuake" [Evening on the bivouac], *Polyarnaya Zvezda* (1823), pp. 215-332.

[12] A. S. Griboyedov, "Gore ot uma" [aptly translated into English by Sir Bernard Pares: "The misfortune of being clever"], Museum monograph printed in *Polnoye sobranie sochineni*, II (St. P., 1913), act II, scene II, ll. 111-14 of the play.

[13] N. I. Grech, "Putevia pisma" [Letters from a trip], *Sochinenia*, II (St. P., 1855), 275-495; cf. pp. 381-382; also "Ocherk poezii dramaticheskoi" [Survey of dramatic poetry], *Repertuar russkago teatra*, May 1840, book V, 1-9.

me this seems unnatural and, therefore, has no appeal."
The other comments show no change of heart.[14]

[14] N. I. Turgenev, "Dnevnik i pisma za 1806-1811" [Diary and letters for 1806-1811], *Arkhiv bratyev Turgenevykh*, i, issue 1 (St. P., 1911), 245, entry for June 1, 1810; 263, entry for Aug. 3, 1810; and 265, entry for Aug. 15, 1810.

2 · CRITICISM

PRIOR to Belinski no original critical studies of the *Quixote* were written in Russia. In Faddei Bulgarin's *Historical Survey of Spanish Literature* there are several pages devoted to Cervantes.[1] Obviously based on French sources and the works of authoritative literary historians like Sismondi, Bulgarin's material is accurate and concise. He gives an account of Cervantes' life and enumerates his more important works, with brief comments about them. The survey as a whole is the first in Russia to deal with Spanish literature from the *Cid*, through the Golden Age, to Romanticism. It mentions all the important figures and their works, and sums up the literary trends of the different periods.

Vissarion Belinski (1810-1848), the great Russian critic, read *Don Quixote* in June 1837, noting in his diary: "I am finishing Cervantes' *Don Quixote*: it is, indeed, the work of a genius!"[2] A later allusion confirms this opinion: "That man of genius, Cervantes, reproduced creatively in his *Don Quixote* the concept of these paper knights for whom pleasant illusion is more precious than the bitter truth. . . ."[3] Another reference is found in his article "On the Russian Novel and the Novels of Gogol." Speaking of the development of literary art, the critic says that at the end of the sixteenth century a complete

[1] F. Bulgarin, "Istoricheskoye obozrenie ispanskoi literatury," *Syn Otechestva*, xxxix, xl and xli. For Cervantes cf. xl.

[2] V. Belinski, *Pisma* [Letters], in three volumes, edited and annotated by E. A. Lytski (St. P., 1914), I [1829-1839] p. 79, letter to M. A. Bakunin, June 28, 1837.

[3] Belinski, "Russkaya literatura v 1840 godu" [Russian literature in 1840], *Sobranie sochineni Belinskago* (St. P., 1896), II, 139-81; cf. p. 145.

reformation occurred: "Cervantes with his incomparable *Don Quixote* killed the pseudo-idealistic currents of poetry, and Shakespeare reconciled it [that is, poetry] and united it to real life forever."[4]

The most complete expression of Belinski's critical evaluation of *Don Quixote* is found in his review of *Tarantas* by Count V. A. Sollogub (1814-1882), a minor Russian author popular in the forties.[5] Sollogub's work deals with two antithetical characters traveling together from Moscow to Kazan in a tumble-down cart (*tarantas*). One of them, Ivan Vasilyevich, reminds the critic of Don Quixote—leading Belinski into an analysis of the knight, a representative portion of which follows:

"What is Ivan Vasilyevich?—He is something on the order of a little Don Quixote. To explain Ivan Vasilyevich's relation to the real, to the great, to the Spanish Don Quixote, it is necessary to say a few words about the latter. Don Quixote is, first of all, the most excellent and the most noble of men. He is a true knight, fearless and irreproachable. Notwithstanding the fact that he is comical from head to toe, physically and spiritually, you cannot regard him as stupid. On the contrary, he is very wise. No, this is insufficient—he is a veritable sage. Whether because of his own nature, or his education, or the conditions of his life, we do not know—but, at any rate, fantasy took the upper hand in him and made him a clown and the laughing-stock of all nations and all ages. The reading of extravagant tales of chivalry caused something to go askew. Dwelling entirely in a world of dreams, completely outside the influence of contemporary reality, he was deprived of all contact with real life, and consequently conceived the idea of becoming a knight-errant— a knight-errant at a time when there was not a single knight to be found and when only the illiterate populace believed in enchanters and miracles. Despite all the cruel disappointments to which a most unchivalrous reality sub-

---

[4] Belinski, *Sochinenia* . . . (Kiev, 1908), I, 94-143; cf. p. 99.

[5] Belinski, "Tarantas, putevia vpechatlenia, soch. Grafa V. A. Sollogua" [Tarantas, traveling impressions by Count V. A. S.], *ibid.*, IV, 5-50.

jected him, he remained faithful to his Dulcinea and his vow—to protect the weak against the powerful. If only this bravery, this magnanimity, this faithfulness, if only all these fine, lofty, noble qualities had been used at an appropriate time and in the proper way, Don Quixote would have been a truly great man! His very nature was paradoxical, and he would never have seen reality in its true guise. He would never have used the priceless treasures of his heart to his own advantage and at the proper moment. If he had been born in the days of chivalry, he most probably would have devoted himself to its destruction. . . . But, since even before his birth all traces of knighthood had disappeared, knighthood became the object of his mania, his *idée fixe*. When for a moment he did happen to free himself from illusion, he astounded everyone by his extraordinary mind, by his common sense. He talked like a sage. Even when the hoax engineered by influential persons seemed to realize his dream of knightly aspirations, he, in the capacity of a judge, revealed not only a great mind, but even great wisdom. Nevertheless, he remained essentially a madman, a clown and a public laughing-stock. We do not propose to reconcile this contradiction, but it is clear to us that such paradoxical characters are not only not rare, but, on the contrary, they are very numerous. They are to be found always and everywhere. They are wise, but only in the world of illusion; they are capable of sacrifice, but for a phantom; they accomplish something, but only trifles; they are gifted, but futilely; everything is comprehensible to them except the one thing that is all-important—reality. They are gifted with an extraordinary capacity for conceiving a nonsensical idea and finding it affirmed by the most contradictory manifestations of reality. The more nonsensical the idea, the more intoxicated they become by it, and regard all sober individuals as intoxicated, mad, and sometimes even immoral, malicious and dangerous. Don Quixote is a highly generic character who will never grow old. It is in this that the greatness of Cervantes' genius is revealed in its entirety."[6]

This analysis is excellent. Belinski has fully grasped the essence of the *Quixote* and understood the public's reaction to the hero's antics. But at this stage he shifts his point of view. He lifts the basic idea out of the novel and transfers it to an abstract plane. Don Quixote becomes the *type* that lives in a world of illusion. Disregarding the actual stimuli in Don Quixote's life, Belinski discusses the knight's behavior according to his own philosophical tenets, making Don Quixote the subject of dangerous generalization. Having done this, he returns the knight to the book. The new Don Quixote, or Don Quixote as Belinski sees him, is vastly different from Cervantes' figure, and subsequent comparison between Ivan Vasilyevich and the hidalgo becomes of little value. Belinski suggests, for example, that the following traits of Ivan Vasilyevich are similar to those found in Don Quixote: Ivan Vasilyevich's virtue is negative. It consists of the absence of evil. ". . . his mind . . . is capable of being stimulated by the thoughts of others, but it is incapable of conceiving any idea or of understanding anything independently and originally. It is even incapable of making the ideas of others his own." "He begins, but never finishes." His soul is wanting in wholehearted enthusiasm, conviction, passion and profound emotion.[7]

There are two definite errors in Belinski's article. He speaks of Don Quixote's display of unusual wisdom in the capacity of a judge, whereas it was Sancho who presided. Furthermore, he writes: "We must admit that the author of the *Tarantas* very wisely and cleverly gave his little Don Quixote a fellow-traveler—not Sancho Panza, but a man who is the very incarnation of common sense, Vasili Ivanovich, a bear-like but none the less respectable Kazan merchant. Ivan Vasilyevich is the unrecognized, self-appointed genius, cherishing reform tendencies for the masses. Vasili Ivanovich represents the people, who with their simple but sound common sense knock the wax wings off the self-appointed genius. The common sense

[6] *Ibid.*, pp. 11-12.   [7] *Ibid.*, p. 14.

of the masses seems despicable to a true genius, and sooner or later the masses succumb to his lofty madness. Nevertheless, they are a whip that whips mercilessly."[8] In this passage, Belinski does not seem to appreciate that Vasili Ivanovich, simply by virtue of being an "incarnation of common sense," is a parallel of the real Sancho.

But one must not be too severe with Belinski. After all, he was primarily reviewing the *Tarantas*, and it is fortunate for Cervantes criticism that in his enthusiasm he digressed from his problem. This digression gave Russia its first critical study of *Don Quixote*, and it is an excellent one at that. Discounting the material irrelevant to the true Don Quixote, Belinski's discussion is sound, and in some ways superior in content and quality to the more famous essay by Turgenev, *Hamlet and Don Quixote*.

[8] *Ibid.*, p. 16.

3 · RADISCHEV
AND ODOYEVSKI

A. N. Radischev (1749-1802), the radical social critic and satirist, is the first Russian author to be definitely influenced by Cervantes. His extensive reading included *Don Quixote*, as is evident from his references to the novel. In his *Life of Ushakov*, for instance, one reads: "It so happened that during our sojourn in Leipzig a major-general was passing through with his wife. They were accompanied by his brother-in-law . . . , a young man fond of harmless jokes and always ready to laugh at the expense of a stupid fellow. He found just such a victim in the person of our *hofmeister*. Taking advantage of the man's passion for bragging, the youth brought him out into the open, as the saying goes. Hitherto we had not been aware of the fact that our hofmeister considered it a compliment to be regarded a knight, and that if he did not have the opportunity of indulging in glorious exploits, he did have a boldness of another type which certainly deserves being included in Don Quixote's adventures."[1]

The arrival of a commanding officer in *A Journey from St. Petersburg to Moscow* reminded Radischev of Don Quixote: "From afar one could hear the cries of the drivers and the trampling of the horses. . . . The speed of the horses and the rotation of the wheels . . . so filled the air with dust that an impenetrable cloud screened His Highness' carriage from the view of those awaiting him. Here, indeed, Don Quixote would have found something extraordinary. The moving cloud of dust . . . suddenly

[1] A. N. Radischev, "Zhitie Ushakova," *Polnoye sobranie sochineni* (Moscow, 1907), I, 119.

stopped, opened, and revealed to us the dust-laden gray figure [of His Highness] resembling a true offspring of a black."[2]

The scene of the wedding feast described in the pseudo-chivalric poem *Bova* contains the following allusion to Cervantes' characters: "And now, from lands far and near, famous knights in full armor flock together. . . . There are knights not inferior to that illustrious Don Quixote. With the shepherd's horn they proclaim, 'Dulcinea of Toboso, the most beautiful maiden in the wide world.' But as you gaze upon this beauty, you behold beneath the powders, rouges and bleach a monkey, a cat or a vacuous Moscovite belle."[3]

Another episode in *A Journey from St. Petersburg to Moscow* reflects Don Quixote's encounter with the galley slaves. A traveler, who is a dreamer fighting for progressive ideas abolished in the reaction under Catherine, meets a group of chained prisoners. Like Don Quixote, he approaches and inquires the reason for their fate.[4] He discovers that they have been taken as slaves into the army by unscrupulous officials. "Free men, innocent of crime, are sold in chains like cattle!" he exclaims. "Oh, laws! Only too often does your wisdom lie merely in the letter! Is this not a flagrant ridicule of law? Nay, more. Is it not a ridicule of the sacred name of liberty?"[5] The hero draws near the prisoners and tells them how to evade such compulsion. The guards quickly descend upon him and drive him away, but the mischief has been done.

It will be recalled that Don Quixote meets some galley slaves as he is traveling and he, too, is struck by the fact that they "van de por fuerza y no de su voluntad."[6] Upon

---

[2] *Ibid.*, I, p. 351.

[3] *Ibid.*, I, pp. 383-405, cf. p. 398.

[4] The resemblance to Don Quixote is so strong that A. Veselovski remarks, "He is Don Quixote all over again." *Etyudy i kharakteristiki* [Etudes and characteristics] (Moscow, 1912), II, 218.

[5] Radischev, *Pol. sob. soch.*, I, p. 344.

[6] Cervantes, *El ingenioso hidalgo Don Quixote de la Mancha* (Madrid, 1922), II, p. 196.

discovering the reason for their plight, he says, "Me parece duro caso hacer esclavos a los que Dios y naturaleza hizo libres." Both protagonists try to free the poor devils, and in both cases officials attempt intervention, but Don Quixote escorts the galley slaves to liberty by his sword, and the Russian hero shows the recruits the way to freedom by his word. The scene, if not the actual form of Radischev's book, which is the same as that of the *Quixote*, was plainly influenced by Cervantes.

A second major literary figure of the period who shows a decided Cervantes influence is Prince Vladimir F. Odoyevski (1803-1869), a man of encyclopedic learning, in whose writings the thinker dominates the artist. A Romantic novelist, he is the author of *Segeliel, the Don Quixote of the Nineteenth Century*.

Odoyevski was well acquainted with Cervantes' *Quixote*, which he considered a model of excellent poetic creation. At the time that he was working on *Segeliel*, he wrote an article on the art of writing novels,[7] in which he says: "A poetic work is a living organism. It comes to the poet unexpectedly. Somnambulistically it haunts him, torments him. . . . When a poet writes, he forgets about himself, he lives in the figures created by him. Even his own thoughts, unnoticed by him, blend with those of the characters he is portraying. . . . A fine example of this is the image of Don Quixote." He discusses an aspect of this work further on in the same article: "Interesting to any reader and powerful in impression are those abstract thoughts which are incorporated in the created figure and represent its characteristics. For example, profound and even abstract ideas are so embodied in Don Quixote that they belong naturally to the character delineated and form an organic part of him. If they were separated from this character they would be dry and inaccessible to the majority of the readers. That is why these thoughts, even the apothegms, are not dull, but comprehensible to

[7] S. F. "Kak pishut u nas romany" [How we write novels in Russia], *Sovremennik* (1836), III, 48-51.

everyone. They penetrate into the soul and produce their impression."[8]

There is an allusion to Cervantes in another work of Odoyevski: "Of course, I am not offended at being compared with Hoffmann. On the contrary, I consider such a comparison a sign of respect, for Hoffmann will always remain, *in his own way*, a genius, like Cervantes and Sterne, and I do not exaggerate if I consider the terms genius [*genialnost*] and creative ability [*izobretatelnost*] synonymous."[9]

Finally, the quotation from the introduction to the *Quixote* which prefaces Odoyevski's *Giordano Bruno* should be cited: "Je puis bien t'avouer, lecteur oisif, que quoique cette histoire m'aît coûté quelque peine à composer, cette préface que tu lis m'en a coûté encore davantage." Odoyevski planned to use this quotation again for the second edition of his works.[10]

Odoyevski was congenial with Cervantes ideologically and artistically. Like Cervantes, he was attracted by the character of a dreamer, a crusader in conflict with society. Like Cervantes, he was interested in representing idealism co-existent with reality. Both authors were masters of satire. In his *Conversation of Two Friends*, Odoyevski says that literature should educate society, and that satire is one of the best mediums. Pursuing this idea, he cites the great social influence of the works of Cervantes, Molière, Swift and other satirists.[11]

Segeliel, the Don Quixote of the Nineteenth Century, Odoyevski's ambitious dramatic poem, was never completed. Most of what was written is fragmentary and remains in "autographs" which were not accessible to the

[8] *Ibid.*, p. 50.

[9] V. F. Odoyevski, *Primechania k Russkim Nocham* [Notes to the Russian Nights] (Moscow, 1913), 14.

[10] P. N. Sakulin, *Iz istorii russkago idealizma, Kn. V. F. Odoyevski, myslitel—pisatel* [From the history of Russian idealism, Prince V. F. O., the thinker and writer] (Moscow, 1913), i, part ii, 7 and 224.

[11] V. F. Odoyevski, "Razgovor dvukh priatelei," *Moskovski Telegraf* (1825), part ii, no. v, supplement, p. 77.

present writer. One portion of the work was printed in
A Miscellany for 1838 but unfortunately that, too, was
unavailable. However, the general ideas and outlines for
parts of the poem, as well as some scattered sections of
it, are found in Sakulin's *An Episode from the History of
Russian Idealism—Prince V. Odoyevski.*[12]

The poem begins with the fall of Lucifer, who is accompanied by the protagonist, Segeliel. Segeliel's hope
for Lucifer's repentance brings about his banishment to
the earth. His pity for mankind and sorrow for Lucifer
make the punishment seem a boon. His debut on earth is
a failure, however, for his advice leads two mortals to
their death in a quagmire. Odoyevski then planned to
have Segeliel undergo a series of metamorphoses—in the
person of Savanarola, Leonardo da Vinci and the like—
and wander upon the earth, but this section was never
written. He did, however, make three sketches of an episode showing Segeliel in contemporary society. One of
them presents the hero at a fashionable ball where, taking advantage of the great assemblage of people, he tries
to influence them and lead them into the path of right-
eousness. But he is misunderstood. Later, the guests discuss his behavior and the consensus of opinion is that he
is "a very stupid fellow," "a pedant," "an intriguer," or, at
best, "an empty dreamer." Another variation of this episode takes place in a garden, where Segeliel urges two
youths to cast off the placidity and indifference that is in-
fecting the new generation. He urges more extensive
learning and greater enthusiasm. Lucifer insinuates himself into the conversation and refutes Segeliel by saying
that learning is nothing, that talent is the all-important
factor. The hero's attempt at enlightenment is again frustrated. In the third variation Segeliel selects business as
the best means of helping humanity. He becomes an ideal
clerk, but in this metamorphosis, too, he is a failure.

"The basic thought of this poem," says a reviewer of

[12] Other information in N. Izmailov, "Pushkin i Knyaz V. F.
Odoyevski," in *Pushkin v mirovoi literature* (Moscow-Leningrad,
1926), 296-301.

the *Miscellany for 1838*, "is to show the social status of an individual filled with love for mankind brought to an extreme. The author wished to combine in one personality all the philanthropic dreams of our age and to contrast them with the real conditions of life. In short, he sought to do for philanthropy, this knighthood of our times, what Cervantes did for knighthood, the philanthropy of his age, representing its noble and comical aspects."[13] Thus, as the reviewer points out, the influence of the *Quixote* lies in the fundamental concept of the work. In its execution other influences took part—Goethe's *Faust*, Milton's *Paradise Lost*, Klopstock's *Messiada*, for example—giving the original theme misleading contours. *Segeliel* might be called "Variations on the Quixote Theme" by a nineteenth century artist, for Segeliel's metamorphoses are nothing more than "variations," and there is a basic similarity between Don Quixote and Odoyevski's hero.

Segeliel is Don Quixote stripped of his seventeenth century Spanish trappings, viewed in a universal sense. Love for humanity characterizes both heroes. Just as Don Quixote goes out into the world to help mankind, so Segeliel comes eagerly to the earth out of pity for mankind, with a desire to alleviate its plight. Their motives are purely altruistic. Both have an ideal for which they sacrifice themselves willingly, and which they do not abandon even in the face of ridicule and abuse. They seize every opportunity, appropriate or not, eloquently to preach their ideal, which in both cases is a concept of good. Segeliel, like Don Quixote, is misunderstood by all and is called a madman. The moral proximity of the two heroes is the result of the fundamental influence of the *Quixote* upon the conception of *Segeliel*.

[13] *Literaturnoye pribavlenie k Rus. Inv. na 1838* [Literary supplement to the Russian inventory for 1838], no. 16, 310-12.

4 · PUSHKIN

A. S. PUSHKIN (1799-1837), the greatest of the Russian Romantic poets, possessed insatiable literary curiosity, artistic sensitivity and receptivity, combined with extraordinary talent and linguistic ability. He knew Latin, Greek, French, English, Italian and Spanish.[1] To discuss even briefly all the authors whom Pushkin read and his reactions to them would be a long study in itself. Some aspects of this subject have been treated by experts in the excellent volume published on the hundredth anniversary of the poet's death.[2] Surprising is the absence of material dealing with Spanish influences on Pushkin, particularly that of Cervantes. In Pushkin's correspondence and literary commentaries there are numerous references to Spanish literature. In his poetry are found Spanish themes, Spanish backgrounds and the influence of Spanish works.

Among the first of the Spanish themes developed by Pushkin was that of Don Juan. On November 4, 1823, he wrote to Count Vyazemski that he was composing a dramatic poem, *Don Juan*.[3] Its sources are uncertain: Molière's *Festin de Pierre* is rejected as a direct source because of the difference in character delineation and the introduction of the scenes between Doña Ana and Doña Laura. Byron's *Don Juan*, so satirical in tone, has little in common with Pushkin's version, which is rather traditional. The libretto of Calzioni's ballet *The Stone Guest*,

---

[1] *Pushkin o literature, podbor tekstov, komentarii i vstupitelnie statyi N. V. Bogoslavskogo* [Pushkin on literature, selection of texts, comments and introductory articles by N. V. B.] (Moscow-Leningrad, 1934), p. 658.

[2] *Révue de Littérature Comparée*, XVII (1937).

[3] A. S. Pushkin, *Pisma* [Letters], (Moscow-Leningrad), I, 58, letter 63.

seen by Pushkin on September 2, 1818,[4] is unknown to the present writer, leaving the problem open. Belinski[5] and Annenkov connect Pushkin's work with Mozart, for like Mozart the poet envisages Don Juan as "a man of great genius who concentrated all his gifts on one thing."[6] The original inspiration may have been derived from Mozart, but, as to the actual composition, one is inclined to agree with Maikov: "The foundation of *The Stone Guest* was the traditional Spanish legend of Don Juan, reworked many times into dramatic form by the Spanish dramatists, and later by Molière. Pushkin was guided by the substance of the legend, not by the dramatic versions of it. He preserved from the legend only the main characters and the situation. The actual development of the drama belongs to our poet. It is, however, permeated with the Spanish spirit and reproduces the national Spanish traits."[7] This contention sounds plausible when Pushkin's habit of going to the source of any theme that he selected is considered, and the fact that the eight years during which Pushkin was working on this dramatic poem correspond to the period of his study of Spanish literature and the language.

Pushkin's translation of Southey's *Roderick, the Last of the Goths* can be included here.[8] As Annenkov and Yakovlev suggest, the poet must have studied the Cid cycle, either in the original or in translation, before un-

---

[4] L. Grossman, *Pushkin v teatralnykh kreslakh, kartiny russkoi stseny, 1817-1820* (Leningrad, 1926), p. 148.

[5] Yu. Veselovski, "Belinski i Pushkin," *Etyudi po russkoi i inostrannoi literature* (Moscow, n.d.), I, 52-93.

[6] P. V. Annenkov, "Materialy dlya biografii Pushkina" [Materials for Pushkin's biography], in *Sochinenia Pushkina* (St. P., 1855), p. 290.

[7] L. N. Maikov, "Razsmotrenie dramy Pushkina so storony eyo istoricheskago kharaktera v otnoshenii khudozhestvennosti" [Examination of Pushkin's drama from the point of view of its historical character and artistry], a posthumous article published in a homage volume *Pamyati L. N. Maikova* (St. P., 1902), pp. li-lv; cf. p. liii.

[8] Zhukovski, who had translated a great deal of Southey, may have interested Pushkin in *Roderick*, for there are earlier references to it in their correspondence.

dertaking his own translation, as a comparative study of the two shows variations.[9]

Other works in which Spain figures either as the theme or background are *The Spanish Romance* (1824), *Before a Noble Spanish Lady* (1830) and *Inesilla! I Am Here* (1830), inspired by Barry Cornwall. In addition to this obvious reflection of Spain in Pushkin's works, there is also evidence of a more subtle penetration by Spain in general and Cervantes in particular into the creative processes of the poet; namely, in his plans for a major work with a Cervantes theme, in the character of Tatyana Larina, the heroine of *Eugene Onegin*, and in the ballad *A Poor Knight* and *Gipsies*.[10]

Artistically and intellectually Pushkin had much in common with Cervantes. He shared Cervantes' love for the indigenous genius of a people, the *pueblo*, as is evident from his frequent selection of legendary and epic themes (e.g. *Rodrigo, Ruslan and Ludmila, The Story of Tsar Sultan*) and in the folkloric richness of his idiom. Pushkin's own critical attitude toward contemporary society and his keen awareness of the value of satire (*Eugene Onegin, The Queen of Spades*) and parody (*The Story of the Village Goryukhino*) made him an understanding reader of Cervantes. Gogol records that Pushkin chided him for his flippant attitude toward Cervantes and Molière, pointed out their great significance as satirists, and urged Gogol to make a thorough study of their works.[11] Pushkin's friend Madame Smirnova also commented on his particular fondness for Cervantes' novel. "Pushkin adored *Don Quixote*, that model of truthfulness . . . ," she writes.[12]

[9] P. V. Annenkov, *op. cit.*, p. 387; N. V. Yakovlev, "Pushkin i Southey," *Pushkin v mirovoi literature* (Moscow, 1929), 145-59.

[10] In a notebook of poems written by the Lycee students, Delvig, Pushkin, Illichevski and Yakovlev, there is one entitled "O Don Kikhote," *Sbornik Pushkinskogo Doma na 1923 god* (Petrograd, 1922), MS in Sobr. 45. As this MS has not been available, it has not been established which of the four is its author.

[11] Annenkov, *op. cit.*, pp. 369-70.

[12] N. P. Dashkevich, "A. S. Pushkin v ryadu poetov novago vremeni" [Pushkin in the ranks of the poets of the new era],

A close acquaintance with Cervantes and his works is revealed in critical comments by Pushkin, most of which are intimately connected with his literary theory. For example, "During the Middle Ages, while in France poetry was still germinating, in Italy and Spain branches of romantic poetry were in full bloom. Italy had the epic; half-African Spain, the tragedy and the novel."[13] Here, according to Pushkin, was born the new poetry in Europe, the source of nineteenth century Romanticism. "Romantic poetry, whose humble progeny we are, flowered luxuriantly and magnificently in all Europe. Italy had its triple poem; Portugal, the *Lusiada*; Spain, Lope de Vega, Calderón and Cervantes; England, Shakespeare; France, Villon. . . ."[14] Understandable, indeed, is his wrath at an article in the *Moscow Telegraph* that included Dante, Ariosto, Cervantes, Calderón and Lope in the ranks of the classical school.[15] Pushkin's admiration for the great forerunners of Romanticism was shared by his contemporaries and friends, W. Kuchelbeker and N. Polevoi.[16]

Turning to Pushkin's creative works, an indirect influence of *Don Quixote* is found in the *Tales of Belkin*. Pushkin disclaims authorship of the *Tales*. He attributes it to a certain fictitious Belkin, just as Cervantes attributed the *Quixote* to Cid Hamed Benengeli. This literary device was transmitted from Cervantes to Pushkin by Sir

---

Sbornik otdelenia russkago yazyka i slovesnosti Imperatorskoi Akademii Nauk, xcii (St. P., 1914), 273.

[13] *Pushkin o literature*, pp. 333 and 428.

[14] Pushkin, *Sochinenia* (St. P., 1855), i, 265. Another interesting remark is his reply to Polevoi's "Don Quixote put an end to knight errants in Europe." He urges Vyazemski to take care of Polevoi who "occasionally falls into inaccuracies!" Pushkin, *Pisma*, i, 132, letter dated May 25, 1825.

[15] *Sochinenia Pushkina, perepiska pod redaktsiei i primechaniami V. I. Saitova* [Pushkin's works, correspondence edited and annotated by V. I. Saitov], ii (St. P., 1908), 18, letter dated March 1827.

[16] W. Kuchelbeker, "O napravleniakh nashei poezii, osobenno liricheskoi v posledneye desyatiletie" [On the tendencies of our poetry, particularly the lyric, in the last decade], *Mnemoza*, part ii, pp. 29-44; N. Polevoi, a review of "Friedrichs von Schiller Sammtliche Werke," *Moskovski Telegraf* (1825), xiv, 289.

Walter Scott (*The Antiquary*)[17] or possibly by Washington Irving (*Knickerbocker's History of New York*).

The theme of an individual maladjusted in civilization seeking refuge in primitive life was very popular with the devotees of Rousseau and Byron. Pushkin developed it in *Gipsies*, a work which contains Cervantian influences complementary to those which are derived from Rousseau and Byron. In his advice to Gogol, Pushkin spoke of the *Novelas ejemplares* in a tone of complete familiarity.[18] His acquaintance with these tales of Cervantes is further suggested by his possession of two editions of the *Novelas* in Spanish, and by his own translation of *Gitanilla*.[19]

Comparative study of Cervantes' *novela* and *Gipsies* reveals the following parallels: Both works deal with a youth of a good family who is so fascinated by a Romany maid that he seeks admission to her band. Like Andrés, Aleko is received by an old male member of the group, who warns him of the difficulties of their mode of life. As in the case of Cervantes' hero, Aleko remains with the gipsies, since his love and passion outweigh reason. Like Andrés, he strives to adjust himself to his new life and to suppress the heritage of civilization.

The extent of Cervantes' influence is limited to this— to the kernel of the story. The development of the plot, the portrayal of the characters, the spirit of the work, and the artistic presentation have nothing further in common with *Gitanilla*.

Kelyin, the Russian Hispanist, also felt the influence of *Gitanilla* on this poem, but he could not establish it, except in the scene where the old gipsy receives Aleko. "The resemblance is so indubitable," he says, "that it strikes one immediately. There [in *Gitanilla*] and here

[17] D. Yakubovich "Predislovie k Povestyam Belkina" [Introduction to the Tales of Belkin], *Pushkin v mirovoi literature*, p. 163. This device was then used by Lermontov in his *Geroi nashego vremeni* [The hero of our times] and by Gogol in his *Vechera na khutore bliz Dikanki* [Evenings on a farm near Dikanka].

[18] V. Annenkov, *op. cit.*, p. 367.

[19] *Pushkin o literature*, p. 658.

[in *Gipsies*] we have an old man, a gipsy, lecturing a 'man of the town.' "[20]

Gipsies furnishes an excellent example of how influences were blended in Pushkin. Here is found, in one incident, a fusion of the influence of Cervantes, Byron and Chateaubriand. The plot of the story, which produces the scene, is derived from Cervantes; the hero has a definite Byronic cast; and, as Lozinski suggests,[21] the scene in its details resembles Chateaubriand's episode between père Soüel and René.

The first work by Pushkin to show the direct influence of *Don Quixote* is the narrative poem *Eugene Onegin*. Briefly, the plot is as follows: Onegin, a St. Petersburg dandy now living in the country, is introduced to the lovely Tatyana Larina, the prospective sister-in-law of his new friend Lenski. The girl promptly falls in love with him, but he rebuffs her, saying that he has no inclination for marriage. Later, out of sheer contrariness, Onegin flirts with Lenski's fiancée. The result of this frivolity is a duel and Lenski's death. Further stay on the estate is impossible, and Onegin goes away. Several years afterwards, Onegin reappears in St. Petersburg and is invited to the home of a friend. His hostess proves to be Tatyana. The situation becomes the more emotional when Onegin realizes that he is madly in love with her. Although Tatyana still loves Onegin she rejects him and remains with her husband.

This story serves as a vehicle for social and literary satire. Pushkin, the founder of the new classical Realism, had little regard for the sentimental novel, still so popular among the upper class. He takes it to task by showing what folly may result from the reading of those absurd, artificial romances.

Tatyana Larina, the charming, sad-eyed heroine, lives in the country where life is so dull that she seeks diver-

[20] F. V. Kelyin, *Nazidatelnia Novelly Servantesa* [Cervantes' exemplary novels], introduction (Moscow-Leningrad, 1943), i, 12.
[21] G. Lozinski "La littérature français et Pouchkine," *Révue de littérature comparée*, xvii (1937), 48-49.

sion in books. The only type of literature found in the Larin library is the sentimental. She tastes it and becomes so intoxicated that all natural pleasures and desires are excluded from her mind. She "falls in love" with the seductive illusions of Richardson, just as Don Quixote does with the equally extravagant absurdities of *Amadís de Gaula*. For her, as for Don Quixote, books create a new world, a new vital reality. As he selects for his pattern the fantastic knight Amadís, so Tatyana chooses the lacrimose Clarissa, Julia and Delphine. Thus Don Quixote becomes a bold knight-errant; Tatyana a melancholy, lovelorn damsel. His life is to be dedicated to knight-errantry; hers to infatuation and the sufferings of unrequited love. She awaits the moment to *aimer éperdument*, and it comes with Onegin's arrival. In this Byronic young man she finds all the exalted qualities of her favorite literary heroes. An aesthetic image adored by her becomes flesh and now she herself can live a life derived from fantasy, literature—a thoroughly quixotic *tour de force*.

Here the critic Pisarev, in his well-known essay "Pushkin and Belinski," draws a clever parallel: "She [Tatyana] imagined that she was in love with Onegin and actually became infatuated with him. She began to burn with passion and commit follies comparable to the somersaulting of the enamored Don Quixote in the Sierra Morena."[22] She declared her love to him, Pisarev continues—most unconventional behavior for a nineteenth century country lady, but quite proper for Delphine or Clarissa and, therefore, for Tatyana. Onegin refused her proposal and delivered a tiresome sermon.

"These flattering and, unfortunately, sincere words of Onegin must have affected Tatyana in the same manner that Don Quixote's victory over the barber and his acqui-

---

[22] D. I. Pisarev, "Pushkin i Belinski," *Sochinenia D. I. Pisareva* (St. P., 1900), v, 1-123; cf. p. 46. Later Flaubert's Madame Bovary goes through a similar emotional cycle. Tatyana's perturbation, however, is restored to equilibrium, while Emma's gets out of hand and shatters her own life and that of those near her.

sition of the brass basin, which he directly renamed 'the Helmet of Mambrino,' affected the unfortunate Don Quixote. Don Quixote's winning of the trophy obviously confirmed him in the sad error that he was a knight-errant, that he really could and must perform great deeds. So Tatyana, having heard all of Onegin's compliments, became even more convinced of the fact that she was in love, that she was suffering, and that she closely resembled the unfortunate heroine of some irritating novel. Every subsequent word of Onegin presented the unfortunate Don Quixote (Tatyana) with new Helmets of Mambrino."[23]

Onegin's rebuff served only to confirm her delusions. With malicious wit Pisarev points out that, according to Tatyana, a heartbroken maiden should pine away and die, but her physical constitution decreed otherwise. Since nature refused to cooperate, she adopted another attitude—that of indifference to the world about her. She permitted herself to be married off. The match was not a bad one by any means. Once married, she played the part of a good wife to the point of exasperation.[24]

"To the very end," concludes Pisarev, "Tatyana remained the very same Knight of the Sad Visage that we saw in her letter to Onegin. Her unwholesomely developed imagination constantly created for her genuine feelings, genuine needs, genuine obligations—a completely sincere program for life. And this artificial program she fulfilled with the same stubbornness that is usually characteristic of persons dominated by some monomania."[25]

Pisarev's observations reveal an obvious similarity in the conduct of the two characters. Tatyana was created according to a formula derived directly from the *Quixote* —fusion of life and literature. However, *Eugene Onegin* is more than the story of a young lady who, like Don Quixote, lived under a misapprehension or lived a myth. It is more than a satire on Russian life. It is, as is the *Quixote*, a parody of the literary genre that directly pre-

[23] *Ibid.*, p. 48.   [24] *Ibid.*, p. 47.   [25] *Ibid.*, p. 46.

ceded it. Just as Cervantes satirized the books of chivalry
with their extravagant heroes, so Pushkin parodied the
sentimental novel with its spineless (and equally extravagant) heroines. In this lies the organic relationship between the two works. In each case, the protagonists of
the earlier genre are transplanted to a later period, subjected to similar maladjustments, and are ultimately
cured of their delusions.

In the model, the treatment of this leit-motif is solid,
grave and dramatic, adorned with bourgeois elegance.
Tatyana lacks Don Quixote's splendor, subtlety and profundity, so pregnant with universal implications. She is
lighter and more romantic, as is her creator and his
period. This is not a deprecation. Pushkin did not strive
here for Cervantian monumentality. He merely developed a suggestion, blended it with other borrowings—
Byronic, for example—and produced something star-
tlingly new, beautiful and perfect; something that is, in
the end, typical of Pushkin, his age and his country.

The ballad *A Poor Knight* is another, different manifestation of Cervantes' influence on Pushkin.[26] It has none
of the light, graceful banter of *Eugene Onegin*. In the
ballad the tone is reverent, devout, and its imagery majestic and powerfully succinct. Much of this spirit is unfortunately lost in the translation below:[27]

> Lived a knight once, poor and simple,
> Pale of face with glance austere,
> Spare of speech, but with a spirit
> Proud, intolerant of fear.
> He had had a wondrous vision:
> Ne'er could feeble human art
> Gauge its deep, mysterious meaning,

[26] Annenkov (*op. cit.*, p. 387) suggests that this poem is a translation of some Spanish *romance* found by Pushkin in his prepara-
tory research for *Rodrigo*. This seems hardly likely, for the poem
antedates *Rodrigo* by three years and directly follows *Eugene
Onegin*. Furthermore, a *romance* that would fit this poem has not
been found.

[27] This version is from Constance Garnett's translation of F.
Dostoyevski's *The Idiot*, New York, 1928, pp. 250-51.

It was graven on his heart.
And since then his soul had quivered
With an all-consuming fire,
Never more he looked on women,
Speech with them did not desire.
But he dropped his scarf thenceforward,
Wore a chaplet in its place,
And no more in sight of any
Raised the visor from his face.
Filled with purest love and fervor,
Faith which his sweet dream did yield,
In his blood he traced the letters
A. M. D. upon his shield.[28]
When the Paladins proclaiming
Ladies' names as true love's sign,
Hurled themselves into the battle
On the plains of Palestine,
Lumen coeli, Sancta Rosa!
Shouted he with flaming glance,
And the fury of his menace
Checked the Mussulman's advance.
Then returning to his castle
In far distant countryside,
Silent, sad, bereft of reason,
In his solitude he died.

The similarity between Pushkin's knight and Don Quixote is patent. Both heroes are poor but proud and fearless knights of a sad or austere countenance. Both are possessed by a vision or idea beyond the ken of the ordinary mind, involving a pure love for an idealized, spiritual lady, as well as a deep love of humanity. The cycle their ideals traverse is the same. Brilliant at first, their vision inflames them, impels them to great and fearless exploits. Then it fades; for Don Quixote it becomes the twilight of sadness and sanity, for the Poor Knight a twilight of sadness and insanity. This moving crepuscule

[28] "N. F. B." (Nastasya Filipovna), used here by Dostoyevski, is replaced by "A. M. D." of the original poem.

is soon resolved in the healing darkness of silence and death.

Pushkin wished to write a poem about a medieval knight, a Crusader. Images from literary reminiscences crowded upon the poet, and again his attention fell upon Don Quixote, but now he saw the character in a new light. He saw him as a knight of great spiritual profundity, an ascetic, a mystic who devoted himself to a life of a high order, who dwelt upon a plane other than our own. It is this figure who hovered over Pushkin as he created his Poor Knight, resulting in an evocation of Don Quixote which was later used significantly by Dostoyevski in *The Idiot*.[29]

A study of the genesis of any one of Pushkin's works reveals an amazing fertility of conception, superb imagination and brilliant ability in execution. A single word uttered by a character can set his genius ablaze, and yield a work completely new, completely foreign to the material that suggested it. In the development of a poem, numerous other literary "suggestions," of which he received many, are synthesized and distilled away.

Pushkin had an idea for a major work based on *Don Quixote*. It enticed him, but he wished to wait until he had leisure to do it justice. This theme he gave to Gogol, who had already won Pushkin's praise. Gogol relates: "But Pushkin made me consider the matter more seriously. For a long time he had been urging me to undertake a long work, and finally, once after I had read to him an excerpt of a small scene, which astounded him more than anything ever read by me, he said, 'How does it happen that with this ability to understand a person, to present him alive with but a few strokes, you do not undertake a long work? It is a sin!' Directly after these words he began to point out to me my weak construction, the faults which might bring my literary life to an early end. As an example, he named Cervantes, who, although he had written several very remarkable and fine *nouvelles*, if he had not written the *Quixote*, would never

[29] Cf. pp. 124 ff.

have reached the place that he now occupies among writers. And in conclusion to all this, he gave me his own subject, out of which he himself had wished to develop something on the order of a poem, and which, according to his own words, he would have given to no one else. This was the subject of *Dead Souls*."[30] This, of course, is Gogol's version, and therefore must be taken with a grain of salt.[31]

Compared to Pushkin, Gogol was a pauper in ideas. He hounded the poet for themes to such an extent that Pushkin remarked, "I have to be more careful with this Little Russian. He is robbing me so mercilessly that I cannot even cry for help!"[32] Actually, Pushkin had no need to fear. Although Gogol might rob him of an original idea, he could never produce anything remotely akin to Pushkin's own work. Gogol's genius was of a different sort.

[30] Annenkov, *op. cit.*, p. 367.

[31] B. Lukyanovski, "Pushkin i Gogol v ikh lichnykh otnosheniakh" [Pushkin and Gogol in their personal relations], *Besedy* (Moscow, 1915), 32-50.

[32] N. Yakovlev, "N. V. Gogol, biograficheski ocherk" [Biographical sketch], *Polnoye sobranie sochineni N. V. Gogolya* (Berlin, 1921), I, 13.

5 · GOGOL

It has never been clearly established that Nicolai Gogol (1809-1852), author of the greatest satire in Russian literature, actually traveled in Spain. According to certain reports, he did speak Spanish and may have visited the country at some time between June and November 1837.[1] If these facts are true, Gogol becomes the first major Russian author to have known Spain at firsthand.

Manifestation of Gogol's interest in Spain is found in a letter to Count A. Tolstoi: "Please let me have the title of the Spanish history that you are reading. I, too, would like to read it. Old Spain, it would seem, could have had everything, and lost it all, but new Spain, in its present state, is well worth examining. It is the beginning of something new. In the *Contemporary* I skimmed through the recently published letters of a Russian, Botkin,[2] who has been to Spain. In many respects they are very interesting, especially those in which he speaks of the freshness of the people's powers and character. . . ."[3] Several days later, referring to Botkin's letters, he says: "I am reading them with great curiosity. Everything in them is interesting, perhaps because the author had undertaken mentally to figure out for himself what comprises the con-

---

[1] A. O. Smirnova, *Zapiski, dnevnik, vospominania, pisma* [Notes, diary, reminiscences, letters] (Moscow, 1929), pp. 312-13; V. I. Shenrok, *Materialy dlya biografii Gogolya* [Materials for Gogol's biography], I (Moscow, 1892), pp. 335-37 and III (Moscow, 1895), pp. 196-98 and 295.

[2] V. P. Botkin, "Pisma ob Ispanii" [Letters about Spain], *Sochinenia* (St. P., 1890), I, pp. 35-283.

[3] *Pisma Gogolya* [Gogol's letters], edited by V. I. Shenrok, IV (St. P., 1896), p. 42, letter to Count A. P. Tolstoi, dated Aug. 8, 1847.

temporary Spaniard, and has approached the question with humility and without prejudice. . . ."[4]

Whether he himself traveled in Spain or not, the influence of Spain and of Cervantes is clearly discernible in Gogol's masterpiece, *Dead Souls*. There is also an echo of Cervantes' *Coloquio de los perros* in his *Notes of a Madman*, in which two dogs, Fidelio and Maggie, converse and correspond. A mad office clerk (who, incidentally, imagines himself to be a non-existent king of Spain, Ferdinand VIII) overhears them gossiping and is startled not only by their talk but by the fact that they write letters to one another. Curiosity possesses him and here, like Cervantes' ensign Campuzano, he steps out of the role of an observer and becomes a participant in the weird situation. He seeks, finds and steals the dogs' letters and reads them. (You will recall that Campuzano eavesdropped.) The content of the Fidelio-Maggie notes is critical, dealing with the social life of the human beings about them. The similarity of this to the theme of Cipion and Berganza's conversation is apparent. In both works, Cervantes' and Gogol's, the heroes' strange adventure into the canine world is made comprehensible to the reader by the authors' indication of the heroes' psychological abnormality at the time. Although the device of endowing animals with human speech has a long literary and popular tradition, here, in Gogol's *Notes*, certain obvious details point to the fact that it was inspired by Cervantes, either directly or indirectly transmitted from Cervantes to Gogol by Hoffmann or Tieck.[5]

The influence of Cervantes on *Dead Souls* is far stronger. The background of the conception of this novel

[4] *Ibid.*, p. 43, letter to P. V. Annenkov, dated Aug. 12, 1847.
[5] F. V. Kelyin (*Nazidatelnia Novelly Servantesa*, pp. 12 and 13) likewise notes the use of this Cervantian device, but he only mentions it in a footnote, whereas in the text he dwells on a fantastic parallelism that he believes to exist between Gogol's madman and the Licenciado vidriera. Toying with the fact that both protagonists are mad and that there is a Spanish element in the Russian's mania, he senses a parallel (which after thorough study remains difficult to grasp) that he attributes to literary reminiscences.

is very interesting. The young writer Gogol left his home town in the South to go to St. Petersburg in quest of success and fame, but there he met with a series of disappointments. His *Hans Küchelgarten* failed to win for him any poet's laurels. His high-pitched voice disqualified him for the stage. His lack of proper connections shut him off from the great figures of the day. Nevertheless, after much frustration, Gogol gained admittance into the society of the *literati*, where he met the poet Pushkin, Zhukovski, the author of the second important Russian translation of the *Quixote*, the Hispanophile Sobolevski and the composer Glinka.

This group often gathered in the salon of Madame Smirnova and there read manuscripts of works in progress, discussed and criticized them. At these gatherings Gogol read some of his short works, which impressed Pushkin very much. The poet saw in Gogol's peculiar talent, outlook and spirit a potential affinity to Cervantes. As has been mentioned earlier,[6] Pushkin one evening directed Gogol's attention to Cervantes, and gave him a theme which the poet had considered developing himself. Madame Smirnova records the incident as follows: "Pushkin spent four hours with Gogol and gave him a theme for a novel, which like *Don Quixote* is to be divided into episodes. The hero will travel through the provinces. Here Gogol will make use of his own traveling experiences."[7]

Gogol's response to this suggestion was as enthusiastic as it was imaginative. Before long, he had grandiose plans for a trilogy which was to embody a sweeping panorama of human depravity, purification and final salvation. The original aesthetic concept was engendered under the inspiration of Dante and Cervantes, the former suggesting the tripartite arrangement of the material, the latter influencing the basic pattern and the character of the hero of the first part, *Dead Souls*.

Gogol began his work on the book with the comment,

[6] Cf. pp. 45-46.
[7] Shenrok, *Pisma Gogolya*, III, 72.

"In this novel I would like to show Russia, be it only from one approach."[8] He intended "to portray in a comic manner the abuses and the roguery of provincial official life and the crudeness of the landowners' customs and manners, just as the external aim of Cervantes was to ridicule knight-errantry."[9] This literary aim found very satisfactory expression in an episodic plot of the type used in *Don Quixote* and in a satirical tone akin to that of the model. Like Cervantes, Gogol sent his hero out to travel and presented his experiences in episodic form. It is from these episodes that the reader derives a clear picture of the protagonist's ambitions and character. As for a satirical depiction of society, Gogol exploited Cervantes' scheme to the utmost.

The plot of *Dead Souls* concerns Chichikov, a clever swindler with a very checkered past, traveling through Russia for the purpose of acquiring a fortune. The scheme that he has devised entails the purchase of dead serfs (termed in Russian "souls") who, although they have died, have not been stricken from the census rolls. These he plans to mortgage and thereby build up the wealth and prestige he covets. With this in mind, Chichikov arrives in a small town. Posing as a man of importance, he calls on all the local dignitaries and so charms them with his *savoir-faire* that he soon becomes a social lion. Under the cover of this excitement, he lays his schemes, becomes familiar with the district and shops for dead souls with reasonable success. All goes well until the rascally Nozdrev and the gossip Korobochka start rumors that magnify and multiply until the swindler is undone.

Chichikov reveals Cervantes' influence in two ways: in his aesthetic function and in his personality. His role as the unifying and motivating element of the novel obviously comes from Don Quixote's, and his character is an

---

[8] *Sochinenia N. V. Gogolya*, edited by V. V. Kallash, IX (St. P., n.d.), 80-81.

[9] N. I. Danilevski, *Rossia i Yevropa, vzglyad na kulturnia i politicheskia otnoshenia* [Russia and Europe, a glance at their cultural and political relations], (St. P., 1895), p. 549.

accurate inversion of that of the hidalgo. Just as Don Quixote is completely good, so Chichikov is completely bad. Here lies the fundamental inversion, and from it, logically and naturally, are derived all his other qualities, which are true negatives of the positive.

This inversion is indicated in Chichikov's external appearance. Don Quixote, the elderly, odd-looking, poorly attired gentleman, emerges in Chichikov as an unremarkable young man, dressed according to the latest and most expensive fashion. Furthermore, Don Quixote's *hidalguía* suggests the knight's good heredity, in contrast to Chichikov's obscure antecedents. His formal education served only to develop an innate unscrupulousness and cold connivance for the purpose of achieving his desired ends. With years, the guiding ideal of Chichikov becomes the victimizing of society for his own benefit, instead of Don Quixote's ideal of liberation of humanity from injustice.

Love, Don Quixote's most powerful motivation, is unknown to Chichikov. Self-love such as his cannot even be considered a phase of the same emotion. To Ivan Pavlovich Chichikov humanity is not to be loved, but to be exploited. Women? They are a means to an end. If he were to marry, it would be for his own comfort and satisfaction, for the "little Chichikovs" who would represent his realization of the universal urge for immortality. This primitive manifestation of the longing finds its perfect antithesis in Don Quixote's bid for immortality through heroic fame and glory.

Chichikov's moral depravity stands as a direct contrast to Don Quixote's spiritual perfection. Behind Chichikov's mask of hypocritical respectability lie craftiness, treachery and dishonesty. All these qualities are directed to his own betterment. He assiduously courts his employer's daughter, not for love, but for a promotion in the office. He is an irreproachable customs inspector, but only in order to win an important post and confidence and thus reap a really profitable crop of bribes. Passing from one intrigue to another, our hero mounts the road of success, until he is unexpectedly faced with exposure. True to type, he takes refuge in flight. Even here, the original antithesis is sustained: Chichikov's cowardice is an inversion of Don Quixote's bravery.

The only character traits of Don Quixote that Gogol retains in their original form are the knight-errant's strength of will and perseverance. These qualities both heroes possess in abundance and, by virtue of them, pursue their self-imposed missions, undaunted by failure, privation or fatigue—one rising to sublime heights of beauty, the other sinking to the lowest depths of spiritual ugliness, both evoking the same reaction in the onlooker, regret. "If only such will and perseverance were used for a good cause!" exclaims Murazov of Chichikov. "If only all of these fine, lofty, noble qualities had been used opportunely . . . !" comments Belinski on Don Quixote.[10]

Although Cervantes centers his book on Don Quixote and Sancho, the scope of the novel includes infinitely more. It presents a faithful picture of contemporary Spanish life and reveals its weaknesses. In this application of literary art, Gogol, the gifted satirist, was very much at home. Like Cervantes, he points out the roguery of the official classes, who obtain and keep their positions by underhanded methods. He also criticizes the pastimes of the upper class. His heated conversation between two "very delightful ladies" poses the same question as Cervantes' picture of life in the duchal palace: Have these people nothing better to do? Social criticism may have been unconscious in Cervantes; in Gogol it is deliberate.

Pertinent here is an excerpt from the critic Danilevski: "In both artists the depth of their poetic conceptions extended beyond their initial intent. Most probably the authors did not realize how far they were carried away. Don Quixote turned out to be a living impersonation—rising to heroism—of the noblest spiritual qualities, for which a field for productive normal activity was lacking because of the emptiness of Spanish life. Only a century previ-

[10] V. Belinski, Review of *Tarantas*, p. 11.

ously, Spanish heroism had been displayed in the brilliant activity of the *conquistadores*, but in Cervantes' time a Spanish hero had no practical outlet. The realm of fantasy alone remained for him. Chichikov is a hero in his own right. He is a hero of practical life—clever, firm, evasive, undespairing. He is a Ulysses deprived, on the one hand, of all idealism in his efforts—and, indeed, whence would this idealism come in a life which has renounced native fundamentals and has not as yet assimilated the foreign ones (since the latter is impossible)?— on the other hand, unable to direct his activity towards something that is really practical and beneficial. This inability proceeds from the barrenness of Russian life, from its narrowness, and its lack of freedom. Persons with a practical type of mind had to resort to ambitions that were purely personal, crudely egoistic, to the trickery of roguery, and to precisely that roguery connected with governmental offices which penetrated all of Russian life."[11]

A. Veselovski also saw the bond between *Dead Souls* and *Don Quixote*. In his book *The Western Influence in Russian Literature*, he writes: "The original concept of *Dead Souls* is based on the model of *Don Quixote*, the plot of which skillfully and with sad irony Gogol parodied in such a way that, instead of eternal pursuit after ideals of knighthood and virtue, there was the same ever-active pursuit directed towards profit, deception and exploitation."[12] He draws attention to another similarity. In both books the heroes travel along a lonely road running through the more deserted plains of the country. But, in contrast to Don Quixote's Sancho, "in whom the common sense of the people and sobriety of judgment gleams through uncouthness, we had the utterly down-trodden squires Petrushka and Selifan, whose minds and sense

[11] Danilevski, *Rossia i Yevropa*, p. 549.
[12] A. N. Veselovski, *Zapadnoye vlianie v novoi russkoi literature* [Western influence on new Russian literature] (Moscow, 1916), p. 192.

have been atrophied by serfdom."[13] This is hardly a parallel, however, for the role that Petrushka and his companion play in *Dead Souls* is insignificant, whereas Sancho is his master's counterpart.

Veselovski makes still another suggestion about Cervantian influence on *Dead Souls*. He speculates on the change in Cervantes' attitude towards his hero in the second part of the novel. He thinks that Cervantes is kinder to the hidalgo in the second part, and even surrounds him with something like a halo of Christianity. Turning to *Dead Souls*, Veselovski says, "Although the second and third parts of Gogol's 'poem' do not exist, in Gogol's mind, if not in Pushkin's, there must have been a feeling that redemption should take place in subsequent parts."[14] In this intention, the critic maintains, lies an influence of the *Quixote*. It is true that Gogol had thought of redemption but, as has already been indicated, that conception came to him through Dante.

In the last third of the book Gogol makes an interesting allusion to *Don Quixote*. Referring to a new phenomenon appearing in Russia, Konstanzhoglo says: ". . . but now there has appeared in the Russian character a Don Quixotism which has never been there before! Enlightenment will occur to him (some Russian) and he will become a Don Quixote. He will establish such schools as would never occur even to a fool! From this school will come a person good for nothing, neither for the village nor for the town. . . . He will go in for philanthropy. He will become a Don Quixote, a lover of humanity. He will build a million useless hospitals and edifices with columns. He will ruin himself and then fling it all to the winds. Here you have philanthropy!"[15]

This rather tongue-in-cheek analysis of "Don Quixotism" is but one more indication of Gogol's sustained

[13] A. N. Veselovski, "Pamyati Gogolya" [In memory of Gogol], a speech delivered at the Moscow University, on Feb. 21, 1902, *Etyudy i kharakteristiki* (Moscow, 1912), п, 201-46.

[14] *Ibid.*, p. 239.

[15] N. V. Gogol, "Mertvie Dushi" (Dead Souls), *Izbrannie proizvedeniya*, "OGIZ" publications, 1946, p. 466.

awareness of Cervantes and his hero. Gogol had a variant of this passage which usually appears in the Russian texts. "There again you have a smart one. What do you think he has cooked up? Almshouses, brick buildings for the village! An enterprise of Christian charity! If you wish to help, then help every peasant fulfill his duty, and do not tear him away from his Christian duty. Help a son shelter his ailing father and do not give him the opportunity of shirking the responsibility. Give him the chance to shelter his neighbor and his brother. Give him money to do it, help him as much as you can, do not put him off or he will cast off all Christian obligations. There are Don Quixotes all over the place. Every man in the almshouses costs two hundred roubles a year! Why, on this money I could support ten men in the village." Skudronzhoglo (Konstanzhoglo's name in the variant) got into a temper and spat. . . . "And here is another Don Quixote of enlightenment. He has founded schools! Well, what, for example, can be more useful to a man than to know how to read or write? But how did he arrange it? I have peasants coming from his village, 'What's all this, sir?' they ask. 'Our sons are completely out of hand, they will not help us. They all want to be clerks. . . . ' "[16]

[16] *Ibid.*, p. 467.

PART II

THE AGE OF REALISM

1850-1880

THE coming of the great age of Realism in Russian literature reveals an increased interest in Spain and a wider diffusion of Cervantes' works. There are important new translations of the *Quixote*—some complete, others abbreviated versions for children—as well as translations of some of the *novelas* and *entremeses*. Comments on and allusions to Cervantes and his works are much more abundant than they were in the preceding period. Cervantes criticism, also more extensive, is approached from the Romantic, historico-sociological and scholarly points of view. Furthermore, such major literary figures as Turgenev, Dostoyevski and Ostrovski show the influence of the *Quixote* in some of their own work.

Spain attracted many more travelers from Russia during this period. Some recorded their impressions of the country in travelogue form; others expounded the turbulent Spanish political and social situation. Vasili P. Botkin's *Letters on Spain*[1] is the most important travel account. It is a thorough, comprehensive work, revealing genuine interest in everything Spanish, combined with a marvelous ability to convey images and sensations to the reader. Though the visit recorded was brief, it was rich in impressions, for it was made after Botkin had spent a long time in serious preparative study of the Spanish language, Spanish literature, history, politics, economics and art. His tour—from Irún, through Madrid, Córdova, Seville, Cádiz, Gibraltar, Málaga and Granada—provides the framework for the more valuable portion of his work

---

[1] V. P. Botkin, "Pisma ob Ispanii" [Letters about Spain], *Sochinenia* (St. P., 1890), I, 35-283. Trip was made in 1840. An earlier edition of these letters appeared in St. P., 1857.

—his astute and sensitive commentaries on Spanish political, religious and economic conditions.

Besides Botkin, mention should be made of the superficial but entertaining travelogue by D. Grigorovich (1822-1899),[2] K. A. Skalkovski's comments on diverse aspects of Spanish life,[3] and the travel impressions of Count E. Salias de Tournemir (1840-1903),[4] perhaps the most captivating account of all. Young Salias was endowed with a winning personality, a good command of Spanish, curiosity, a sense of humor and a spirit of adventure—not to mention a versatile pen. His descriptions form a charming gallery of pictures, bright and alluring in their simplicity and vivacity, set into frames of history, romance, folklore and personal experiences. Artistic appreciation and an unbridled spirit of youth pervade the whole of Salias' account, as well as the entertaining short stories that are based upon his experiences in Spain.

The treatise *Christianity in Spain during the Moslem Domination*[5] and the articles "Father Merino: An Attempt on the Life of the Spanish Queen in 1852"[6] and "Mozarabic Rituals in Toledo"[7] were the fruits of K. Kustodiev's visit to Spain. A priest, he was primarily interested in the religious aspect of the country, but he re-

[2] D. Grigorovich, "Ugolok Andaluzii, iz putevykh zametok" [A corner of Andalusia, from travel notes], *Vremya* (1861), v, 364-434.

[3] K. A. Skalkovski, *Mesyats za Pireneami, putevia vpechatlenia v Ispanii, Yegipte, Aravii, i Indii, 1869-1872* [A month beyond the Pyrenees, travel impression of Spain, Egypt, Arabia and India, 1869-1872] (St. P., 1873).

[4] E. A. Salias, "Ispania, putevia ocherki" [Spain, traveling sketches], *Russki Vestnik* (1874), iv, 735-90, vi, 756-86; ix, 45-77. Salias, using the pseudonym "Vadim," published other installments of this series of articles much earlier in the newspaper *Golos*. His short works *Los novios, Una niña, Las Españas* and *Andaluzskia legendy* [Andalusian legends] also contain many of his travel impressions.

[5] K. Kustodiev, *Khristianstvo v Ispanii pod vladych. musulman, istorich. ocherk* (Moscow, 1867).

[6] Kustodiev, "Svyaschennik Merino, pokushenie n zhizn ispanskoi korolevy v 1852," *Russki Vestnik* (1866), lxii, no. 3, 142-71.

[7] Kustodiev, "Muzarabskoye bogosluzhenie v Toledo," *Pravoslavnoye Obozrenie* (1870), no. 8, 211-33; and no. 9, 352-70.

ported on contemporary events in a short article, "Badajoz, Notes about Spain."[8]

In 1867 a six-page article entitled "Sketches of Spain"[9] by an anonymous traveler appeared in *Notes for Reading*.

The writer P. D. Boborykin spent some time in Spain during the period of political unrest, 1867-1873, and wrote two articles of a journalistic nature explaining the situation to his compatriots. One was headed "Before a New Storm: Letters from Madrid,"[10] and the other, "Intellectual Currents of Spain."[11] A series of letters written by another anonymous Russian traveler during 1872-1873[12] belongs to the same category, as does the colorful reporting by G. Vyrubov for the *St. Petersburg Journal.*[13]

In 1876 the illustrated *Library of Travels: Spain and Its Wealth and Poverty. South American Pampas* was published.[14] Although a thousand copies were printed, not a single one was available to the present writer. The same was the case with P. de Chigachev's account of Spain[15] and A. I. Voekov's *Sketches from a Trip Through Spain.*[16]

[8] Kustodiev, "Badakhos, iz zametok ob Ispanii," *Pravoslavnoye Obozrenie* (1867), XXIII, no. 6, 194-210.

[9] "Ocherki Ispanii" in *Zapiski dlya chtenia* (1867), nos. 2-3, 42-48.

[10] P. D. Boborykin "Pered novoi burei, pisma iz Madrida," *Sanktpeterburgskia Vedomosti* (1869), nos. 203 and 231.

[11] Boborykin, "Umstvennoye dvizhenie Ispanii," *Sbornik Nedelya* (1872), 53-74.

[12] "Pisma ob Ispanii" [Letters about Spain], *Otech. Zapiski* (1872), vol. 204, no. 9, pp. 209-34; vol. 205, no. 11, pp. 145-72; vol. 205, no. 2, pp. 506-20; vol. 208, no. 6, pp. 355-68.

[13] G. Vyrubov, "Neskolko dnei na teatre ispanskoi mezhdunarodnoi voiny [Several days on the scene of the Spanish Civil War], *St. P. Vedomosti* (1874), nos. 257, 258, 272 and 273.

[14] *Biblioteka puteshestvi, Ispania, yeya roskosh i nischeta. Pampasy Yuzhnoi Ameriki* (St. P., 1876), cited by V. I. Mezhkov, *Russkaya Istoricheskaya biblioteka za 1865-1867 goda,* VI (St. P., 1886), 343.

[15] Arturo Farinelli, *Viajes por España y Portugal, desde la edad media hasta el siglo XX, divagaciones bibliográficas* (Madrid, 1920), p. 432.

[16] R. Foulché-Delbosc, *Bibliographie des voyages en Espagne et en Portugal* (Paris, 1896), I, no. 644. Mention should be made

There were many other distinguished Russian travelers who left no record of their journeys in Spain; for example, Prince A. Mescherski,[17] V. V. Stasov,[18] the famous art critic and defender of the "new school" of Russian music, and Anton Rubinstein,[19] who gave several concerts in Spain.

Diplomatic relations, established during the previous century, continued, and occasionally reports of these embassies were published for the public.[20]

All such reports and travel accounts helped, of course, to acquaint Russians with Spain and roused in them a keener interest in the country. They discarded French intermediaries, and turned to study and observe the land of Don Quixote directly, producing a more extensive and varied literature dealing with Spain. The most popular subjects were current events—domestic[21] and colonial[22]—and prominent figures of the day—General

here also of the translation of George Borro's travelogue, "Putevia zapiski Borro, angliiskago missionera v Ispanii," *Biblioteka dlya Chtenia* (1858), I, 11-194.

[17] Farinelli, *op. cit.*, p. 409.

[18] F. Chaliapine, *Pages from My Life: An Autobiography*, trans. by H. M. Buck, revised, enlarged and edited by Katherine Wright (New York-London, 1927), p. 208.

[19] Catherine D. Bowen, *"Free Artist": The Story of Anton and Nicholas Rubinstein* (New York, 1939).

[20] "Posolsvo Kn. Dolgorukova i Myschetskago vo Frantsiyu i Ispaniyu v 1867," *Semeinie Vechera, Starshi vozrast* (1868), no. 5, 272-90.

[21] "Kratki ocherk noveishei istorii Ispanii" [A brief survey of the recent history of Spain], in the monthly supplement to *Birzh. Vedomosti* (1866), nos. 7-8, pp. 1-19; Viktor Lussien, "Ispania v 1868 godu" [Spain in 1868], *Syn Otechestva* (1868), no. 251; I. T., "Ispania nakanune perevorota" [Spain on the eve of an upheaval], *Voyenny Sbornik* (1868), LXXIV, no. 12, pp. 285-318; L. Polonski, "Politicheskia partii v Ispanii i novoye korolevstvo" [Political parties in Spain and the new reign], *Vestnik Yevropy* (1871), VI, no. 11, pp. 423-49; A. Trachevski, *Ispania XIX veka* [Spain of the XIX century], I (Moscow, 1872); S. S. Shashkov, "Sudby Ispanii" [Spanish destinies], *Delo*, VII, 63-95.

[22] "Ostrov Kuba" [Cuba], *Syn Otech.* (1869), no 31; "Prazdnik negrov v Gavane" [Negro holiday in Havana], *Illyustrirovannaya Gazeta* (1869), no. 10; "Provozglashenie republiki sredi tsvetnogo naselenia ostrova Kuby" [Announcement of the Republic], *Vsemir. Illyustr.* (1869), no. 39; "Epizod iz istorii vozstania na ostrove

Prim,[23] Ferdinand VII,[24] Don Carlos,[25] Isabel II,[26] Amadeo,[27] Castelar,[28] Alfonso XII,[29] and others.[30] There were also books and articles dealing with well known Spaniards of the past, such as Philip II,[31] Loyola,[32] Murillo,[33]

Kube" [Episode in the history of the Cuban uprising], *Vsemir. Illyustr.* (1869), no. 42; "Vostanie na ostrove Kube" [An uprising in Cuba], *ibid.* (1871), no. 156.

[23] "General Prim," *Illyustr. Gazeta* (1866), vol. 17, no. 10, p. 149; vol. 27, no. 3, pp. 46-47; "Don Juan Prim," *Vsemir. Illyustr.* (1871), no. 5, p. 27.

[24] I. G. Golovin, "Istoria Ferdinanda VII, korolya ispanskago" [History of Ferdinand, the Spanish king], *Blagonamerenny* (Leipzig, 1859), no. 4, pp. viii and 1-103.

[25] "Don Karlos Burbonski," *Illyustr. Gaz.* (1869), XXIII, no. 4, p. 55 and XXIV, no. 37, p. 184; *Vsemir. Illyustr.* (1869), no. 37 and (1872), no. 176; "Cherty iz zhizni Don Karlosa" [Aspects of Don Carlos' life], *Zhivopisny Sbornik* (1869), VI, no. 8, pp. 241-51; "Begstvo dona Karlosa iz Ispanii" [Don Carlos' flight from Spain], *Birzh. Ved.* (1876), no. 59; "Don Karlos i grazhdanskaya voina v Ispanii" [Don Carlos and the Civil War in Spain] *Delo* (1876), no. 3, pp. 429-50, and no. 5, pp. 77-104; S. Gavrilov, "Tainy Ispanii, Don Karlos po noveishim izsledovaniam" [The secrets of Spain. Don Carlos in the light of recent investigation], *Mosk. Birzh. Gaz.* (1872), nos. 32 and 33; "Ugolovny protsess i kazn Don Karlosa, infanta ispanskago" [The trial and execution of Don Carlos, Spanish Infante], *Birzh. Ved.* (1869), nos. 349 and 351.

[26] "Isabella II," *Illyustr. Gaz.* (1869), XXIII, no. 6, p. 91.

[27] "Ferdinand Maria Amadei, korol ispanski," *Vsemir. Illyustr.* (1870), IV, p. 842; "Amadei I, korol ispanski," *Illyustr. Gaz.* (1871), XXVII, no. 2, pp. 28-30.

[28] "Emilio Castelar," *Illyustr. Nedelya* (1873), no. 47, p. 743; *Illyustr. Gaz.* (1869), XXIII, no. 7, p. 104.

[29] "Don Alfons," *Illyustr. Nedelya* (1875), no. 10, p. 148; *Vsemir. Illyustr.* (1875), XIII, p. 50.

[30] "General Koncha," *Vsemir. Illyustr.* (1874), XI, no. 282, p. 346; *Illyustr. Nedelya* (1874), no. 34, pp. 529-30. "Gonzalez Bravo," *Illyustr. Gaz.* (1868), XXII, no. 37, p. 188. "Marshal Pavia," *Vsemir. Illyustr.* (1869), I, no. 4, p. 59. "Marshal Serrano," *Vsemir. Illyustr.* (1869), II, no. 29, pp. 44-46; *Illyustr. Nedelya* (1874), no. 35, pp. 547-48. "Admiral Topete," *Illyustr. Gaz.* (1868), XXII, no. 47, p. 347; *Vsemir. Illyustr.* (1869), I, no. 4.

[31] M. N. Petrov, *Ocherki iz vseobschei istorii* [Sketches from world history] (Kharkov, 1868), chapter X is devoted to Philip II; and there were translations made of Prescott's *History of the Reign of Philip II* (St. P., 1868) and *The Conquest of Mexico* (St. P., 1885).

[32] S. Sobolevski, "Ignati Loyola," *Semeinie Vechera*, 1869, no. 9.

[33] "Murilio," *Zhivopisnoye Obozrenie* (1875), no. 48.

Ribera,[34] Fortuny,[35] and Jordan.[36] Some of the works on earlier periods include *The Spanish Inquisition*,[37] *Spain a Century Ago and Today*,[38] *The Former Spanish Court and the Grandees*,[39] *Discoveries in Spanish History*.[40] A. S. Khomyakov's *Notes on World History*[41] contains many interesting pages dealing with the West Goths in Spain, Moslem domination of the peninsula, Spanish colonization in America, the split between the Eastern and the Western Churches and the role of Spain in this issue. In his discussion of this rupture, the reader is made aware of Khomyakov's Slavophil animosity towards Catholicism. There were also numerous works about other aspects of Spain, e.g. *An Ethnographical Study of the Spanish Basques*,[42] *The Slavs in Andalusia*,[43] *The Fashions of the Period of Philip the Beautiful*.[44] In a separate category are studies of a religious nature, such as *Early Teachers of Christianity in Spain*,[45] *Freedom of Worship*

[34] "Ribera," *Vsemir. Illyustr.* (1875), XIII, 310.

[35] "Mariano Fortuni," *Pchela*, 1875, no. 4, p. 55.

[36] "Khordan," *Illyustr. Gaz.* (1865), XV, no. 6, p. 91.

[37] "Epizod iz istorii inkvizitsii," monthly supplement to *Birgh. Ved.* (1866), nos. 7-8, pp. 18-26; M. N. Granovski, *Sochinenia* (Moscow, 1866), has a discussion of the Inquisition in the Supplement.

[38] "Ispania sto let nazad i teper" [Spain a century ago and today], *Birzh. Ved.* (1875), no. 293.

[39] "Byvshi ispanski dvor i grandi" [Former Spanish court and the grandees], *Birzh. Ved.* (1869), no. 164.

[40] V. Bilbasov, "Otkrytia v ispanskoi istorii" [Discoveries in Spanish history], *Zarya* (1869), no. 12, pp. 45-117.

[41] A. S. Khomyakov, *Polnoye sobranie sochineni* (Moscow, 1904), III.

[42] Tishanski, "Ispanskie baski: etnograficheski ocherk" [Spanish Basques, ethnographic sketch], *Russki Mir.* (1875), nos. 121, 122 and 124.

[43] K. Shainokh, "Slavyane v Andaluzii," translated from the Polish by B. Shostakovich, Moscow, 1874; excerpts in *Vsemir. Trud* (1868), VI, no. 11, pp. 168-91.

[44] "Ustav o modakh v tsarstvovanie Filippa Krasivago," *Vaza*, 1875, no. 21, pp. 246-48.

[45] Arkhimandrit Arseny, "Drevneishie propovedniki Khristianstva v Ispanii," *Strannik* (1876), IV, pp. 21-41.

in Contemporary Spain,[46] *Protestantism in Spain,*[47] and the works of Father Kustodiev.[48] These all were original works by Russian authors, it must be remembered, as distinct from the translations of works on Spanish subjects of the preceding period.

This information was supplemented by new material on Spain written in Spanish, French and German, and accessible in Russian libraries.[49] A glance at a page of a library catalogue reveals titles like the *Memorial histórico español* (Madrid, 1851), Castro's *Exámen filosófico sobre las principales causas de la decadencia de España* (Cadiz, 1852) and the *Crónica de San Juan de la Peña* (Zaragoza, 1876).[50] The Imperial Library contained valuable Spanish manuscripts dealing with Spanish history which were not even possessed by Spain.[51]

Comments on Spain, its celebrities and its problems appear in the private correspondence and writings of many literary figures—for example, in those of Grigoryev,[52] Herzen,[53] and Dostoyevski.[54]

[46] P. A. Adoratski, "Istoricheski ocherk voprosa o svobode veroispovedanni v sovremennoi Ispanii," *Pravoslavny Sobesednik* (1876), no. 6, pp. 181-215 and no. 7, pp. 264-70.

[47] A. Sudakov, "Valdensy i protestanstvo v Ispanii," *Tserkovnaya Letopis Dukhovnoi Besedy* (1874), no. 36, pp. 166-70, no. 37, pp. 184-92 and no. 38, pp. 204-8.

[48] Cf. p. 58.

[49] *Katalog biblioteki Imperatorskago Novorossiiskago Universiteta* (Odessa, 1878-1884), i, 892-93, nos. 1-40.

[50] *Ibid.*, nos. 26, 30 and 34.

[51] Juan Valera, *Correspondencia* (Madrid, 1913), ii, pp. 287-89.

[52] V. Sadovnik, "A. A. Grigoryev, biograficheski ocherk" [A. A. Grigoryev, a biographical sketch], *Sobranie sochineni A. Grigoryeva*, i (Moscow, 1915), p. xxiv; A. Grigoryev, "Poezia Nekrasova" [Nekrasov's poetry], *Sob. soch. A. G.-va*, no. ii, issue 13 (Moscow, 1915), p. 34; A. Grigoryev, *Materialy dlya biografii* [Material for a biography] (St. P., 1917), pp. 175, 207 and 211. Murillo is the subject of these allusions.

[53] A. Herzen, *Polnoye Sobranie sochineni i pisem* [Complete works and letters] in 22 volumes, edited by M. K. Lemke, Petrograd, 1919, xii, p. 112 (Abencerraje); xiv, 332 (Aguado); v, 491-99, 548, vii, p. 382, vii, 40, x, 66, xiii, 456, xv, 273 and 293, xvi, 179, xviii, 134, xx, 69 (Donoso Cortés, comments not very favorable); ix, 20-22 (Herzen saw the canvases of Velásquez and Murillo in London and wrote an enthusiastic letter on the subject to

Some outstanding examples of Spanish art found their way into Russia. Juan Valera wrote to Leopoldo de Cueto on January 3, 1857: "Neither in the Louvre, nor in the Dresden Gallery, nor anywhere else outside of Spain is the Spanish school as well represented as it is here [in the Hermitage]. Of the Murillos alone there are twenty-two. . . . Of Alonso Cano the best is a *Virgin* with the Christ Child in her arms. Of Morales there is a *Mater Dolorosa*. . . ." He then enumerates the canvases by Antolínez, Ribera and Velásquez, and ends by saying, "There are also, in that room, pictures by Coello, Juan de Juanes, Baltasar del Prado, Ribalta, Castillo, Zurbarán, Carreño and I do not remember how many others."[55]

At this time Spanish literature took its place in the university curricula. Several Russian professors[56] introduced courses on European literature, including the Spanish. Evidently to supplement such study, translations of M. Carrière's *Art in Connection with the Development of Human Culture and Ideals*[57] and Ticknor's *History of Spanish Literature*[58] were made. Available also were

Ogarev, Sept. 4, 1857); i, 100; xiv, 527 and 685; xvii, 23; xxi, 321; xiv, 24.

[54] F. M. Dostoyevski, *Polnoye sobranie sochineni F. M. Dostoyevskago* [Complete works] (St. P., 1895), ix, 359, 365, 367, 391 and 443 feature Spain and Castelar.

[55] Juan Valera, *op. cit.*, pp. 284-85.

[56] A. N. Veselovski (1836-1906), professor of the University of St. Petersburg, A. I. Kirpichnikov (1845-1903), of the University of Kharkov and later of Kiev, and N. I. Storozhenko (1836-1909), of the University of Moscow, were the prominent pioneers.

[57] *Iskusstvo v svyazi s obschim razvitiem kultury i ideala chelovechestva*, translated by E. Korsh (Moscow, 1874). Volume v, which covers the Renaissance and Reformation, has a section devoted to Cervantes, creative art in Spain, national drama during the Reformation period, the Spanish theater as a development of popular poetry, Lope and the flower of court poetry, and Calderón.

[58] *Istoria ispanskoi literatury po Tiknoru*, translated by P. Kulish (St. P., 1861). University libraries doubtlessly had texts for these courses, but the library catalogue of the period available was one from a university where this program was not active. Even here, however, is found a German translation of the *Quixote* by J. H. Einenert (Tubingen, 1826) and a Spanish version of *Guzmán de Alfarache*. (*Katalog Biblioteki Imperatorskago Novorossiiskago Universiteta*, vol. i, nos. 32 and 26 respectively).

Veselovski's *Ancient Theater in Europe*,[59] with chapters on the Spanish theater from Juan del Encina through Calderón, and Kirpichnikov's *Spain and Portugal during the Renaissance*.[60] Random examination of issues of the current journals find popular articles on "The Development of the Spanish Language and the First Monuments of Spanish Literature"[61] and on contemporary writing in Spain.[62] Two scholarly works made an appearance as well: I. I. Sreznevski's edited text and translation of *La vida y hazañas del Gran Tamorlán*[63] and Buslayev's critical study of *El Mío Cid*.[64]

Producers, playwrights and dramatic critics of this period were keenly interested in European classic plays and welcomed Russian renditions. This resulted in many translations of Spanish dramas: Lope de Vega's *El perro del hortelano*,[65] *La dama melindrosa*,[66] *El castigo sin venganza*, *Fuente Ovejuna*,[67] and *El mejor alcalde el rey*,[68]

---

[59] A. N. Veselovski, *Starinny teatr v Yevrope*, Moscow, 1870.

[60] A. I. Kirpichnikov, "Ispania i Portugalia v epokhu vozrozhdenia," in *Vseoschaya istoria literatury* published by Korsh and Kirpichnikov, III (St. P., 1888).

[61] "Razvitie ispanskago yazyka i pervie pamyatniki ispanskoi literatury," *Biblioteka dlya Chtenia* (1850), VI, 1-28.

[62] N. K-v, "Sovremennaya ispanskaya literatura" [Contemporary Spanish literature], *Otechestvennia Zapiski* (1866), CLXVI, no. 10, pp. 267-83, no. 11, pp. 512-21, and CLXIX, no. 21, pp. 99-118. E. Denegri, "Ocherki novoi ispanskoi literatury" [Sketches of the recent Spanish literature], *Delo* (1873), no. 9, pp. 94-123; (1874), no. 2, pp. 107-33. Lemke, "Istoria ispanskoi literatury," *Otechestvennia Zapiski* (1856), CIV, no. 7, pp. 51 ff. The same journal has an article "Sbornik novykh ispanskikh romansov" [Collection of new Spanish romances] (1856), CVII, no. 6, pp. 72-75, and a review of a performance of T. Mure's play "Miguel Cervantes," *ibid.* (1856), CVI, no. 6, pp. 148-50.

[63] *Sbornik otdelenia russkago yazyka i slovesnosti Imperatorskoi Akademii Nauk* XXVIII, part 1 (St. P., 1881), introduction, pp. i-vii and text, pp. 1-455.

[64] F. V. Buslayev, *Ispanski narodny epos o Side* (St. P., 1864). Some of the romances on the *Cid* were published in Russian translation by Galakhov in *Russkaya Khrestomatia* (16th edition, St. P., 1876), II, no. 92.

[65] Translated by Timkovski in 1843 and Pyatnitski in 1851.

[66] Translated by Pyatnitski in 1854.

[67] Both plays done by Yuryev in 1876.

[68] Translated by Pyatnitski in 1877.

Calderón's *El alcaide de si mismo, El alcalde de Zala-mea, A secreto agravio, secreta venganza, La cisma de Inglaterra, La hija del aire, El médico de su honra* and *La vida es sueño*,[69] and all of Cervantes' interludes.[70] There was also a translation made of the contemporary work of Tamayo y Baus, *La locura de amor*.[71]

Spain continues to figure as a literary motif or background in Russian literature, as is seen in the plays *Calderon*[72] by Ilyin, *Love of the Spanish Girl*,[73] Polonski's *Janizaro*,[74] and A. N. Maikov's poems "King Ferdinand Was a Knight,"[75] "The Queen's Confession,"[76] "Cruel Was King Don Pedro,"[77] and the group of six poems[78] derived, according to Maikov, from a Spanish anthology. In music it appears in A. S. Dargomyzhski's last opera, *The Stone Guest*, which had a libretto by Pushkin, and in the compositions of Anton Rubinstein, *Danse Espagnole, Toreador et Andalouse* and *Don Quichotte*.

TRANSLATIONS

In 1866 a new translation of the *Quixote* was made by V. Karelin. It was prefaced by a short biography of Cervantes that is as imaginative as it is inaccurate. Karelin says that Cervantes studied law at the University of Salamanca, and there became intimate with his teacher López de Hoyos; that Cervantes' miserly and cruel master in Algiers kept him captive with great strictness, in chains and under severe guard. . . . In Lisbon Cervantes had a love affair with a well-known married lady. . . . He then

[69] L. B. Turkevich, *op. cit.*, pp. 156-57.
[70] Cf. pp. 68-70.
[71] By V. R. in *Russki Vestnik*, Dec. 1874, vol. 114, reviewed by Postorony in *Moskovskia Vedomosti*, 1874, no. 291.
[72] "Kalderon," tragedy in three acts, by Ilyin, Moscow, 1844, reviewed in *Biblioteka dlya Chtenia*, 1844, vol. 67, part 6, pp. 5-9.
[73] Produced in 1850-1851 with E. N. Zhuleva as Rita (*Yezhe-godnik Imperatorskikh Teatrov*, sezon 1895-1896, vol. vi, p. 407).
[74] Ya. P. Polonski, "Otryvok iz dramy Khanizaro" in *Russkie Propilei, materialy po istorii russkoi mysli i literatury*, edited by M. Gershenzon, Moscow, 1915, pp. 372-89.
[75] A. N. Maikov, *Polnoye sobranie sochineni* (St. P.), i, 188.
[76] *Idem*, ii, 21.　　[77] *Idem*, ii, 52.　　[78] *Idem*, i, 210-11.

married a lady of high birth and illustrious name. . . . It was his marriage that transformed the soldier into the writer, thus making the *Galatea* a product of the honeymoon. . . .[1] These samples of Karelin's biographical material require no further comment.

As for the translation, it is complete, with the exception of the dedications and the prologue. The author claims that it was made from the Spanish, but the rendition of the text and the gallicized forms of the proper names suggest a French rather than a Spanish source. Karelin's work is redeemed, however, by its excellent style, which conveys much of the charm and flavor of the *Quixote*. The proverbs and *dichos* so vital to the book are rendered by often well-chosen Russian parallels.

There are quite a number of omissions in the text, and grammatical changes and errors that resulted from Karelin's excessive liberty with the original are far too numerous, occasionally distorting the meaning. Notwithstanding these minor flaws, Karelin's translation is really a very good one in that it revealed to Russian readers the true spirit of the *Quixote*. During this period, it went through three editions—the first in 1866, the second in 1873, and the third, with the critical article "Don Quixotism and Demonism,"[2] in 1881.[3]

A second edition of *The Story of the Famous Don Quixote of La Mancha*,[4] translated under the editorship of M. Chistyakov, was issued in St. Petersburg in 1883.

[1] V. Karelin, "Migel Servantes Saavedra i yego kniga Don Kikhot Lamanchski" [Cervantes and his book Don Quixote de la Mancha], *Don Kikhot Lamanchski, sochinenie Miguelia Servantesa Saavedry, perevod V. Karelina* (St. P., 1873), pp. v-xxix; cf. pp. vi-xiii.

[2] Cf. pp. 85-89.

[3] For other details concerning these editions, consult Appendix, nos. 18, 19 and 20.

[4] V. I. Mezhkov, *Pyatoye pribavlenie k sistematicheskoi rospisi knigam prodayuschimsia v knizhnikh magazinakh Ivana Ilyicha Glazunova* [Fifth supplement to a systematic description of the books sold in the bookstores of I. I. Glazunov], covers the years 1883-1887 inclusive. (St. P., 1889), p. 744, no. 11736; cf. also Leopoldo Rius y de Llosellos, *Bibliografía crítica de las obras de Miguel de Cervantes Saavedra* (Madrid, 1895), I, no. 833.

Nothing more is known about this translation except that by 1914 it had gone through five editions. Neither is it mentioned by Smirnov in his *Russian Translations of the Quixote*.[5] It is but 354 pages long, which suggests the possibility of its being an abbreviated version.

In 1879 A. N. Ostrovski, the father of the Russian theater, translated Cervantes' Interludes, a project he had wanted to undertake for some time.[6] The work was done quickly—seven to ten days to an interlude[7]—and consequently the quality of the translation is poor. Ostrovski planned to have them published, but with some revision, which he evidently did not make because of bickerings with the publishers.[8] The result was that when Burdin, the actor, asked for two Interludes for his performance, Ostrovski had to refuse, offering a variety of excuses,[9] and when Vainberg, the publisher of *The Journal of Belles-Lettres*, bought them, there was not much time to make the version as graceful "as the name of the author deserves."[10] Certainly, the text as it appeared in

[5] A. Smirnov, "O perevodakh Don Kikhota," *Khitroumny idalgo Don Kikhot Lamanchski* (Moscow-Leningrad, 1929), pp. lxxxiii-xci.

[6] *Neizdannye pisma k A. N. Ostrovskomu, Tolstogo, Goncharova, Nekrasova, Dostoyevskogo, Pisemskogo, i dr. iz Arkhiva Ostrovskogo, po materialam Teatralnogo Muzeya imeni A. A. Bakhrushina.* Prigotovil k pechati M. D. Prygunov, Y. A. Bakhrushin, i N. A. Brodski [Unpublished letters of Tolstoi, Goncharov, Nekrasov, Dostoyevski, Pisemski and others to A. N. Ostrovski, edited by Prygunov, Bakhrushin and Brodski] (Moscow-Leningrad, 1932), p. 49, P. I. Vainberg's letter of Dec. 25, 1882.

[7] Appendix, nos. 96-104 for the dates of the translations' completion.

[8] *Neizdannie pisma k A. N. Ostrovskomu* . . . A. S. Suvorin's letter of Dec. 18, 1880, p. 558, V. F. Korsh's letter of April 22, 1882, p. 165, and P. I. Vainberg's letter of Dec. 25, 1882, p. 49.

[9] *A. N. Ostrovski and F. A. Burdin, Neizdannie pisma iz sobrani Gos. Teatralnogo Muzeya imeni A. A. Bakhrushin, pod redaktsiei N. L. Brodskogo, N. P. Kashina, and A. A. Bakhrushina* [Ostrovski and Burdin, unpublished letters, edited by Brodski, Kashin and Bakhrushin] (Moscow-Petrograd, 1923), Burdin's letter of Aug. 27, 1880, no. 494; Ostrovski's letter of Sept. 2, 1880, no. 495; and Burdin's of Sept. 9, 1880, no. 496.

[10] *Neizdannye pisma k A. N. Ostrovskomu* . . . P. I. Vainberg's letters of Nov. 1883, nos. 9, 10, 11, 12, 13, 14, pp. 51 ff.; *Pisma*

the journal is not a credit either to Ostrovski's abilities and reputation or to Cervantes.

A limited edition of the complete works of Ostrovski was published in 1886. All of Cervantes' Interludes, except *El rufián viudo*, were included in one of the volumes, with a preface by the translator in which he says:

"Among the different works for which we are indebted to the peer of Spanish geniuses are his Interludes—the least known of his works, but the most deserving of fame. Readers can see in them how, long ago, with what variety Cervantes' genius was able to grasp and unfold before the public both grandiose and trivial themes. And we dare to assert that it is in the Interludes, more than any other work (except *Don Quixote*), that Cervantes reveals his true self. In these jolly pictures, painted with light strokes, Cervantes' genius is in its own element. Here the endless stream of his inimitable sense of humor flows smoothly. In the depiction of characters—the exalted, the peculiar and the comical—Cervantes has no equal. And since it is they that constitute the main material of what is now commonly called the *sainete*, no one hesitates to recognize them, for their originality and purity, as examples of the ingenuity of Cervantes' talent.

"The language of these plays is natural and true to the persons and situations. It is witty, playful, and glistens with *dichos* and *refranes*. It is Cervantes who originated this type of writing, and it is he who brings it to perfection.[11] Though written at the beginning of the seventeenth century, these Interludes are as interesting to the modern reader as they would have been had their characters been drawn from a contemporary milieu. This proves that there is no subject so trivial as not to acquire great significance in the hands of a real genius. He knows how to place universal and human interest in

---

russkikh pisatelei k A. S. Suvorinu, podgotovil k pechati D. I. Abramovich [Letters of Russian writers to A. S. Suvorin, edited by Abramovich] (Leningrad, 1927), Ostrovski's letter of March 23, 1884, p. 104.

[11] Other Russian writers have made the same error.

simple and insignificant things so as to make them flow along the current of the ages."[12]

The Journal of Belles-Lettres was not in existence long enough to publish all of Ostrovski's translations of Cervantes, and only forty-two copies of the limited edition were offered to the public. Thus the *entremeses*, even in the version so deeply regretted by the translator, failed to reach the Russian public for some time longer.[13]

A translation of *Señora Cornelia* was made by A. Kirpichnikov from Brockhäus' *Colleción de autores españoles*, volume xxv.[14] In comparison with Ostrovski's work, this translation is excellent. However, since the author was a specialist, a professor in Western European literature, one can be more exacting in details. The style of the version is good, sacrificing literal translation, and occasionally meaning, to ease and clarity.

As these translations increased the number of adult readers of the *Quixote*, a need seems to have been felt to make the novel more accessible to children, for condensed versions began to appear with greater frequency. The first *Don Quixote for Children* was made from a French text of Abbott Le Jeune by the writer A. N. Grech (1814-1850), the son of N. I. Grech.[15] Its existence is known only from the fact that a second "revised edition" appeared in 1860.[16] Other editions followed in 1868 and 1880.[17]

The second edition of Grech's abbreviated version received a very unfavorable review in one of the Russian literary journals.[18] The reviewer begins by saying, "If this

[12] A. E. Burtsev, *Bibliograficheskoe opisanie redkikh i zamechatelnykh knig* [A biblographical description of rare and remarkable books] (St. P., 1901), II, 558-59.

[13] Cf. p. 195.

[14] *Siniora Kornelia*, translated by A. K. in *Russki Vestnik* (1872), CI, 237.

[15] Cf. p. 21.

[16] V. I. Mezhkov, *Sistematicheski katalog russkikh knig prodayuschikhsia v knizhnom magazine Al. F. Bazunova* [Systematic catalogue of the Russian books on sale in the bookstore of Al. F. Bazunov] (St. P., 1869), no. 2511.

[17] Cf. Appendix, nos. 13 and 14.

[18] *Russkoye Slovo*, March 1860, p. 149. Author unknown.

is really the second edition, it is by no means a revised one." He claims, and rightly so, that because of its content and basic ideas *Don Quixote* is not in the least suitable for condensation into a children's book—even if it were done by a talented writer. The reviewer feels that Grech, however, is not in the least talented, and that, moreover, the French version from which it is taken is very poor, having obliterated "all vestiges of the high merits of the original." He concludes with the revealing observation that it is not the quality of Grech's condensation, but the title and fame of the original novel that creates the market for this *Don Quixote for Children*.

Other abbreviated versions of this period were made by N. Lvov (1867), N. K. Gernet (1874 and 1882), Filonov (1875) and O. I. Schmidt-Moskvitinova, also known as Rogova (about 1883).[19]

THEATER PRODUCTIONS

THE most important theatrical imitations of *Don Quixote* during the age of Realism are two ballets by Petipa. One —a short ballet in four acts and eight scenes—had its première December 14, 1869.[1] The other, which was a revision of the former—a long ballet in five acts and eleven scenes, with a prologue and an epilogue—was performed on November 9, 1871,[2] twice in 1874, again in 1876,[3] and once during the season of 1881-1882.[4] The music was by Minkus. A libretto was published in 1875.[5] "It was based upon the novel by Cervantes. The old and wealthy Gamache is to be married to Kitri, daughter of an innkeeper, Lorenzo. But Kitri has fallen in love with Basil. After various adventures, the lovers are united

[19] Cf. Appendix, nos. 25, 26, 27, 28 and 29.
[1] C. W. Beaumont, *A History of Ballet in Russia (1613-1881)* (London, 1930), p. 109.
[2] *Ibid.*
[3] *Yezhegodnik Imperatorskikh Teatrov* (1900), supplement III, 66.
[4] *Ibid.* (1912), mentioned in the article "Repertuar Sanktpeterburgskikh Imperatorskikh Teatrov, 1881-1882."
[5] V. I. Mezhov, *Glazunov Catalogue* (St. P., 1882), no. 14922.

71

through the aid of Don Quixote."[6] To date, these two ballets remain the standard Russian choreographies for *Don Quixote*.

Don Quixote also made his way into music. Anton Rubinstein wrote a musical character-piece entitled *Don Quixote*, which was performed in Moscow on January 8, 1871.[7] The composer Tchaikovsky was present at this performance and wrote his impressions of it to a fellow musician, Balakirev: "At the last concert they played 'Don Quixote.' I find this work very interesting and cleverly done, although in its episodic character it resembles somewhat ballet or pantomime music. Its orchestration is above average and very effective in spots. The finale (supposedly a parody on Liszt, I believe) is drawn out. The love theme is rather banal. I like the theme depicting the knight-errant, and the episode with the windmills is superb. All in all, I consider this to be one of the most interesting and most carefully developed of Rubinstein's works."

Ivan Turgenev attended a St. Petersburg performance of *Don Quixote*, and wrote the following note about it to Mme. Viardot: ". . . Puis concert de Rubinstein à l'assemblée de la noblesse; un monde fou; il a joué comme toujours; immense applaudissements. Auer y a joué aussi, mais j'avoue que j'ai surtout admiré ses yeux et toute sa physionomie. Le morceau pour orchestre intitulé *Don Quichotte* est assez bien; seulement l'élément comique, le Sancho Pança, manque complètement. Il a introduit des fragments d'airs espagnols, en les choisissant assez vulgaires. Je crois me rappeler qu'il vous les avait demandé ainsi."[8]

This orchestral work of Rubinstein's was later tran-

[6] Beaumont, *op. cit.*, p. 109.

[7] M. A. Balakirev, *Perepiska M. A. Balakireva s P. I. Chaikovskim* [Balakirev's correspondence with Tchaikovsky], (St. P., n.d.), p. 63, letter dated Jan. 10, 1871.

[8] Ivan Tourgeneff, *Lettres à Madame Viardot*, publiées et annotées par E. Halpérine Kaminsky (Paris, 1907), p. 253, letter dated Feb. 22, 1871.

scribed for two pianos by the German Richard Klein-
michel.[9]

ALLUSIONS

By the middle of the century, Cervantes and his hero
had become familiar to Russian intellectuals. They encountered Don Quixote in the original or in translation,
or they struck up an acquaintance at secondhand, as it
were, by hearsay. Consequently, it is not surprising that
references, allusions, comments and opinions on *Don
Quixote* are much more copious than in the preceding
period. In fact, the term "Don Quixotism" was rapidly
becoming a part of the language. A. S. Khomyakov
(1804-1860), a Slavophil poet and philosopher,[1] and
Valeryan Maikov (1823-1847), critic and editor of the
literary journal *The Contemporary*,[2] afford excellent examples of this familiarity with the knight of La Mancha.

A. A. Grigoryev (1822-1864), a writer and critic noted
for his theory of organic criticism, alluded to *Don Quixote* and Cervantes in two ways—one philosophico-roman-
tic, and the other historico-sociological. Allusions of the
first type appear in several passages of self-analysis.[3]
Grigoryev liked to compare himself to Cervantes' knight,
or boast, "I am an eternal Don Quixote," seeing himself
as an enthusiastic blundering idealist. Comments such as
this prompted Grigoryev's biographer and editor, Sadovnik, to write a short comparative study of the critic and
Don Quixote.[4]

Grigoryev's approach to literature was purely historical
and social. What role do national, social and moral fac-
tors play in creating an artist? The answer to this ques-

[9] J. D. M. Ford and R. Lansing, *Cervantes, a Tentative Bibliography of His Works and of the Bibliographical and Critical Material concerning Him* (Cambridge, Mass., 1931), p. 142.
[1] A. S. Khomyakov, *Polnoye sobranie sochineni* (Moscow, 1904),
viii, 222, 421.
[2] V. N. Maikov, *Sochinenia* (Kiev, 1901), ii, 111.
[3] A. Grigoryev, *Materialy dlya biografii* [Materials for biography]
(St. P., 1917), 167, 170, 204-205, 252, 274, 275, 295.
[4] V. Sadovnik, "Biograficheski ocherk" [Biographical sketch],
Sobranie sochineni A. Grigoryeva, i (Moscow, 1915), xlvii.

tion he expounded in his theory of organic criticism, which insists that literature is an organic product of the national soil, people and period. It did not matter to Grigoryev whether the soil is English or French or German or Spanish or Russian. Art, to be great, must be inseparably bound up in a nation's social, religious, moral and historical nature. It is only this powerful association that can produce geniuses. Furthermore, Grigoryev believed that the strength of this bond varies with the period. At one time it is weak, resulting in a period of artistic sterility or mediocrity; at another it is strong, producing an epoch opulent with artistic gifts.

"In epochs of indissoluble creation," he writes, "artists like Shakespeare, Dante, Cervantes, Molière, do not resort to any *invisibles* to seek higher purposes for their work—higher personal ideas of good and evil, and conceptions of the social good. These conceptions thrive within them, with a powerful organic life that is rooted in the soil from which the artist came. The poet believes in life and in its high laws. He does not even ask himself whether he believes or not. Without this implicit faith, impossible is the creation of such images as those of Dante's *Inferno*, the laughter of Cervantes and Molière, and the moral infallibility of Shakespeare."[5]

In Cervantes, Grigoryev goes on to say, we find spiritual identification with his native soil, with his life and with his time. His conception of life is therefore a part of his artistic and intellectual makeup, and so he need not consciously seek social ideals. They are within him. Here lies the secret of his art and of its immortality.

According to Grigoryev, the poetic, moral and social worlds are blended in Cervantes into a force that endows him with a certain fullness and unity in his vision of life and humanity. This blending gives him an accurate perspective of life, and a keen sense of justice that enables him to create lifelike characters, to make them breathe,

[5] Grigoryev, "O pravde i iskrennosti v iskusstve" [Of truth and sincerity in art], *Sob. soch. A. G-va*, I, issue 2 (Moscow, 1915), p. 51.

live, enjoy and suffer like human beings. Consequently, Cervantes responds to his Don Quixote and Sancho as if they were real men of flesh and blood. He condemns and praises them, he chastises and rewards them for their actions just as he would if they were from his own home town.[6]

Time and again, the critic writes, we encounter expressions of perplexity or admiration at the coincidence in appearance of *Don Quixote, Hamlet* and *King Lear.* Grigoryev has a historical solution for this coincidence. "Historically it is not we individuals who live, but it is trends that live, of which we, as individuals, are to a greater or lesser degree representatives. Hence, the parallelism—striking to the point of obviousness—of events in different spheres of the world's life."[7] Both Shakespeare and Cervantes are bound to their native soil and to their age; consequently there exists between them an organic bond. A certain philosophic, social and historical similarity between the nations that produced Shakespeare and Cervantes explains the coincidence in the creation of *Don Quixote* and *Hamlet.*

The critic Belinski once called Griboyedov's Chatski, the hero of *Woe from Wit,* a Don Quixote.[8] Grigoryev denies any resemblance between the two characters. He claims that to be a Don Quixote one's protest must have a social, historical or moral foundation, and that Don Quixotism is "any protest that perishes in unequal and singlehanded combat." This is not so in Chatski's case.[9] His indictment of society has a personal foundation. If he were not in love with Sofia, the social set-up would not disturb him as much. As it is, society irritates him doubly, because he holds it responsible for Sofia's coolness. The

[6] *Ibid.,* p. 31; cf. also "Lermontov i yego napravlenie" [Lermontov and his tendencies], *ibid.,* i, issue 7 (Moscow, 1915), p. 15.
[7] Grigoryev, "Moi literaturnie i nravstvennia skitalstva" [My literary and moral wanderings], *ibid.,* i, issue 1, p. 55.
[8] V. Belinski, *Sobranie sochineni,* v (St. P., 1901), p. 317.
[9] Grigoryev, "Gore ot Uma Griboyedova" [Griboyedov's The misfortune of being clever], *Sob. soch. A. G-va,* i, issue 5, p. 17; cf. also "Lermontov i yego napravlenie," p. 92.

same point of view appears in other allusions by Grigoryev to Don Quixote.[10]

A. Herzen (1812-1870), a writer of liberal tendencies
and editor of the radical periodical *The Bell*, published
in London, often alluded to Don Quixote.[11] In one of his
literary essays, he compared the Romantic school to the
Knight from La Mancha: "Waterloo decided who should
dominate the field—Napoleon, the classicist, or Welling-
ton and Blücher, the romantics. . . . Romanticism triumphed. Classicism was taboo. Linked with Classicism
were memories which all sought to forget, whereas Romanticism resurrected the forgotten which all wished to
recall. Romanticism spoke incessantly; Classicism was
silent. Like Don Quixote, Classicism sat with the sedate
dignity of a Roman senator."[12]

Herzen's figure of speech approaches the real Don
Quixote, the loquacious, bellicose knight who is striving
to resurrect in an age of iron the "Age of Gold," the age
of fantasy and idealism. The only difference between the
Don Quixote of Cervantes and the Don Quixote identified with Romanticism lies in the fact that the former's
attempt to bring back the past met with no sympathy,
whereas that of the latter was welcome at the beginning
of the nineteenth century.

In the light of this quotation, Don Quixote stands as
the symbol of Romanticism. He is, for Herzen, the representative of a mode of thinking that was so exalted, fantastic and far removed from reality as to cause Ariosto,
Boccaccio and Cervantes to rebel against it. "In poetry
knighthood loses its contemplative importance and
feudal dignity. Ariosto playfully, smilingly, sings of his
Orlando; Cervantes with vicious irony declares to the

[10] Grigoryev, "I. S. Turgenev i yego deyatelnost" [I. S. T. and
his activity] *Sob. soch. A. G-va*, II, issue 10, pp. 30, 68-69; "Real-
izm i idealizm v russkoi literature" [Realism and idealism in Russian literature], *ibid.*, I, issue 4, p. 12.

[11] A. Herzen, *Polnoye sobranie sochineni i pisem* [Complete
works and letters], in 22 volumes, edited by M. K. Lemke (Petrograd, 1919), I, 215, letter to N. Kecher, Dec. 31, 1835.

[12] *Ibid.*, III, "Diletanty-romantiki" [Dilettantes-romantics], 177-
93; cf. p. 180.

world its impotence and untimeliness; Boccaccio un-
frocks the life of a Catholic monk. Rabelais with the bold
frankness of a Frenchman goes even further. . . ." In *Don
Quixote* Cervantes, the realist, rises against and ridicules
Romanticism.[13]

"Don Quixote of the Revolution" is a phrase often encountered in Herzen's later works. From his point of
view, the French revolution of 1848 was hopelessly mis-
managed by antiquated, weak and overeager optimists.
Where he had expected to find a group of vigorous, mature men, he discovered a lot of "Don Quixotes of the
Revolution," senile old men of 1789 lapsing into second
childhood.[14] While all France had learned, progressed
and adjusted itself to new trends, the "Don Quixote of the
Revolution" remained rooted to the spot he occupied in
1789. Herzen bitterly remarked: "The Don Quixote of the
revolutionary circles is worthy of his knightly predeces-
sor." Where is the Cervantes to paint him? he asked.[15]

N. G. Chernyshevski (1828-1899), who was also an
eminent radical and critic, made the following entry in
his diary: "I am still reading *Don Quixote*. Even though
it is in a translation by Chaplet, it is very good, very
sound. And Don Quixote talks ever so wisely. Everything
that he says is superb, even the things about knighthood.
Only there he does not discern the true circumstances."[16]

N. A. Dobrolyubov (1836-1861), another journalist-
critic, has a comment on Don Quixote in his review of
Turgenev's *On the Eve*.[17] He points out that to produce

[13] *Ibid.*, p. 187.
[14] *Ibid.*, xv, 259, letter dated July 20, 1862.
[15] *Ibid.*, vi, 428-29, letter dated Aug. 9, 1851. A similar passage
appears in xv, 260-61, letter dated Aug. 10, 1862. It is interesting to
find a request for a copy of *Don Quixote* which he wished to give
his daughter in a letter of March 30, 1865 (xviii, 71).
[16] N. G. Chernyshevski, *Literaturnoye nasledie, iz avtobiografii
i dnevnika 1848-1853* [Literary heritage, from autobiography and
diary for the years 1848-1853] edited and annotated by N. A.
Alekseyev, M. N. Chernyshevski and C. N. Chernov (Moscow,
1828), p. 300, entry of Oct. 12, 1848.
[17] N. A. Dobrolyubov, "Kogda zhe pridet nastoyaschi den?"
[When will the present day come?], *Sochinenia N. A. Dobrolyubova*
(sixth edition: St. P., n.d.), iv, 256-99.

a rational man of ideas it is necessary to go outside Russia, because Russian idealists are only "comical Don Quixotes." "The distinctive feature of Don Quixote is his lack of understanding of the reason for which he is fighting and of the outcome of his efforts—these very features appear with amazing vividness in the Russian Don Quixotes."[18] The critic does not seem to have understood Cervantes' character at all.

D. I. Pisarev (1840-1868), Dobrolyubov's successor in journalism, was the brilliant spokesman of Russian nihilism, the position of which he aptly summarized as follows: "Our period is definitely not conducive to the development of theories. . . . Our brain demands facts and proofs. Phrases do not overwhelm us. In the most brilliant and harmonious creation we will detect the debility of the premise and arbitrariness in the deductions. Fanatic enthusiasm in an idea or in a principle is not, as it seems to me, a trait of the Russian people. Common sense, considerable humor and skepticism compose the most characteristic quality of the true Russian mind. We tend to lean more towards Hamlet than towards Don Quixote. The enthusiasm and mysticism of a passionate adept is hardly comprehensible to us."[19]

An essay on *Don Quixote* from so materialistic a mind would have been most interesting, but topics of more immediate concern held Pisarev's attention. Comparisons and allusions to Don Quixote, however, occur frequently in his works. In fact, almost every article, excepting his scientific and historical treatises, contains a reference.[20]

[18] *Ibid.*, p. 285.
[19] D. I. Pisarev, *Sochinenia D. I. Pisareva*, in four volumes (St. P., 1900), I, 356.
[20] Pisarev, Review of A. F. Pisemski's "Stoyalaya voda," *Soch. D. I. P-va*, I, 427; "Pisemski, Turgenev i Goncharov," *ibid.*, I, 452; "Progulka po sadam russkoi slovesnosti" [Rambles through the gardens of Russian letters], *ibid.*, IV, 372; "Kukolnaya tragedia s buketom grazhdanskoi skorbi" [A puppet tragedy with a bouquet of civil sorrow], *ibid.*, IV, 164; "Pogibshie i pogibayuschie" [The perished and the perishing], *ibid.*, V, 299; "Zhenskie tipy v romanakh i povestyakh Pisemskago, Turgeneva i Goncharova" [Feminine types in the novels of Pisemski, Turgenev and Goncharov], *ibid.*,

It is significant that Pisarev and Chernyshevski, Nihilists who rejected works of art and embraced skepticism, should have liked Don Quixote, that incarnation of the aesthetic and faith. These writers who strove to improve Russia and life by living a scientific materialism were fundamentally linked to the knight who sought to better Spain and the world by living a literary idealism. They all lived the abstract, imagined or theoretical. The Nihilists, like Don Quixote, had surrendered themselves completely to an idea stemming from a book, *The Origin of the Species*. For them, as for the knight, this materialistic idea was at once the source and impulse of life. Such behavior, however, was not limited to the Nihilists. Rather, it is typical of many Russians and consequently explains Russian responsiveness and understanding of Don Quixote.

Pisarev's article "A Russian Don Quixote" is not about Cervantes' hidalgo, but a prominent Slavophil whom Pisarev maliciously compares to the real Don Quixote. In fact, the whole comparison is so drawn that one could almost imagine that Don Quixote de la Mancha had been reincarnated in I. V. Kireyevski (1806-1856). He, says Pisarev, was a man with a brilliant mind and perception in regard to all but reality, and there his lucid vision, skepticism and cold logic failed. Adjustment to existing conditions was impossible for him, and he therefore turned to dreaming. His dream was what he sought in reality and did not find—"so he idealized it, painted it up to suit his fancy, and became a knight of the sad visage just like the unforgettable Don Quixote, the lover of the incomparable Dulcinea of Toboso. Slavophilism is Russian Don Quixotism. Where stand windmills, there the Slavophils see armed giants. From this come their endlessly verbose and muddled ravings about nationalism, Russian civilization. . . ."[21] Having espoused a cause (an

---

i, 509; "Obrazovannaya tolpa" [The educated mass], *ibid.*, vi, 244. There is another allusion to Don Quixote on p. 247.

[21] Pisarev, "Russki Don Kikhot" [The Russian Don Quixote], *ibid.*, i, 238; for other allusions to Don Quixote cf. pp. 40-41.

erroneous one, in Pisarev's estimation), Kireyevski, like Don Quixote, armed himself with a superb dialectical skill that helped convince himself and others that his idea was not an illusion, but reality.

As numerous as are Pisarev's allusions to Don Quixote, his comments on Cervantes are scarce. Only one, in fact, has been discovered. In speaking of the great pioneers of Russian literature, he says: "We have to concede that Karamzin, Zhukovski, Dmitryev and others have lived out their lives, and have become so hopelessly distant from us as probably no person with really potent talent like Shakespeare, Byron, Cervantes, Pushkin, ever will."[22]

I. A. Goncharov (1812-1891), though a prominent Realist himself, criticized the principles and extremes towards which the contemporary school was heading, and advocated instead the realism of the great classics, including the work of Cervantes. "That reasonable and sober realism of which I speak is just as old as the classics themselves," he writes in one of his letters. "What or who was more realistic than Homer? How much truth in the depiction of details—in feasts, in battles . . . ! Aristophanes, the Roman dramatists, the medieval Dante, Cervantes, Shakespeare—finally, Goethe and our Dickens-Pushkin . . . were all realists and classics."[23]

In a critical essay, Goncharov elaborates the point: "Of course, realism is one of the primary bases of art, but not the realism advocated by the new school abroad, and to some extent here.

"Who would reject aspiration for truth—both in art and in life—recommended by the Realists? They admit that Homer, Cervantes, Shakespeare, Goethe and others, and also our own Fonvisin, Pushkin, Lermontov, Gogol, aimed at truth, found it in nature, in life, and included it

[22] Pisarev, "Moskovskie mysliteli" [The Moscow thinkers], *ibid.*, II, 200.

[23] I. A. Goncharov, *I. A. Goncharov v neizdannykh pismakh k Grafu Valuyevu* [I. A. G. in unpublished letters to Count Valuyev] (St. P., 1906), p. 37.

in their works. Then this is not an innovation at all! . . .[24]

"The new realistic school, in so far as we can understand, seems to reject it [portrayal of types]. This is an attack not only on the so-called 'Romantic school,' but also on Shakespeare, Cervantes and Molière! Who would be interested in the half-mad Lear and Don Quixote if they were mere portraits of some queer fellows, and not types—that is, mirrors reflecting within countless images from the past, present and future of human society . . . ?[25]

"This world of created types has, it would seem, its own special life, its history, its geography and ethnography, and probably will become the object of interesting historico-philosophical critical studies. Don Quixote, Lear, Hamlet, Lady Macbeth, Falstaff, Don Juan, Tartuffe and others have already given birth to new generations in the works of later writers. . . ."[26]

Certain eternal themes always evoke characters who have been successfully created by previous writers to portray these themes. Every subsequent writer cannot help being influenced by them when handling the same ideas. Goncharov develops this theory, using the struggle between generations as an eternal theme, and Griboyedov's Chatski as the best Russian exemplification of it.

"This is why, even today, Griboyedov's Chatski, and with him the play [*Woe from Wit*], are not outmoded, and it is improbable that they will ever be. And when an artist has to deal with the struggle between generations, he will not be able to break away from the magic circle drawn by Griboyedov. He will either produce an extreme, immature type . . . or will create a slightly altered Chatski, just as after Cervantes' Don Quixote and Shakespeare's Hamlet an endless number of their likenesses appeared—and are still appearing."[27]

[24] I. A. Goncharov, "Luchshe pozdno chem nikogda" [Better late than never], *Polnoye sobranie sochineni* (St. P., 1899), i, 83.
[25] *Ibid.*   [26] *Ibid.*, p. 78.
[27] Goncharov, "Milion terzani" [A million tortures], *ibid.*, vi, 148. Other references to Don Quixote are to be found in "Obryv" [Precipice], *ibid.*, viii, 45, 347 and "Oblomov," *ibid.*, iii, part iv, chap. viii.

In the writings of Ya. P. Polonski (1819-1898), an eclectic poet, is found but one allusion to the *Quixote*: "I, like you, prefer a pure, unadulterated poetic motif or image. I was unpleasantly puzzled, I remember, by Sancho Panza's wise speeches in Cervantes' *Don Quixote*, where he too, for some reason, went into the mountains and almost became a governor. Whence comes this sudden administrative sagacity?"[28]

F. I. Buslayev (1818-1897), an educator and exponent of the comparative method of studying literature, makes several allusions to Cervantes, in which he stresses the importance of the native, popular elements in literature and also the interrelation and interdependence of nationalities in art, literature and language.

"Reciprocity of intellectual interest brought the different literatures into competition with one another, and from time to time one or the other came to the forefront of the history of European civilization. Such works as the romances of the Cid, Boccaccio's *Decameron*, Cervantes' *Don Quixote*, were not mere samples of different nationalities, but consecutive stages in human development, in its literary expression, and the more profound the impression of the local peculiarities on these works, the greater the rights claimed by that nation for universal importance. Therefore, nationalism did not conflict with the universal, but coincided with it, serving it as a definite step in the path of progress.

"The extent of the importance of the popular works to Spanish literature even in the fifteenth century, in the epoch when it began to develop within itself elements for the most civilized artistic activity, can be judged from the fact that the Marqués de Santillana, at Juan II's request, collected proverbs and made of them a book of instruction, like the Sermons of Solomon, for reading to the heir Don Enrique of Castile. They were printed in 1496—

[28] S. Balukhaty, "Russkie pisateli o literature" [Russian authors on literature], a citation of unpublished letters to Maikov, Polivanov and Fet, *Arkhiv Instituta Literatury Akademii Nauk* (Leningrad, 1939), I, 473.

Centiloquio—and reprinted nine or ten times in the sixteenth century. Thus, the creation in Sancho Panza of the
simple plebeian type, crude, yet uttering wisdom in proverbs, was not an introduction into literature of forgotten
elements of the *castizo*, but an artistic reproduction of
that which had already sent deep roots into artistic, civilized literature."[29]

After the Renaissance in the West, Buslayev says elsewhere, "There begins a period of amazing reworking of
national materials into artistic forms, done by such great
masters as Shakespeare in England, Torquato Tasso in
Italy and Cervantes in Spain."[30]

"In the West, emancipation from plebeian prejudices
and lack of taste was accomplished by the education of
the upper classes, by the success of the enlightenment of
the foremost personalities, scholars, poets and artists,
who satisfied the higher intellectual and moral demands
of their time. Consequently, if prior to the second quarter
of the eighteenth century, i.e. prior to the epoch of Lo-
monosov's literary activity, our artistic literature was not
free from plebeian taint, if it did not become the representation of the convictions of the best, select, outstanding persons, the cause for it was not the ignorance of
plebeian literature, but the lack of progressive men, who,
like Cervantes, Shakespeare and Molière, originating in
the popular-national (*narodnykh*) sources, would have
liberated themselves from the exclusiveness of the crude
morals of their epoch, and through their higher ideals
would have answered the aspirations of the finest, select
minds of the time."[31]

A. F. Pisemski (1820-1881), a Realist,[32] refers to *Don*

[29] F. I. Buslayev, "Russki bogatyrski epos" [The Russian chivalric
epic], *Sbornik otdelenia russkago yazyka i slovesnosti pri Imperatorskoi Akademii Nauk*, XLII (St. P., 1887), p. 5.

[30] Buslayev, "Lektsii F. I. Buslayeva Yego Imperatorskomu Veli-
chestvu Tsesarevichu Nikolayu Aleksandrovichu, 1859-1860" [Lec-
tures to the Tsarevich Nicholas], *Starina i Novizna*, XII (Moscow,
1907), 10-306; cf. p. 251.

[31] *Ibid.*, p. 187.

[32] The *Quixote* is found among the books that Pisemski recalls

Quixote in his criticism of a literary theory propounded by Buslayev. The latter claims that the novel, unhampered by the limitations fettering other literary genres, must lend itself to didacticism. Theoretically this is so, says Pisemski, but actually works purporting to teach, like those of Eugene Sue and Chernishevski, make no impression on the public. "Such was not the fate of the great old novelists. I am taking them at random: Cervantes, who probably did not intend to teach anyone by his novel, *Don Quixote*, presented only a picture of dying chivalry, yet it is remembered by the entire reading world." Smollett, George Sand, Pushkin, Lermontov, Gogol—all these merely presented facts, leaving it up to the reader to derive and learn from them what he wished.[33] The objectivity that Pisemski noted in Cervantes, Smollett, Sand, and so forth, he developed to a high degree in himself.

M. E. Saltykov-Schedrin (1826-1889), prominent radical journalist and novelist, believed that to create a fine work of art the author must have a well-defined and sound *Weltanschauung*. As an illustration of this point he pointed to Cervantes and his *Don Quixote*.[34]

Finally, it is interesting to come across an allusion to Don Quixote by the composer P. I. Tchaikovsky in a letter to Nadejda von Meck: "What a Don Quixote Wagner is! Why does he strain himself in pursuing the impossible, when in his hands is a great gift from which, if he would only submit to its natural direction, he could extract a whole ocean of musical beauty?"[35]

---

having read when he was a child. "Avtobiografia," *Polnoye sobranie sochineni A. F. Pisemskago* (St. P., 1910), I, 5.

[33] *Ibid.*, p. 33.

[34] M. E. Saltykov-Schedrin, "Snopy Ya. Polonskago" *Polnoye sobranie sochineni* (St. P., 1905-06), VIII, 423.

[35] Catherine D. Bowen and Barbara von Meck, *"Beloved Friend": the Story of Tchaikowsky and Nadejda von Meck* (New York, 1937), p. 170.

7 · CRITICISM

CERVANTES criticism during the period 1850-1880 is in a state of transition, shifting from the philosophic interpretation exemplified by Turgenev's *Hamlet and Don Quixote*[1] to the scholarly approach of Storozhenko. An interesting departure from the purely philosophical technique is to be found in the work of V. Karelin, author of one of the period's best Russian translations of *Don Quixote*.[2]

Assuming the privilege of translators, Karelin prefaced his version with an essay on the subject "Don Quixotism and Demonism."[3] Heretofore, the approach to the *Quixote* had been philosophical, with only occasional leanings towards the sociological. Karelin's study is an attempt to combine and coordinate the two points of view. He first extracts from Don Quixote and Milton's Satan certain "philosophic truths" and then introduces a sociological slant by indicating the place these truths hold in history and social psychology. In so far as the philosophico-ethical characterization goes, Karelin's system is essentially the same as Turgenev's but the element of sociological ethics assumes a new and important role. Furthermore, as K. Derjavin points out, "Karelin is the first to define and characterize quixotism as a psychological feature peculiar not only to individual men, but also to social groups at certain moments of their political life."[4]

As the title "Don Quixotism and Demonism" suggests, Karelin's philosophic observations center upon two fun-

---

[1] Cf. pp. 108-11.

[2] Cf. pp. 66-67.

[3] V. Karelin, "Don Kikhotizm i Demonizm," *Don Kikhot Lamanchski*, translated by the author (St. P., 1893), vol. I.

[4] C. Derjavin, "Crítica cervantina en Rusia," *BAH*, XCIV (Madrid, 1929), 215-38.

damental types of ethical behavior as observed in Don Quixote and Milton's Satan of *Paradise Lost*. These types of behavior are not contrasts, but different manifestations of the same occurrence—the protest of a strong creative personality against uncongenial surroundings. "Don Quixote is the most perfect incarnation of the so-called Don Quixotism, a sickly phenomenon, whereas Milton's hero is the most complete impersonation of the so-called Demonism, a purely robust phenomenon revealing itself demonically in an unwholesome atmosphere. . . ."[5] Both characters are typified by a total renunciation of the sensual, or what Karelin terms the "sensual 'I'."[6] Oblivious of petty sensual interests, they live on a spiritual plane, with all their forces concentrated upon the idea they have adopted. "They are so completely engrossed in their idea . . . that the victory or the fall of this idea is their own victory or defeat, their own joy or sorrow."[7]

In contrast to this form of human behavior, Karelin continues, there stands a form of conduct completely devoted to the sensual interests of the individual, as exemplified by Sancho. Sancho's own "I" is the only thing that matters to him; all else is of no account. "The final aim of Don Quixote and Milton's hero is contrary to this, . . . it involves the well-being not of the subject, but of the object. . . ."[8]

Between these two poles—a purely spiritual existence, as manifested by Don Quixote and Satan, and an absolutely sensual one, as manifested by Sancho—lies the mass of mankind. Some individuals approach more closely to one pole, others to its opposite, yet only the exceptional personalities are at the very extremes.[9] "But, alas, they are so few in number, because life, as we made it, claims its own. 'Tis but one small step from the great to the ridiculous. Consider this Lamanchan Knight of the Sad Visage and you will find in him all that goes to make

[5] Karelin, *op. cit.*, p. 5.   [6] *Ibid.*
[7] *Ibid.*, p. 6.   [8] *Ibid.*, pp. 5-6.
[9] *Ibid.*, p. 6. For a concrete application of this idea, see *Ibid.*, p. 16.

CRITICISM

the great leaders of mankind in all spheres of human activity. He is so very close to them, but it is precisely this proximity that makes him ridiculous."[10]

Cervantes perceived this dangerous proximity between the great and the ridiculous, Karelin believes, and in his *Quixote* revealed its tragedy to the world. Greatness could have been Don Quixote's but the unhealthy atmosphere about him transformed it into ridiculousness by diverting power and potential greatness into abnormal channels.[11] Karelin stresses the fact that Don Quixote selects knight-errantry, suggesting that he sensed that the brilliance of the court is often bought with the tears of those very widows and orphans whom he wanted to protect.[12]

Having once set out on his path of fantasy, Don Quixote makes as great progress as he would have had he entered upon a path of reality. This, says Karelin, is typical of all strong and receptive natures.[13] Though dwelling in a world of unreality, Don Quixote still retains his tremendous spiritual force and intense inspiration—that greatness expressed in boundless and fiery love for humanity. Though a madman with chimeric Dulcineas as apparent drives for his activity, he is really motivated by goodness, truth and human welfare. From this, we can see that for all those elevated and noble aspects of his character that command our sympathies, Don Quixote is indebted to himself, whereas for his comical and pitiful aspects he is indebted to that unwholesome environment in which he lives—the environment "whose purpose was to submerge and kill him instead of applying his high qualities for the benefit of society." Here lies the source of the depressing effect always produced by the *Quixote*.[14]

In conclusion to this portion of his study, Karelin comments on the unusual accuracy with which the type is drawn. Books of chivalry, a pathological product of a diseased society, could not help but make Don Quixote mad. "The novels of chivalry affected his mind only be-

[10] *Ibid.*, p. 8.　　[11] *Ibid.*　　[12] *Ibid.*, p. 12.
[13] *Ibid.*, p. 11.　　[14] *Ibid.*, p. 10.

8 7

cause the society that had originally produced them first muddled Don Quixote's brain" and the novels, its product, completed the process of disintegration.[15]

Why is Don Quixote mad? What elements in society, history, or in the economic set-up may have caused this madness? Karelin claims that social conditions shut off normal outlets for Don Quixote's inclinations and he was forced to seek self-expression elsewhere.[16] This phenomenon is by no means confined to the *Quixote* or *Paradise Lost*, the critic points out. It is ever to be found in life. We, too, have in our midst persons who are completely withdrawn from the sensual ego, persons who are ready to act in the name of an idea. If our atmosphere were a healthy one, they would not come to grief but, like Don Quixote's, it is *not* healthy. Our dreamers are also forced into paths of fantasy—hence the prevalence of Don Quixotism in the present-day world. Parallels to Don Quixote's antics are to be found daily, in all walks of life, and, Karelin says, they will not vanish for years and years to come—if ever.[17] This section of the study is particularly important, for it defines and characterizes Don Quixotism as a psychological phenomenon to be met not only in individuals, but also in social groups—in, for example, the German attitude towards France in the 1870's.[18]

There is much that is valuable in this article, and therefore its importance in Cervantes criticism cannot be denied, but its actual construction could have been better. Karelin is concerned with two aspects of one phenomenon, but every now and then he introduces irrelevant material that detracts from the logical development of the main thesis. His contrast between Don Quixotism-Demonism and "Sanchism" furnishes an example. The idea in itself is good, but as it is presented it is unbalanced and incomplete. He then follows Turgenev's example and attempts to set up two opposing poles, with

[15] *Ibid.*, p. 15.   [16] *Ibid.*, pp. 11-12.   [17] *Ibid.*, p. 16.
[18] *Ibid.*, pp. 16-22, contains this example, as well as many parallels between modern man and Don Quixote.

mankind distributed between them. Then he immediately drops this figure and without further warning turns to Don Quixotism's and Demonism's relation to greatness. Furthermore, a disproportionately small amount of space is devoted to the actual thesis of Don Quixotism and Demonism, for his sociological interpretation, as it stands, is not above reproach.

Fewer repetitions and more reservations and logical deductions would have probably made Karelin's interpretation sounder. Instead, at the slightest provocation, he digresses into clever but none the less long, irrelevant comparisons, such as that of Sancho and Richard III,[19] or into discussions of other aspects of the novel—for example, the value of *Don Quixote*. He dwells at length upon its merits—the humane element that it introduced into the new literature; the progressive ideas it expressed —for example, on the treatment of the Moors and slaves; "the magnificent panorama of customs, manners and beliefs of the national, social and private life of a whole epoch."[20] This has absolutely nothing to do with Don Quixotism and Demonism as aspects of ethical conduct. However, some of these irrelevancies constitute the article's main value, for in them Karelin touches upon *Don Quixote*, the work of Cervantes. He deals with aspects of the novel hitherto neglected by Russian critics. For a student of Cervantes many of these observations and much of Karelin's information is no longer new, but they were new to the Russian reading public of 1860.[21]

Some years later V. G. Korolenko (1853-1921), an important writer of the late nineteenth century, commented on Karelin's work in his diary thus: ". . . Karelin continues speculating on what would have happened had Don Quixote known political economy. He would then have been in danger of 'arriving at some Malthusian solutions,' etc., etc. What a naïve attempt—to measure gigantic hu-

[19] *Ibid.*, p. 32.   [20] *Ibid.*, pp. 26-28.
[21] *Ibid.*, pp. 28-30. For a review of Karelin's essay cf. N. K. Mikhailovski, *Polnoye sobranie sochineni* (St. P., 1913), x, pp. 721-23.

man types with the yardstick of the tiny contemporary
moment! A proof of this is that science, even the 'contemporary' one, has its own Sancho Panzas and that pedant-
ism is just as eternal as Don Quixotism, so profoundly
commented on by Mr. Karelin ("Don Quixotism and
Demonism"). 'Following the original,' Mr. Karelin can
'unerringly guess' what would have happened to Don
Quixote under different conditions of life. In classical
Greece, for example, he would have been something on
the order of Socrates! Again, what a naïve misinterpretation, arising from an equally naïve adherence to the theories of the 'influence of conditions and milieu'! First of
all, Cervantes' Don Quixote is an eternal type, immortal
always and under all conditions. Secondly, he is a Spaniard of the end of the sixteenth and beginning of the seventeenth centuries. Cervantes clearly indicated the reason
for the madness of Don Alonso Quijado, the hidalgo from
La Mancha. But in order to have so distinct a delineation
of the accompanying circumstances in the given character and to produce so lavish a harvest, a deep foundation
of typical qualities of the character were needed. These
qualities are such that under no conditions of education
or milieu would the 'imaginative' and independent Don
Quixote, analyzed by the critic, have become a Socrates!
Not to comprehend this means either a complete disregard of the meaning of the Lamanchan knight's image, or
an attribution to it of an interpretation too narrow as well
as too temporal. Can Mr. Karelin really assert that in the
'conditions of classical antiquity' there were no Don
Quixotes, or that in Cervantes' Spain there were no
people of Socrates' type? No. Don Alonso became a Don
Quixote because he was a Don Quixote by nature from
the very start. He was born with a preponderance of
imagination and independent impulses over analysis and
criticism. The reading of the chivalric romances and
the atmosphere filled with the shades of dying feudalism
are but secondary features, which gave the Lamanchan
hidalgo the coloring of his time and place. . . . They are
merely the clothes of an immortal type.

"It is doubtful that the reason for the appearance of Don Quixotes in mankind . . . will ever be found, even by the most scientific of sciences—'psychological hygiene.' This is so because in his immortal work Cervantes touched those depths of the human spirit where it is a matter of dealing with the vital facts of human nature. Humanity has Don Quixotes, as well as Hamlets and Socrates, and 'psychological hygiene' must recognize this fact completely and unconditionally. As for the reason for Don Quixote's illness . . . well, to this Cervanteses, not versed in 'psychological hygiene,' really have quite an adequate answer."[22]

Belinski's, Turgenev's and Karelin's articles on Don Quixote all presuppose the reader's acquaintance with the novel. They discuss the hero extensively, but little is said about the author or the actual work. In this respect V. G. Avseyenko's study, "The Origin of the Novel," is different.[23] Its purpose is to acquaint the public with Rabelais' and Cervantes' place in literature, with their works and their significance.

Avseyenko (1842-1913) was himself a reactionary novelist of the sixties and seventies. The first section of his essay deals with Rabelais and the French Renaissance, and the second with Cervantes and the corresponding period in Spain. Broad suggestive strokes depict the Spanish Renaissance, bringing into the foreground its political, religious, imperialistic and cultural features, tracing its development from a rapid emergence from the Middle Ages, through a meteoric rise to the zenith— *Don Quixote*. *Don Quixote* contains in it, Avseyenko contends, the highest and most perfect expression of this period, and at the same time the seeds of its disintegration.

Avseyenko then acquaints the reader with Cervantes' activity in diverse branches of literature. Heretofore, the

[22] V. G. Korolenko, *Dnevnik* [Diary], in four volumes (Giz Ukrainy, 1925-1928), I, 190, entry made in 1890.
[23] V. Avseyenko, "Proiskhozhdenie romana: Servantes," *Russki Vestnik* (1877), CXXXI, part 9, pp. 95-124; and CXXXII, part 2, pp. 442-62.

Russian public had known about the *Quixote* and perhaps something of the *Novelas* and the *Galatea*, but *Persiles y Sigismunda* and Cervantes' dramatic works had
never been mentioned. In this study Avseyenko introduces *Persiles y Sigismunda*. Competently he discusses
some of its merits and shortcomings.[24] He considers the
novel's "serious subject matter" to be of particular importance, but here he digresses into philosophic speculations
centering on Cervantes' choice of the Arctic region as a
setting for the tale. He sees in this selection a definite
purpose—a desire to contrast the simplicity and truth of
primeval existence with the decadent life of southern
Europe, the seat of Renaissance culture. It is to those
northern lands that Persiles is drawn in his search for
truth, beauty and goodness. In this Avseyenko is hardly
faithful to the text of the novel. Despite this distortion,
perhaps intentional, the passage is very interesting.

Avseyenko begins his discussion of the *Quixote*[25] with
a commentary on Cervantes' initial aim in writing the
book. Like so many other critics, he believes that the
purpose was to ridicule the novels of chivalry out of existence, but that the idea outgrew its original plan. The
idea, he continues, though it did assume tremendous proportions, developed a remarkable adaptability and flexibility. It lends itself perfectly to countless interpretations, limited not by the printed matter in the book, but
only by the reader's own vision, imagination or intellectual keenness. If one wishes to consider *Don Quixote* a
political and social satire of Spain, ample substantiation
for this thesis can be found. If one insists on its being a
novel of manners, or a presentation of the conflict between the real and the ideal, or an impersonation of faith
—for all these, as well as many other interpretations, *Don
Quixote* can offer plenty of material. This profundity of
content greatly contributed to the novel's success.

The purely literary aspects of the *Quixote* are now introduced by Avseyenko. He is the first Russian critic to

[24] *Ibid.*, cxxxii, part 2, pp. 445-48.
[25] *Ibid.*, pp. 450-62.

stress the aesthetic rather than the ethical value of Cervantes' types. Turgenev and Karelin regard Cervantes' protagonists as synthetic creations, representational puppets. They speak of Don Quixote's symbolism. Avseyenko stresses a completely new feature of these characters—their realism. Though they are creations of "an exceptionally strong imagination," though they are completely new and original, they produce such a convincing impresssion of reality that one feels that one actually does know Don Quixote and Sancho. Avseyenko now proceeds to Cervantes' "artistic tone"—his humor and irony. He believes that Cervantes' humor is comprehensible to most readers and, as such, is a source of great pleasure, but his irony is too refined, too subtle, too consistently sustained to be easily appreciated. Unfortunately, the reader misses it more often than not.

The third literary aspect of the *Quixote* discussed by the critic is its exposition of an aesthetic philosophy, which he considers to have been badly neglected. In fact, he suggests that Cervantes' views, for their soundness and their revolutionary importance in the nineteenth century, deserve a place in textbooks along with the literary theories of Lessing and Hegel.

Before concluding a résumé of Avseyenko's essay, mention should be made of the connection he draws between the author and his work. *Don Quixote* is the product of Cervantes' old age. "Disappointed, sick, crippled and degraded, he felt that his own life, full of suffering, was being reincarnated in this image of the half-mad hidalgo —so severely punished for excesssive faith and desire. Between Cervantes' life and his novel there exists a personal bond which must be explained in order to understand his work fully." Avseyenko then selects some of the biographical material contained in the *Quixote* and demonstrates its importance.[26]

The critic does not forget the other works of Cervantes. He has a few words to say about the *Galatea*,[27] about

[26] *Ibid.*, cxxxi, part 9, p. 106.
[27] *Ibid.*, cxxxii, part 2, p. 451.

some of the *Novelas*,[28] and about Cervantes' dramatic activity. Granting and explaining Cervantes' dramatic limitations, Avseyenko still calls him the real creator of the Spanish theater, substantiating this claim with a good brief picture of Spanish drama before Cervantes' time.[29]

This material is presented in a simple, logical manner. There is nothing new or startling about the essay, but Avseyenko makes no pretense to originality. And after all, he was not writing for today, but for the Russian public of 1877. He had available some important information about the author of a very popular novel. These data had never been given to the public before, so he offered them. His main purpose was to present facts and to show their literary importance.

N. I. Storozhenko (1836-1906), a professor of European literatures at the University of Moscow, contributed another significant study on Cervantes, "The Philosophy of Don Quixote."[30] After surveying the earlier critical attitudes towards Cervantes' novel, he points out the pitfalls to which the philosophical approach can lead: "It is a critic's lawful and inherent right to evaluate from different angles the types created by an artist, to uncover the general meaning of the work, and to draw therefrom this or that moral deduction—but to abuse this right and to ascribe to a given work ideas or symbols, such as a conflict between realism and idealism, poetry and prose, etc., is absolutely wrong."[31]

Instead of crushing Don Quixote into some new mold, Storozhenko considers him in the original, the *Quixote* of Cervantes. When possible and plausible, he uses some of the ideas proposed by the philosophic school, which considered Don Quixote an idealist, an enthusiastic personality. At the same time he does not disregard the more realistic views advanced by Lvov. Never forgetting the

[28] *Ibid.*, p. 444.
[29] *Ibid.*, p. 442.
[30] N. Storozhenko, "Filosofia Don Kikhota," *Vestnik Yevropy* (St. P., 1885), v, 307-24.
[31] *Ibid.*, p. 308.

original novel, he synthesizes, as Derjavin terms it,[32] the two views and gives them a well-rounded form.

Storozhenko introduces his own thesis by first explaining the social conditions and political measures that led up to Cervantes' writing a satire on the books of chivalry.[33] He discusses Cervantes' familiarity with this genre and points out that the Spaniard ridiculed not only the spirit, but also the mannerisms of the novels of chivalry.[34] Furthermore, for a more convincing presentation of a living model showing "the harmful effects of the books of chivalry, Cervantes did not select a stupid fellow who is easily led astray, but an intelligent, well-read man who is full of exalted aspirations. This man, however, has a vulnerable spot—a pathologically developed fantasy and a passionate interest in human sorrow."[35] Don Quixote's reading affects this weakness and causes his derangement. He is an Amadís who falls asleep after one of his combats and then awakens after the disappearance of feudalism. Oblivious to the fact that now "the moral order rests on different principles, that the rights of the weak and oppressed are defended not by the knight-errants, but by laws and institutions," Don Quixote continues in his old sweet way of knighthood.[36] From this discrepancy numerous comical situations arise, cleverly used by Cervantes to show that Don Quixote's "knightly ideals are just as out-of-date as are his weapons, that his bravery and valor are absolutely unnecessary in the sixteenth century, especially in the form in which he offers them to the world, and that, as a result of this, at every step he commits injustices and finally even harms those whom he wishes to help."[37]

Even the most confirmed of philosophical critics would agree with the first portion of Storozhenko's discussion. But Don Quixote's malady or "vulnerability" has always been the one point subdued by them, intentionally or

[32] Derjavin, "Crítica cervantina en Rusia," *BAH*, xciv, 215-38.
[33] Storozhenko, *op. cit.*, pp. 311-12.
[34] *Ibid.*, p. 313.   [35] *Ibid.*
[36] *Ibid.*, pp. 314-15.   [37] *Ibid.*, p. 315.

otherwise. It would seem that an admission of any pathological condition in Don Quixote would perforce detract
from the glamour of the self-abnegation or idealism with
which the philosophical critics endowed him. But this
position is erroneous. Storozhenko's suggestion of Don
Quixote's duality in no way belittles the knight. "If Don
Quixote, in spite of all his nonsense, can arouse in us not
only laughter, but also pity, that is explained by his dual
personality. Don Quixote is not only a fool and a knight-
errant, but also an intelligent, noble and humane person.
In the behavior of this dualism in Don Quixote's character, sustained throughout the whole novel, is brilliantly
expressed the artistic talent of Cervantes." Don Quixote
may be mad, Storozhenko believes, but once he is outside
the enchanted circle of his *idée fixe*, he is a sage.[38]

Upon these observations Storozhenko sets his refutation of ideas propounded by the earlier critics. "Does
such a misinterpretation of reality as Don Quixote's give
one a claim to heroism?" he asks.[39] No. In considering
Don Quixote the incarnation of the idea of self-sacrifice,
and in stressing the altruistic nature of his exploits, philosophic criticism neglects two points. First, "in life, heroism is valued not only by its moral motivation and spiritual force, but also by its rational instrumentation and a
clear consciousness of the purpose of the exploit and of
the benefit it can bring to mankind." Second, Don Quixote is really a reflection of the novels of chivalry. As a
knight-errant, he is motivated in his exploits not only by
altruistic ideas, but also by a thirst for fame and a desire
to distinguish himself for his lady, and at times the latter
motive takes precedence over the former. Storozhenko
offers plenty of evidence drawn from the *Quixote* for
this, and concludes: "The author of *Don Quixote* did not
ridicule enthusiasm for goodness and truth, but the extravagant form of its manifestation, its caricature, induced by the novels of chivalry, which was not at all
suitable to the spirit of the times."[40]

[38] *Ibid.*, p. 317.   [39] *Ibid.*, p. 316.   [40] *Ibid.*

The last third of the essay is devoted to a variety of topics, some of which are new to the Russian public. Like Avseyenko, he dwells on the biographical significance of the novel.[41] He then sums up Cervantes' literary theories,[42] and his religious,[43] social and political views,[44] documenting his discussion with well-chosen selections from the *Quixote*. In these pages lies the basis for the thorough studies on the social, religious and historical significance of the *Quixote* later to be written by Shepelevich and other Hispanists.

A. N. Veselovski (1836-1906), a professor of European literature at the University of St. Petersburg, approaches the *Quixote* from the aesthetic point of view in his article "The Knight of the Sad Visage."[45] The secret of the work's immortality and eternal appeal Veselovski attributes to its happy blending of realism, humor, comedy and a portrayal of seventeenth century Spain. Cervantes, he feels, was able to perform this marvelous literary feat not by virtue of his erudition or the national traditions of the Spanish Renaissance, but by virtue of his own life experience.[46]

Cervantes' original purpose, to satirize the current literary vogue, weaves throughout the entire work, but this attack on actuality is in effect its defense, according to Veselovski. In attacking the contemporary literary taste, he sought to cure and revivify it. As the tale developed, the implications of the first idea expanded. It even acquired a sociological twist, giving the work the coloring of a novel of manners. "It showed an individual's honorable pay-off to life and man, amidst lawlessness and arbitrariness, caste system and inequality, intolerance and cruelty, which were constructed on a different basis." Without pretending to be a moralist-prophet, Cervantes unrolled this pregnant idea, tracing step by step the ex-

[41] *Ibid.*, pp. 316-20. [42] *Ibid.*, pp. 321-22.
[43] *Ibid.*, pp. 322-23. [44] *Ibid.*, pp. 323-24.
[45] A. N. Veselovski, "Vityaz pechalnago obraza" [Knight of the Sad Visage], *Etyudy i kharakteristiki* (Moscow, 1912), I, 36-45.
[46] *Ibid.*, p. 40.

ploits of the defender of mankind and truth to his tragic
end. Sancho called Don Quixote the "caballero de la
triste figura," for he sensed the melancholy beauty of
these words, which reminded him of the bitter destiny
suffered by the Crusaders of the good old days. Cervantes, a knight at heart, appreciated this epithet and so
did succeeding generations. It was thus that Cervantes
dealt the death blow to the adulterated chivalry of the
libros de caballería and elevated genuine chivalry to its
pedestal.[47]

The article "The Merits of Cervantes and Shakespeare
in Psychiatry," also belonging to this period, appeared
in the *Archive of Legal Medicine* in 1868. This journal
has not been available, but Shepelevich says that the
article is merely a brief reference to an essay by González,
"*El Siglo médico*," and deals with Don Quixote's madness.[48]

[47] A reference to Cervantes is found in Veselovski's "Iz istorii
romana i povesti" [From the history of the novel and nouvelle],
*Sbornik otdelenia russkago yazyka i slovesnosti Imperatorskoi Aka-
demii Nauk*, XL (St. P., 1886), no. 2, p. 14.

[48] L. Shepelevich, "Russkaya literatura o Servantese" [Russian
literature about Cervantes], *Yubileiny sbornik v chest N. I. Storozhenko* (Moscow, 1902), p. 165. For further material on Shepelevich cf. pp. 161-72.

8 · TURGENEV

THE work of the Russian novelist Ivan Turgenev (1818-1883) was intimately connected with Western European culture, and the influence of Spanish culture in particular is traceable to Turgenev's friendship with the Louis Viardot family. During his years in France, Viardot's Spanish wife, the singer Pauline Viardot-García, and her mother introduced Turgenev to Spanish life, customs and literature. They, too, were probably responsible for his undertaking a study of Spanish.

On October 19, 1847, Turgenev wrote, "I have taken a teacher of the Spanish language—el señor Castelar."[1] The identity of this gentleman with the illustrious name remains a mystery. He was probably a Spaniard then living in Paris; the famous Emilio Castelar was at the time some fifteen years old and presumably studying in Spain. Not only did Turgenev sit over grammar books learning his lessons, but he went daily to the García home where he spent pleasant evenings sitting with Viardot's family around the *brasero*, conversing in Spanish. In the same letter in which he described these evenings to Mme. Viardot, he promised her that in four months he would "talk only in that language."[2] He was delighted with his new hobby and the very next day he informed Pauline Viardot that his studies were progressing "bien, très bien, mais très bien."[3] And, indeed, within two months he was able

[1] Ivan Turgenev, *Neizdannye pisma k Pauline Viardot* [Unpublished letters to Pauline Viardot] (Moscow, 1900), p. 13.

[2] Turgenev, "Pisma k Madame Viardot" [Letters to Madame Viardot], *Russkia Vedomosti*, July 28, 1911, Turgenev's letter dated Nov. 26, 1847.

[3] *Ibid.*, Turgenev's letter dated Nov. 27, 1847.

to read Spanish with ease, for Turgenev had a "knack for learning."[4]

Turgenev's interest in Spanish, once aroused, went beyond the acquisition of the spoken language. As a writer and critic, he was eager to use his knowledge for closer acquaintance with Spanish history and culture.[5] He began with Calderón—*La devoción de la Cruz, La vida es sueño* and *El mágico prodigioso*. He also read the *Histoire de la guerre en Espagne dépuis 1807* by General Sarrazin and *Doña Isabel de Solís* by Martínez de la Rosa. Quite in keeping with his views on modern literature, Turgenev considered Martínez infantile.[6]

The date of Turgenev's first acquaintance with Cervantes is unknown. He must have read *Don Quixote* prior to the summer of 1855, for *Rudin* (published in that year) contains a specific reference to it and manifests its influence.

Rudin, the hero of this story, exemplifies the tragedy of the preceding generation, a generation genuinely fine, but wanting in comprehension of the significant values of real life. The plot of the novel is briefly this: The educated and idealistic Rudin unexpectedly appears as a

[4] *Ibid.*, Turgenev's letter dated Nov. 26, 1847.

[5] I. S. Rozenkranz's article "Turgenev and Spanish Literature," *Slavia, casopis pro slovansku filologii* (Prague, 1927), vi, 609-12, is a fairly complete list of extracts from Turgenev's correspondence referring to his study of the Spanish language, to his reading of Spanish literature, to his use of Spanish words, phrases and proverbs, and to his translation of *Rinconete y Cortadillo*. There is, however, one uncertain point. Without indicating the source of information Rozenkranz says, "He was well acquainted with the famous novel of Cervantes, *Don Quixote*, and with Louis Viardot, the husband of the singer, he undertook the translation of this novel into French" (p. 612). No reference to this intention has been found by the present writer. Viardot had translated the *Quixote* in 1836-37 and the *Novelas* in 1838, and no other versions done with Turgenev are known. Rozenkranz may have mistaken here Turgenev's intention to translate *Don Quixote* into Russian for the actual performance (Avrahm, Yarmolinsky, *Turgenev: The Man, His Art and His Age*, New York, 1926, p. 148).

[6] I. Turgenev, *Letters d'Ivan Tourgeneff a Mme. Viardot*, publiées et annotées par Halperine-Kaminsky (Paris, 1907), p. 87, letter dated July 4, 1849.

guest at the charming estate of some idle Russian gentry. His effusive and eloquent personality arouses intense likes and dislikes. Natalya, his hostess' daughter, is dangerously fascinated by him. With youthful enthusiasm, Natalya offers to sacrifice everything to be with him, but Rudin does not grasp the full import of the girl's proposal. Where she expected to find a heroic lover, she finds an impractical Don Quixote. Compelled to leave the estate, Rudin plunges into a series of foolhardy adventures which culminate in his futile death.

In Rudin Turgenev portrays the type of man whose nature and education have removed him from the realities of life, a man who has constructed for himself the world of an idealist, a man of sincere interests, full of aspirations for truth. With all his familiarity with philosophic postulates, with all his lofty comprehension of the needs of mankind, Rudin, like Don Quixote, is powerless when confronted by reality. Heroic in theory, Rudin is a coward in love. Sadly, but without remorse, he does the only correct thing—he rejects Natalya in submission to her mother's will. Submission is the easier in that it also restores to him the thing that he cherishes above all, freedom.

The freedom motif emerges when Rudin prepares to depart from the estate. He asks his admirer Basistov: "Do you remember what Don Quixote says to his squire when he is leaving the court of the duchess? 'Freedom, my friend Sancho,' he says, 'is one of the most precious possessions of a man, and happy is he to whom Heaven has given a bit of bread and who need not be indebted to anyone.' What Don Quixote felt then, I feel now. . . ."[7] Rudin is quite right in drawing this parallel, for the Lasunski home offers him the promise of a happy life, just as at the duchess' court lay the apparent fruition of all of Don Quixote's and Sancho's dreams. In both cases, however, the heroes soon realize that the price for this security and satisfaction is their freedom. Like Don Quix-

[7] Turgenev, *Rudin*, translated by Constance Garnett (New York, 1894), p. 195.

ote, Rudin turns his back on all this, takes his freedom and goes forth to lead a life equally fantastic, equally irrational, equally altruistic. Without family, without money, without a destination, Rudin wanders through the country in much the same manner as Don Quixote.

Rudin's quixotic tendencies, suggested throughout the book, are best revealed in his conversation with Lezhnev at the end of the novel, in which he describes his life after his departure from the Lasunski home. In the course of his wanderings he had met an eccentric science-enthusiast, whose resources Rudin tried to apply to humanitarian causes. He tells Lezhnev, "My plans, brother, were great; I dreamed of various improvements and innovations."[8] He entered upon this venture with high hopes, but constant self-examination killed his faith in the enterprise and, as a result, two years' work came to nothing. "There is in Rudin's actions something of Don Quixote de la Mancha," comments Fedoseyev, "but in his speculations something of Hamlet."[9] Rudin then joined Kurbeyev, and they decided to pool their resources "for the public benefit, by converting one of the rivers in the province of K. into a navigable stream."[10] After sacrificing for this scheme all that he had, Rudin failed. But these disappointments did not kill his idealism. Like Don Quixote, he falls, then rises and goes right ahead with imperturbable faith. He falls again, only to rise anew. After the ill-fated experiment with the river project, he tried to make himself socially useful by becoming a professor of Russian literature;[11] but here, too, disappointment awaited him. After numerous such attempts Rudin dies in the French Revolution—significantly fighting heroically for the cause of freedom.

In addition to these parallels between Rudin and Don Quixote, there are less important ones, such as his man-

[8] *Ibid.*, p. 239.
[9] G. Fedoseyev, "O realizme Turgeneva" [On Turgenev's Realism], *Otyabr*, x (Oct. 1933, Moscow), 205-12; cf. p. 208.
[10] Turgenev, *Rudin*, p. 243.
[11] *Ibid.*, pp. 247-48.

ner of speaking, which is characterized by fervor, passion and sincerity. No person is too sophisticated for him to instruct. Though Rudin does not saddle a Rosinante, he goes forth like Don Quixote to preach and debate. He talks to Pigasov, Basistov and Natalya in the same manner that he uses to the German dressmaker. He speaks with a fluency and erudition worthy of Don Quixote. Like the hidalgo, he is more skilled in dialectics and exposition than in description or narrative. In courtesy, generosity and candor Rudin is a true son of Don Quixote.

The explanation for this similarity between Rudin and Cervantes' hero must be sought by an examination of the sources of Turgenev's creative impulses. As the author himself says, "Not possessing a great deal of free inventiveness, I was always in need of the solid ground of others upon which I might walk."[12] The character of Rudin consists of many elements, among which are personalities in Russian philosophical circles of the 1830's and 1840's and Don Quixote as well. Where the influence of the living models ends and that of the Cervantian begins is impossible to determine, but the result is a character who is unquestionably related to Don Quixote.

Writing of Rudin, the critic Pisarev says: "It is of utmost importance to dethrone the empty *talker*, to show that he is talking nonsense . . . that he can only be a pompous orator. Such a lesson will sober up a whole generation, which, once sobered, will examine surrounding phenomena. The generation of Rudins—Hegelians, preoccupied only with the supremacy of system in their ideas and the intricate mystery of their phrases—reconciled us to the absurdities of life, justified them by various lofty opinions, and, harping all their lives on aspirations, did not stir from one place, and did not know how to improve even the peculiarities of their own personal life.

"It is just as important to uncrown this type as it was for Cervantes to bury, by means of his Don Quixote, the novels of chivalry, that last heritage of medieval life. The

12 Yarmolinsky, *op. cit.*, p. 148.

type of a fine *phraseur*—who is absolutely and sincerely fascinated by the stream of his own eloquence, for whom words supplant actions and who, living within his own imagination, vegetates in real life—is completely exposed by Turgenev. . . ."[13]

Cervantes continued to be very much on Turgenev's mind during these years.[14] In 1861, he delivered his famous speech on *Hamlet and Don Quixote*, to be discussed in detail later in this chapter, and subsequently he made a translation of *Rinconete y Cortadillo*.[15]

Bazarov of *Fathers and Sons* was conceived in this same period. The model consciously used by Turgenev was a certain nihilistic provincial doctor; unconsciously, however, he breathed a quixotic spirit into Bazarov. Indicative, too, is the fact that the similarity existing among all of Turgenev's heroes is particularly strong between Bazarov and Rudin, who was plainly influenced by Cervantes. Turgenev was completely unaware of the kinship between Rudin and Bazarov until it was called to his attention. In describing the genesis of Bazarov, he tells how he selected the doctor for his model.

"The impression this personality produced upon one was very strong but indistinct. At first, I could not give myself a very clear account of him, and I watched intently everything that surrounded me, as though desirous of believing in the truthfulness of my own sensations. I was confused by the fact that nowhere in our literature did I find what was so apparent to me everywhere. Naturally, doubt rose. Am I going after a shadow . . . ? I communicated my idea to him [a prominent Russsian critic], and with dumfounded amazement heard the following comment, 'You have, I believe, portrayed a similar type

[13] D. I. Pisarev, "Pisemski, Turgenev, Goncharov," *Sochinenia Pisareva*, I, 459.

[14] Yarmolinski (*op. cit.*, p. 148) suggests that at this time Turgenev considered "turning *Don Quixote* into Russian." His source of information is not known to the present writer.

[15] P. V. Annenkov, *Literaturnia vospominania* [Literary reminiscences] (St. P., 1909), pp. 585, 587, letters dated Feb. 21, 1866, and Feb. 28, 1866, respectively.

in Rudin.' I was silent. What was there to say? Rudin and Bazarov—the same type?"[16]

Bazarov, the personification of nihilism, can be considered in the following relation to Don Quixote: It is not customary to regard negation as a form of idealism, and therefore one's first impression of Bazarov does not recall Don Quixote. One is only aware of the strength of his convictions, of his faithfulness to his credo, and of his self-sacrifice in the name of this idea. Such qualities are definitely uncommon in Turgenev's heroes. When they do appear, they are traceable to a foreign source, and here, it seems, to the *Quixote*.

The reading of books of chivalry was a vogue of the period in which Cervantes' hero lived. The hidalgo represents this fashion and its results. Nihilism was one of the important intellectual movements of the 1860's, denying, among other things, sentiment, emotion and art. This intellectual attitude and its effect are exemplified in Bazarov.

Don Quixote embraces the ideal of the novels of chivalry, persuades Sancho to become his squire and sets out with him into the world to realize his beliefs. Bazarov saturates himself with nihilistic principles, wins over Arkady Kirsanov as his disciple and, with faith and fervor equal to that of Don Quixote, sets out to disseminate and practice these precepts. With eloquence worthy of the knight of La Mancha himself, Bazarov teaches Arkady the fundamentals of nihilism, and defends them in arguments with Pavel Kirsanov.

One of the prerequisites of chivalry, in Don Quixote's opinion, is a lady with whom the knight must be passionately in love, a lady who motivates his deeds. In this respect Bazarov's position seems to be a point of departure. Nihilism denies love, hence the reason for Bazarov's attitude towards Odintsova. He meets this enticing and intelligent widow at a dance. Despite his notions concerning relations with women, the normal young man

[16] Turgenev, "Po povodu 'Otsov i Detei' " [Concerning "Fathers and Sons"], *Polnoye sobranie sochineni* (St. P., 1913), 101-2.

within him speaks. And Bazarov, the nihilist, tries to stifle such heretical impulses by intellect. When, after leaving the ball, Arkady comments on the lady's charm, Bazarov replies, "What a magnificent body!—shouldn't I like to see it on the the anatomy table!"[17] Yes, he is a hypocrite. Yet were he to admit even to himself that he is interested in the lady, he would come in conflict with his credo. Later on, there is a violent struggle between the healthy male and the nihilist that comes to a crisis when Odintsova provokes a confession of love from Bazarov.[18] Fortunately for his idealism, the matter comes to nothing. He masters his emotions and reverts to his old mode of existence. There is, however, a tinge of doubt or regret in his mind, which is revealed in his comment on Arkady's proposed marriage.[19] Thus it can be demonstrated that this point of apparent divergence between the two characters, Bazarov and Don Quixote, is fundamentally a link, for in their contradictory attitudes towards women is distinctly manifested an identical pursuit of and loyalty to their respective ideals.

Don Quixote endures many privations and never realizes that they are quite unnecessary. Bazarov, too, brings upon himself unwarranted suffering. He denies himself the comforts of his parental roof, the joys of love and marriage and the pleasures derived from art. Just like Don Quixote, he embraces an ideal, goes out and fights for it; when he discovers that it is a "phantom," he dies. Don Quixote on his deathbed admits that the pursuit of his ideal was madness. Bazarov does not, although a distinct note of disillusionment is heard.

Before evaluating Turgenev's celebrated speech *Hamlet and Don Quixote*,[20] attention should be called to three phases of the novelist's critical and personal background. The first is his contact with the preceding period in the

[17] Turgenev, "Otsy i deti," *Polnoye sobranie sochineni* (St. P., 1913), II, 90.
[18] *Ibid.*, pp. 107-15.   [19] *Ibid.*, pp. 212-15.
[20] Turgenev, "Hamlet i Don Kikhot," *Pol. sob. soch.* (St. P., 1913), X, 451-75.

persons of P. A. Pletnev[21] and Pushkin. The second is his Berlin education, which imbued him with Hegelian philosophy and criticism, and implanted within him the germs of Westernism and cosmopolitanism. The third is his close friendship with the Louis Viardot family, previously mentioned. The first two contacts account for his critical attitude, the last for his intimate knowledge of the *Quixote* and of Spain.

One further trait in Turgenev's character must be stressed here—his lack of self-assurance. He was never his own master. His early years were dominated by his mother and the remainder of his life by his infatuation with Mme. Viardot. In creative work he was afraid to depend on his own inventiveness and sought out models,[22] constantly calling for the approbation of his friends to assure him that his work was worthwhile. This weakness bothered the novelist who, no doubt, would have liked to resemble that epitome of independence, Don Quixote. His longing is evident in the models that he selected for his heroes.[23] The models were strong, but, more often than not, in his hands they became weak puppets. As Mirsky remarks, Turgenev strove for Don Quixotes, but produced Hamlets.[24]

Turgenev was not the first to link *Don Quixote* to *Hamlet*. Friedrich Schlegel anticipated him in this, but Schlegel did not concentrate on the heroes of the two works. He discerned a certain property that appears in the works of Cervantes, Shakespeare and Goethe—a duality, which he explains in his discussion of *Wilhelm Meister*. The duality that appears in Goethe's work proceeds, Schlegel felt, from the fact that it was created at two distinct moments, springing from two different ideas. At first, it was conceived as a purely artistic novel but, once conceived, it extended itself beyond the limits set

---

[21] P. A. Pletnev (1792-1865), Pushkin's friend, literary agent and successor as editor of the journal *Sovremennik*, a poet in his own right, was Turgenev's professor at the University of St. Petersburg.

[22] Cf. p. 103.   [23] Cf. p. 105.

[24] D. S. Mirsky, *A History of Russian Literature* (New York, 1934), p. 248.

for it by the author. It outgrew the first draft. To the
original scheme is added "the formative teaching of living
art, and it becomes the genius of the whole. Just this type
of remarkable duality is apparent in the two most complete masterpieces in the entire realm of romantic art—
in *Hamlet* and in *Don Quixote*. . . . To these alone is
Goethe's universality comparable."[25] This is the essence
of Schlegel's analysis. He discusses briefly the art of the
authors, but he does not go into the similarities or differences that a related technique can produce when it is
handled by the three writers under consideration.

Turgenev overlooks technique, and begins where
Schlegel leaves off. He, too, stresses the fact that the
Quixote outgrew the author's first intention, and then
shows how this expansion is manifested. Cervantes' genius, Turgenev has said elsewhere,[26] produced a truly great
work, conceived in the very depths of his poetic personality, a personality that was well acquainted with contemporary life and reflected it not in part, but in the whole.
It created a work which by its grace reflects the Middle
Ages (the epoch), and by its hero represents the spirit
of the South (the locality and the people), a bright,
joyous, naïve spirit—receptive, but not capable of penetrating into the depths of life; one, nevertheless, that reflects all of life's phenomena.[27]

Don Quixote's ideal and his attitude towards it is such
a reflection. His "enthusiasm for this cherished thought,
his sublime faith in it, his firm moral constitution, endow
all his actions, thoughts, judgments, even his pitiful figure, with a certain aureole of magnificence and brilliance,
regardless of the humiliating circumstances into which he
constantly falls." He knows but this one ideal, to which
he is always constant. This biases him mentally, but what

[25] F. Schlegel, *Seine prosaischen Jugendschriften* (Vienna, 1906),
ii, 381.
[26] Turgenev, "Faust, Tragedia Goethe," perevod M. Vronchenko
[*Faust*, a tragedy by Goethe], *Pol. sob. soch.*, x, 263-307; cf. p.
265. In this interpretation of greatness, Turgenev coincides with
Grigoryev and Taine.
[27] Turgenev, *Hamlet i Don Kikhot*, p. 465.

of it? He needs nothing else. He understands the principal thing in life, that something which was concealed from Turgenev and from many of us—his purpose on the earth.[28]

Cervantes' depiction of Don Quixote's love for Dulcinea expresses a fundamental peculiarity of human behavior. "We, too," says Turgenev, "in our life's journey have seen people dying for equally non-existent Dulcineas or for equally coarse and often sordid nonentities, in which they discern the realization of their ideal, and the transformation of which they also ascribe to the influence of evil—we nearly said 'enchanters'—evil chance or individuals."[29]

Turgenev finds further observation of human nature in the hero's impetuosity. This trait makes the hidalgo appear comical, but the episodes in which it is manifested are only a comical frame about a picture pregnant with meaning—he who, in sacrificing himself, first stops to calculate and weigh all consequences, is hardly capable of self-sacrifice.[30] Mass psychology is reflected in Sancho's fidelity. The secret of Sancho's attachment to Don Quixote lies in "the peculiarity of the masses—in the tendency towards happy and honest blindness, in the propensity for disinterested enthusiasm, and in the scorn of daily bread."[31] "A great, universally historical peculiarity!" exclaims Turgenev. "The mass always ends up by following, believing implicitly those persons whom it had formerly jeered, whom it damned and persecuted, but who, undaunted by its persecutions and even by its damnations, mindless of its laughter, go unswervingly forward, with their eyes fixed upon their goal. They seek, they fall, they rise, and finally find. . . ."[32]

Turgenev offers a clever interpretation of Don Quixote's encounter with the swine. This adventure is not an anticlimax, but a vital episode which is characteristic of life. "Such trampling always occurs in the lives of ideal-

---

[28] *Ibid.*, pp. 452-53.
[29] *Ibid.*, p. 461.
[30] *Ibid.*, p. 457.
[31] *Ibid.*, p. 459.
[32] *Ibid.*, p. 460.

ists and always at the end. It is the last toll that they have to pay to coarse chance, to indifferent and vulgar misunderstanding. . . . It is the slap of a pharisee. Then they can die. They have gone through fire, have won immortality, and it is opening up before them."[33]

At the conclusion of his analysis of *Don Quixote*, Turgenev draws attention to the hero's deathbed speech, in which he, for the first and last time, mentions his nickname, "Alonso, el bueno." "This is the only word that has meaning in the face of death," says the writer. "All will pass, all will vanish, but good deeds will not disappear in smoke; they are more enduring by virtue of their brilliant beauty."[34]

Thus Turgenev interprets the *Quixote* as an expression of the phenomena of human life, and of the behavior of a certain intellectual type. He concedes that these ideas were perhaps not inserted by the author consciously, but he does believe that they made their way into the work as an inherent product of Cervantes' "poetic personality." "It seems to us that in these two types (Don Quixote and Hamlet) are embodied two opposite fundamental peculiarities of human nature—the two poles of an axis about which it revolves. We think that all people belong more or less to one of these two types; . . . All people live consciously or unconsciously by an ideal, which they accept in totum, or subject it to minute examination; the ideal may be within the man—as his 'I'—or without—something that he considers superior." Don Quixote represents faith in something eternal, in something outside the individual—in truth, which is attainable only by constant devotion and sacrifice. Hamlet represents egotism, skepticism, analysis, and therefore incredulity. Hamlet thinks too much. "The man who sets out to sacrifice himself with careful forethought and consideration of all the consequences . . . is hardly capable of self-sacrifice. . . . Only he who is led by the heart reaches the ultimate goal." Don Quixote loves man, believes and can inspire the same feeling in the masses. "It seems to us, therefore,

[33] *Ibid.*, p. 469.   [34] *Ibid.*, p. 472.

that the principal thing in life is sincerity and strength of our convictions—the result lies in the hands of faith. This alone can show whether we have been contending with phantoms or real foes, and with what armor we have covered our heads. Our business is to arm ourselves and fight."[35]

At the time of its publication, the value of this article was great. It was the second of its kind, dealing with a figure well-loved by most Russians and has inspired much comment.

There is an important article on *Don Quixote* by A. Lvov[36] which is actually a refutation of Turgenev's speech. Unfortunately, it has not been available, and it must be estimated through the comments of other critics. According to Derjavin,[37] Lvov claims Turgenev's speech to be "lleno de divagaciones erróneas y poco argumentadas." "La división de la humanidad en dos tipos es para Lvov una tentativa inútil y convencional." "Confundió por completo Tourgenev la convicción en lo ideal con la fe en la verdad." Furthermore, Lvov does not consider Don Quixote in the Turgenevian light of idealistic heroism and leadership. For him, the hidalgo is simply a madman. Not only is Don Quixote not an altruist, but the exact contrary—an egoist. Lvov says that Don Quixote fights windmills from egoistic motives—to enrich himself.[38] In regard to Don Quixote's love for Dulcinea,

[35] *Ibid., passim.* Cervantian allusions of Turgenev's not quoted here appear in "Pisma I. S. Turgeneva k Grafine E. E. Lambert" [Turgenev's letters to Countess Lambert], with introduction and notes by G. P. Georgyevsky, in *Vtoroye prilozhenie k Otchetu Imperatorskago Moskovskago Rumyantsevskago Muzeya 1914 goda* (Moscow, 1915), p. 8; and in his "Rech o Shakespeare" [Speech about Shakespeare], in "Pisania I. S. Turgeneva ne vklyuchennia v sobranie yego sochineny," *Russki Propiley* (Moscow, 1916), III, 163.

[36] A. Lvov, *Hamlet i Don Kikhot* (St. P., 1862), cited by Constantin Derjavin.

[37] C. Derjavin, "Crítica cervantina en Rusia," *BAH*, XCIV (1929), pp. 215-38.

[38] A. Yevlakhov, "K trekhsotletiyu Don Kikhota" [For the Three Hundredth Anniversary of Don Quixote], *Mir Bozhi* (1905), no. 5, pp. 47-69; cf. p. 60.

which Turgenev called "ideally chaste," Lvov maintains that Don Quixote loves only his ideal—the thought of Dulcinea.[39]

The critic A. Skabichevski (1838-1910) commented on Turgenev's speech thus: "Unfortunately, Turgenev on the one hand overgeneralized his categories by including in them all people, without exception. . . . This, of course, is too much. . . . On the other hand, he narrowed down the limits of these very categories. Although he avers that all people, without exception, belong either to the Hamlet or to the Don Quixote type, yet upon reading the article one unconsciously gets the impression that the discussion deals exclusively with the cultured and highly educated class."[40] Skabichevski is obviously quibbling here.

Leo Tolstoi (1828-1910), who had read *Don Quixote* himself, wrote of Turgenev: "In my opinion there are three phases in his life and his literary works: (1) Faith in beauty (of women, love, art). This is expressed in a great many of his works. (2) Doubt about this, and about everything. And this is expressed both touchingly and charmingly in *Enough*. (3) An unformulated—apparently purposely so, from fear of grasping it (he himself says somewhere that only the unconscious is strong and vigorous in him)—an unformulated faith that motivates him both in his life and in his writings, a faith in goodness, in love and self-sacrifice, which is expressed in all his self-sacrificing types, and most strikingly and charmingly in his [speech on] *Don Quixote*, where the mood of paradox and the peculiarity of the form freed him from his diffidence about assuming the role of a preacher of goodness."[41]

In a short article,[42] A. G. Hornfeld, a twentieth century

---

[39] *Ibid.*, p. 62.

[40] A. Skabichevski, "Geroi razrushiteli i geroi sozidateli" [Heroes-destroyers and heroes-creators], *Sochinenia A. Skabichevskago v 2 tomakh* (St. P., 1903), II, 893-916; cf. p. 897.

[41] L. N. Tolstoi, *Polnoye sobranie sochineni*, LXIII (Moscow-Leningrad, 1934), p. 149, letter is to Pypin.

[42] A. G. Hornfeld, *Boyevye otkliki na mirovie temy* (Leningrad, 1924), pp. 18-28. The article was written in 1913.

critic and psychologist, examines Turgenev's parallel and
enters some reservations and corrections. He suggests
that here the novelist is attempting to solve his own personal problem. Finding a great similarity between himself and Hamlet, he hates the Danish prince, whereas,
seeing no likeness between himself and Don Quixote, he
conceives a great affection for him. Hornfeld then turns
to Turgenev's statement that there are no pure Hamlets
or Don Quixotes, and says that Turgenev is blind to the
quixoticism that is abundant in Hamlet. "He does not
appreciate him as a great idealist, a champion of truth
. . . as a representative of mankind."

Concerning Turgenev's contention that Don Quixote
represents a high type of human development, Hornfeld
admits that a high type he is, but so is Hamlet, and actually of the two the latter is superior. Turgenev says that
Don Quixote wants to exterminate evil: That is a simple
task for one whose mind is befogged by innocence and
phantasmagoria, whereas Hamlet, striving for the same
end, is also well aware of its true magnitude and man's
impotence. While Hamlet, the critic continues, shares
Don Quixote's desire to uproot evil, he is, in addition, the
bearer of eternal thought. "By it, by its restless motion, by
its restless search, by its agitation, Hamlet's life and
death, actions and fate, are determined. He vacillates.
Thank heaven for that, since it holds promise of great
deeds! We act too much and think too little, therefore we
are like Don Quixote, but we must not forget that we
must think, and that Hamlet's thoughts deal with the
highest problems of human existence. . . . Don Quixote's
problem is solved by him alone, while Hamlet's requires
the cooperation of all mankind."[43]

P. I. Novitski,[44] another modern critic, makes this de-
batable comment on Turgenev's thesis: "In his speech
Turgenev was solving his own internal problem; he was

[43] *Ibid.*, p. 28.
[44] P. I. Novitski, *K. sotsiologii zhanra i obraza* [To the sociology
of genre and image] in the introduction to a Russian translation
of *Don Quixote* (Moscow, 1932), vii-xxxvii; cf. pp. xxiv-xxv.

fighting the timidity, skepticism, of his generation. He utilized the concepts of Shakespeare and Cervantes for the moral rejuvenation of his social milieu. Therefore, he had to condemn Hamlet's spiritual 'intelligentsian' flabbiness, and extol Don Quixote's pure enthusiasm."

G. Fedoseyev, a Soviet critic who, like Novitski, approaches literature mainly from a socio-economic angle, writes: "Turgenev wishes to find the 'fundamental principle' for the solution of the cardinal question about the essence of activity, its conditions and precedents, and decides that humanity is divided into two parts—Don Quixotes and Hamlets. . . . The author puts aside the entire gallery of characters created by him, closes his eyes to real life, to create an abstraction of two eternal human characters. . . . These abstractions are peculiarly Turgenevian; the author's liberal-noble survey of the world reproduces in them his own social nature, and not the whole scale or the entire variety of human types. Turgenev found in this excellent, though incorrect, abstraction only temporary peace from the paradoxes distressing him."[45]

Thus do the critics of succeeding generations respond to Turgenev's *Hamlet and Don Quixote*. They may quarrel with his interpretation of Cervantes' hero, but they still find him provocative.

[45] F. Fedoseyev, "O realizme Turgeneva" [On Turgenev's realism], *Oktyabr*, x (1933, Moscow), 205-12; cf. p. 209. Other references to Turgenev's speech appear in Avseyenko's "Proiskhozhdenie romana" [Origin of the novel], *Russki Vestnik* (1877), vol. 132, part 12, pp. 442-62; A. Yevlakhov, *op. cit.*, pp. 49 and 57; P. Kogan's "Hamlet," *Kratki sistematicheski slovar vsemirnoi literatury* (St. P., 1906), pp. 95-100; and V. Ivanov's "Crizis individualizma" [Crisis of individualism], *Voprosy Zhizni* (1905), v, 47-60.

9 · DOSTOYEVSKI

ESPECIALLY interesting is the relation of Fyodor Dostoyevski (1821-1881) to Cervantes. Though distant geograph-
ically and chronologically, the two great novelists were
exposed to many comparable conditions. Both men were
natives of a country in which religion and patriotism
were inseparable. Both were sons of the city and of socially decadent families. Dostoyevski was also a *ciru-
jano's* son. Despite their fame as writers, they had to
struggle with the literary market for remuneration. Both
came into conflict with other great figures of their respective periods—Cervantes with Lope, and Dostoyevski
with Turgenev and Tolstoi. Imprisonment is another experience the two held in common. These parallels, though
not of prime importance, are significant. Cervantes was
the first novelist to create an abnormal individual as his
hero—a task which he accomplished to perfection. Dostoyevski, his most gifted modern counterpart, produced
abnormal types so excellently conceived that they stand
the test of psychiatric analysis.

Dostoyevski was attracted by the ideological and philosophical aspects of *Don Quixote*, and his interpretation
of them and his comments upon them approach closely
those of the Kantian critics Bouterweck, Sismondi and
his compatriot Turgenev. For him the *Quixote* was a commentary on life and a revelation of the human mind and
heart.

In his *Diary of an Author*, Dostoyevski writes: "Once,
while wandering with his faithful squire Sancho in pursuit of adventure, Don Quixote—that illustrious knight of
the sad visage, the most generous of all the knights that
ever lived, the simplest in soul and greatest in heart of all

115

men—was suddenly beset by a bewildering idea that made him ponder long and hard."[1] His perplexity lay in the physical impossibility of a knight of the chivalric novels killing a host of warriors within a very short time. Don Quixote solved the problem to his own satisfaction by deciding that the soldiers of this army could not have had human flesh. Dostoyevski continues: "Here the great poet and observer of the heart marked one of the deepest and most mysterious aspects of human nature. Oh, this is a great book, not the kind written today. Such books are sent to mankind but once in several centuries! And observations of the deeper aspects of human nature such as the one above one finds on every page. Take, for example, the fact that Sancho, the personification of common sense, prudence, shrewdness, by chance became the friend and fellow traveler of the maddest man in the world. He, and no one else! He deceives Don Quixote constantly, fools him like a child, and at the same time fully believes that he [his master] has a lofty intellect. He is fascinated to the point of tenderness by the greatness of his heart; he believes implicitly in all the fantastic dreams of the great knight; and not once does he doubt that Don Quixote will ultimately win for him the island. How desirable it would be for our youth to become thoroughly acquainted with these products of world literature! I do not know what is taught in literature classes, but I am sure that an acquaintance with this magnificent and saddest of books ever to have been created by the genius of man would elevate the soul of youth with lofty thoughts, would awaken in his heart great questions that would tend to divert his mind from paying homage to the eternal and stupid idol of mediocrity, self-satisfied conceit and vulgar reasonableness. Man will not forget to take this *saddest* of books to the Last Judgment. He will point to its infinitely profound and fatal mystery of man and mankind. He will show how man's purity, wisdom, simplicity, be-

[1] F. M. Dostoyevski, "Dnevnik pisatelya" [Diary of an author], *Polnoye sobranie sochineni F. M. Dostoyevskago*, xi (St. P., 1895), 304-8.

nignity, manliness and, finally, his lofty intellect—all
these, not infrequently (alas, how very frequently!) go
to waste, without benefit to mankind, and are even ridiculed by it, only because all these highly noble and magnificent gifts, with which man is often endowed, lack but
one last gift—namely, the *genius* to manage all the
wealth of these gifts and all their greatness—to manage
and to guide all this power along the road of truth and
not of fantasy and madness, along the path that will
benefit humanity! But geniuses are allotted to clans and
peoples in such meager numbers, and so rarely, that we
frequently witness the spectacle of the evil irony of fate
which often destines noble men and ardent friends of
humanity to jeers, laughter and stoning, only because at
the critical moment they could not penetrate the true
meaning of things and find a *new word.* This spectacle of
futile destruction of such great and noble forces can, indeed, drive some people to despair. It can no longer
arouse laughter, but bitter tears, and can enrage with lasting doubt a heart heretofore pure and credulous.

"Incidentally, I merely wished to indicate that curious
feature which along with hundreds of other equally
penetrating observations Cervantes noticed in the human
heart and pointed out. The most fantastic of men, who
believed to the point of madness in the most fantastic
ideas imaginable, suddenly fell into doubt and perplexity
which almost shattered all his faith. And it is curious that
it was not the absurdity of his basic mania, not the absurdity of the existence of knights wandering about for
the good of mankind, not the absurdity of those enchanted miracles related in the 'most truthful books' that
could shake his faith. No, on the contrary, it was a mere
side issue, a secondary, absolutely trivial circumstance
that threatened his ideal. The visionary suddenly *became
homesick for realism!* It was not the fact that magic
armies made their appearance that disturbed him. Oh,
this was not open to doubt. How could those great and
marvelous knights manifest their prowess if they were
not subjected to all these trials, if there were no envious

giants and evil enchanters? The ideal of knight-errantry is so great, so wonderful and beneficial, and it had so charmed the noble Don Quixote's heart, that to reject belief in it was absolutely impossible for him, was tantamount to treachery to the ideal, duty and love for Dulcinea and mankind. (When, upon his return from his second excursion in which he was conquered by the clever and sane barber Carrasco, the objector and satirist, he did reject it [his ideal]; when he was cured of his mania and became sane, he died then and there, quietly, with a sad smile, consoling the weeping Sancho, loving the entire world with all the great power of love imprisoned in that holy heart of his, realizing, however, that in this world there was nothing left for him to do.) No, it was not the ideal that confused him, but only the very precise and mathematical observation that regardless of how the knight waved his sword, and regardless of his strength, still it was impossible to conquer an army of a hundred thousand in a few hours, even in a day—killing every single man. Yet so it is written in the 'truthful' books. Then a lie is written. But if there is one lie, then all is a lie. How can the truth be saved? And so, to save the truth, he thinks up another idea, but one that is twice as fantastic as the first, more crude and nonsensical. He devises hundreds of thousands of infuriated men with the bodies of mollusks, bodies through which the knight's sharp sword can pass ten times more nimbly and briskly than through those of ordinary men. *Realism* is thereby satisfied, and *truth is saved*, and now, of course, it is possible to believe without a doubt in the first fundamental dream. . . ."

There are a number of other places in Dostoyevski's *Diary* where Don Quixote's name appears. He speaks of extraneous matters and brings in the figure of the Spanish knight by way of comparison. Count Chambort, for instance, "that genuine knight, almost a Don Quixote, an ancient knight with the vow of chastity and poverty, a worthy figure, . . . refused the power and the throne only because he wished to become the king of France not for himself, but for the salvation of France; but since, in his opinion, salvation was not compatible with the compromises demanded of him . . . he refused to rule. . . . I have just compared Count Chambort to Don Quixote, but I know no higher praise. A more profound and a more powerful work than this one (*Don Quixote*) is not to be found. It is thus far the final and greatest word of the human mind. It is the bitterest irony that man is capable of expressing. And if the world were to come to an end, and there in the Beyond—someplace—they were to ask man, 'Well, did you understand your life, and what have you concluded?'—then man could silently hand over *Don Quixote*. 'Here is my conclusion about life, and you —can you criticize me for it?' I do not insist that the man would be absolutely correct, but . . . "[2] and Dostoyevski significantly leaves the sentence unfinished.

In "Metternichs and Don Quixotes," another article in the *Diary*, Dostoyevski compares Russia and the Russian diplomats to the knight from La Mancha: "Russia never could produce its own genuine Metternichs and Beaconsfields. On the contrary, during its entire European existence, it lived not for itself, but for others, namely, for the 'interests of all mankind.' And really, there were instances . . . when she produced Metternichs, but always . . . the Russian Metternich unexpectedly turned out to be a Don Quixote and therefore amazed Europe. Naturally, they laughed at Don Quixote, but now it seems that the time has expired and Don Quixote no longer amuses, but terrifies. The truth of the matter is that undoubtedly he has realized his situation and will not go forth to tilt with windmills."[3] Russia's unselfishness, as represented by her diplomats, prompted Dostoyevski to compare his motherland to Cervantes' knight, and in the remainder of the article he frequently refers to Russia as "Don Quixote."

To cite but one more quotation: Speaking before the Russian Socialists, Dostoyevski said: "The ancient legendary knight believed that all obstacles, all phantoms

---

[2] *Ibid.*, x, 113-14.   [3] *Ibid.*, xi, 53.

and monsters would fall before him, and that he would
conquer all and attain everything if only he would keep
his pledge of justice, chastity and poverty. You will say
that all this is a legend and song that only Don Quixote
can believe, and that the laws of actual national life are
not in the least the same. Well, my dear sirs, I will hereby
corner you and accuse you of being a perfect copy of
Don Quixote, of having the same idea, too, in which you
believe and through which you wish to rehabilitate mankind!"[4]

Early in his career, Dostoyevski created two quixotic
characters—Devushkin and Golyadkin. Makar Devushkin, the protagonist of *Poor Folk*, Dostoyevski's first
work, is an elderly man of very scant means who takes
under his wing a needy girl, Varvara. He cannot afford
this gesture, but he gladly endures great privation for
her. He gives her his protection and surrounds her with
love and solicitude. This contrast between his existence
at the margin of life and his belief in his having "the
power to rise as a defender, protector, a knight (a knight
who is two-thirds a father, and one-third a lover)" is ap-
propriately designated by the critic W. Giusti as "don-
quixotesque."[5] The hero is not modeled after Don Quixote, and the book as a whole bears no resemblance to
Cervantes' novel, yet it has this one quixotic feature, a
spontaneous product of Dostoyevski's own imagination.

The same type of character recurs in *The Double*, another work of Dostoyevski's first period. Golyadkin, the
hero, imagines that his wealthy employer's daughter is in
love with him and needs his protection. This is utter nonsense. Here, again, a poor deluded man aspires to protect
a lady supposedly in distress by means which he has not
at his disposal—with a resulting contrast between the no-
tion of self-sacrifice and actual circumstances.

This appearance of quixotic figures in Dostoyevski's

[4] *Ibid.*, xi, 21. Other references to Don Quixote and Cervantes
will be found on pages 447 and 466 of volume xi.
[5] W. Giusti, "Sul donchisciottismo di alcuni personaggi del Dos-
tojevskij," *La Cultura*, x (1931), 171-79; cf. p. 172.

first novels must not be overlooked, for it reveals a kinship in point of view and predilection in the two authors, springing possibly from similarity in environment, mentality or temperament. Nothing in Dostoyevski's letters of the time, which are so full of comments and references to literature, suggests any acquaintance with the *Quixote*, yet here are two works strongly reminiscent of Cervantes.

A long period of time elapsed before Dostoyevski produced another quixotic character—Prince Myshkin. In the interim he spent ten years in Siberia. Intense suffering sharpened his innately sensitive spiritual constitution, and returned him to life and letters profoundly changed. In 1860 ". . . Dostoyevski reads Turgenev's essay entitled *Hamlet and Don Quixote*. It is curious to note how two opponents as irreconcilable as Dostoyevski and Turgenev agree fundamentally on Cervantes' works and come to the conclusion that *Don Quixote* contains the basic sense of life. . . .

"The reading of the *Quixote* and, in all probability, of Turgenev's essay as well, contributed to the transformation of the type of 'weak in heart' (such as Devushkin) and of the 'double type' (such as Golyadkin) into the humanly complete figure of Prince Myshkin. Doubtless, this development in Dostoyevski is primarily a result of that internal cause (his predisposition to create don-quixotic characters) which we have already noted; nevertheless, Cervantes' hero was definitely in Dostoyevski's mind during this period of transformation."[6]

In 1867 Dostoyevski began work on *The Idiot*. In the first seven drafts of this novel the protagonist, the Idiot, is a figure commonly termed "Dostoyevskian"—feverish, sensual, wallowing in moral filth.[7] In the eighth, the hero emerges a totally different type, distinctly Christlike and quixotic, eventually representing a synthesis of three, possibly four, models, all having very much in common

[6] W. Giusti, *op. cit.*, p. 174.
[7] *Iz arkhiva F. M. Dostoevskago, Idiot* [From F. M. Dostoevsky's archive, Idiot], edited by P. N. Sakulin and N. F. Belchnikov (Moscow-Leningrad, 1931), pp. 1-53, *passim*.

—Christ, Don Quixote, Pushkin's Poor Knight and, it has been suggested, Chatski.[8]

Dostoyevski himself discusses Myshkin's genesis in a letter to his friend and critic S. A. Ivanova: "About three weeks ago I began another novel. . . . The idea of the novel is to present a positively beautiful character. There is nothing more difficult, especially nowadays. Writers, not only ours, but also European, who have attempted to depict a positively excellent character have always given up because this is a tremendous problem. The excellent is the ideal, but neither our ideal nor that of civilized Europe has developed sufficiently. There is only one positively beautiful figure—Christ—and, therefore, the appearance of this immeasurably, infinitely wonderful personality is indeed an unquestionable miracle. . . . But I have gone too far. I will merely mention that of the beautiful characters in Christian literature, Don Quixote alone is the most complete. But he is excellent only because at the same time he is comical. Dickens' Pickwick (a conception infinitely weaker than Don Quixote, yet vast) is also ridiculous, and succeeds by virtue of this fact. Pity is evoked for that ridiculed and beautiful figure, ignorant of its worth, and consequently sympathy is aroused in the reader. This stimulation of pity is the secret of humor. . . . In my work there is positively nothing of the kind (this type of humor) and, therefore, I am dreadfully afraid that it will be an absolute failure."[9]

In the final version of *The Idiot*, the original tale of depravity inspired by the Umetski case[10] is completely eclipsed by the tragic theme of goodness. Now Dosto-

[8] A. L. Bem, *U istokov tvorchestva Dostoyevskago* [At the sources of Dostoyevsky's works], Prague, 1936, p. 25 ff. E. J. Simmons in his excellent book *Dostoevski*, N.Y., 1940, suggests also the image of the inspired idiot, which is so deeply rooted in Russian tradition (p. 214).

[9] "Fyodor Mikhailovich Dostoyevski v pismakh 1867-1870 godov" [Dostoyevski in his letters of 1867-1870] *Russkaya Starina* (July 1885), XLVII, 137-66; cf. p. 144.

[10] V. S. Dorovatovskaya-Lyubimova, " 'Idiot' Dostoyevskago i ugolovnaya khronika yego vremini" [Dostoyevski's "Idiot" and criminal annals of his times], *Pechat i revolyutsia* (1928), III, 31-53.

yevski presents a positively beautiful character, impractical, struggling against the world and finally overwhelmed by it. The book thus becomes a vehicle for a
theme very similar to what Dostoyevski considered the
fundamental idea of the *Quixote*.[11]

A. L. Bem considers Chatski, the hero of Griboyedov's
Woe from Wit, the primary model for Myshkin. He introduces his thesis by showing the place *Woe from Wit*
occupied in Dostoyevski's creative consciousness, and
then says: "What, in Dostoyevski's mind, linked Chatski
to Don Quixote and Pushkin's Poor Knight? . . . First of
all, the fantastic inclinations of the hero (I use this word
in the meaning given to it by Dostoyevski), an absence of
a sense of reality, an existence in a world of fantasy and
created images, an incomprehension of environment and
people. Therefore, upon contact with reality there is a
breakdown, a tragedy of a *dreamer*, which leads to profound disappointment or even ruin. . . . Like Don Quixote . . . Chatski also was unable to 'correct and direct' the
wealth of his talents along the 'real and not fantastic'
road. As with Don Quixote, his powers and abilities are
senselessly lost to humanity. . . .

"Thus far in the personal sphere, failure in love, Chatski's fate reveals features related to . . . Don Quixote de
la Mancha, and Dostoyevski could not but note them in
Chatski. . . . His Prince Myshkin has the same lack of a
sense of reality. . . . His tirade at the Epanchin soirée, . . .
is highly reminiscent, in its psychological aspect, of Chatski's performance at the Famusov party. The monologue
at the end of the third act surprises the reader particularly by its contrast with the setting in which he pro-
nounces it. . . . Here is a clear manifestation of 'Don
Quixotism,' fascination of the spirit by its own fantasy,
inability to understand its surroundings.

"One more feature unites Chatski to Don Quixote. This
feature is love for a woman created by their own fancy.
Chatski sees Sofia Pavlovna just as he wishes to see her.
Subtly Griboyedov shows how Chatski does not notice

[11] Cf. pp. 116-17.

the obvious predilection which Sofia shows for Molchalin. To preserve her image for himself, he conjures up various rivals; only Molchalin does he stubbornly reject. Like Don Quixote, he creates his own Dulcinea and does not see Aldonsa. According to Dostoyevski's admirable interpretation of the image of Don Quixote, the idealist-dreamer, in order to save his illusion, piles lie upon lie, for 'falsehood is saved by falsehood.' . . .[12]

"The 'idiot' Prince Myshkin and the so-called 'madman' Chatski are equally close to Don Quixote, whose image was so dear to Dostoyevski. And, of course, it is understandable that he recalled Chatski when he was creating the 'Don Quixote' in the person of the Prince."[13]

Chatski, belonging to the same generic group as do the other characters mentioned by Bem, has much in common with Don Quixote and the Poor Knight. Griboyedov even called his hero a "Don Quichotte." Bem's analysis, as it stands, seems, however, to be a *tour de force*. Chatski may have entered into the creation of Myshkin only in so far as he is a representation of an enthusiast out of tune with his surroundings.[14] Spiritually and ideologically, he is really far removed from Myshkin and his other models. Even his attitude towards women, to which Bem points, has a texture different from Myshkin's. It is passionate, blinding him to actual circumstances, whereas that of Myshkin, Don Quixote, and the Poor Knight is chaste, pure—sexless.

Dostoyevski appreciated the connection between Pushkin's Poor Knight and Don Quixote,[15] and made outright use of the former. In his novel the Epanchins come to see Myshkin at Pavlovsk, and, in a conversation, Kolya Ivolgin remarks about Aglaya: "A month ago you were looking through 'Don Quixote,' and you cried out those words, that there was nothing better than the 'poor knight.' I don't know whom you were talking of, whether it was Don Quixote or Yevgeny Pavlovitch or some other person, but you were talking of some one and the con-

[12] Cf. p. 118.
[14] Cf. p. 81.

[13] A. L. Bem, *op. cit.*, pp. 27-30.
[15] Cf. pp. 42 ff.

versation lasted a long while."[16] The reference is to Myshkin, which the young people seek to cover up, but Mme. Epanchin insists on an explanation of the allusion, claiming that there is some "fresh foolishness" intended.

" 'There's no foolishness in it, nothing but the deepest respect,' Aglaia suddenly brought out, quite unexpectedly, in a grave and earnest voice. . . .

" 'Deepest respect,' Aglaia went on as gravely and earnestly in response to her mother's almost spiteful questions, 'because that poem simply describes a man who is capable of an ideal, and what's more, a man who having once set an ideal before him has faith in it, and having faith in it gives up his life blindly to it. This does not always happen in our day. We are not told in that poem exactly what the "poor knight's" ideal was, but one can see it was some vision, some image of "pure beauty," and the knight in his loving devotion has put a rosary round his neck instead of a scarf. It's true that there is some obscure device of which we are not told in full, the letters A.N.B. inscribed on his shield. . . .'

" 'A.M.D.,' Kolya corrected her.

" 'But I say A.N.B., and that's what I want to say,' Aglaia interrupted with vexation. 'Anyway, it's clear that the poor knight did not care what his lady was, or what she did. It was enough for him that he had chosen her and put faith in her "pure beauty" and then did homage to her for ever. That's just his merit, that if she became a thief afterwards, he would break a spear for her pure beauty. The poet seems to have meant to unite in one striking figure the grand conception of the platonic love of medieval chivalry, as it was felt by a pure and lofty knight. Of course all that's an ideal. In the "poor knight" that feeling reaches its utmost limit in asceticism. It must be admitted that to be capable of such a feeling means a great deal, and that such feelings leave behind a profound impression, very, from one point of view, laudable, as with Don Quixote, for instance. The poor knight is the same Don Quixote, only serious and not comic. I didn't

[16] Constance Garnett's translation of *The Idiot*, p. 246.

understand him at first, and laughed, but now I love the "poor knight," and what's more, respect his exploits.' . . .

" 'Well, he must have been a fool anyway, he and his exploits, was her mother's comment."[17]

Here Aglaya has brought out the points that appealed to Dostoyevski in these two characters, and furthermore has indicated their connection with Myshkin.

Doubtless Christ was the chief model for Myshkin[18] and Don Quixote the secondary one. The problem of defining the influence of the latter is, however, somewhat difficult because of the resemblance of Don Quixote himself to Christ. It is, therefore, in the variants of the primary model that one can determine the influence of Don Quixote on Myshkin. It appears in the motivating force of the character, in his attitude towards society, his manner of facing adverse circumstances and in the role of women in his life.

The lives of all three, Christ, Don Quixote and Myshkin, are impelled by a desire to help mankind. The awakened spirit of Myshkin, when he emerges from the Swiss sanitarium, is serene and idealistic, seeking to do good to mankind and endow it with all the moral beauty with which he himself is imbued. He comes up against a world of vice and sorrow, and his catastrophe, like Don Quixote's, lies in the fact that he is not aware of this reality. He loves man. Rogozhin's calling him "brother" affords him supreme pleasure. He is deluded (Christ was never deluded) into believing Parfyon's present character is not the true expression of his nature. He gives this man all that he has of holy goodness, but to no avail. Nastasya Filipovna, Ippolit, Burdovski, Lebedev, Ganya—in fact, almost everyone—scorn his noble efforts, or respond with a meanness which may be comparable to the sound pummeling given to Don Quixote in his pursuit of his ideal. In the case of the latter, the assault is physical, but in that of Myshkin it is spiritual and far more painful. The

[17] *Ibid.*, pp. 248-49.

[18] A splendid analysis of Christ's influence on Myshkin is to be found in Simmons' *Dostoevski*, pp. 212 ff.

potential of both Don Quixote and Myshkin is tremendous but they both lack the ability to make effective use of their talents. As Myshkin's name suggests, he has the potential of a lion (lev) but the effectiveness of a mouse (myshka).

Myshkin's attitude towards the world—gentle and submissive, derived from Christ—is in direct contrast to Don Quixote's militant one, but there is one aspect of it that draws him away from Christ and unites him to the hidalgo. Christ was meek not through innocence. He was cognizant of the ways of man. Both Myshkin and Don Quixote, in spite of all their abstract wisdom, are infants when confronted with the human factor. Christ was a realist with a mission, whereas Don Quixote and Myshkin are dreamers with ideals. Christ's purpose in life was within Him. He was the ideal, and therefore the ideal was flexible. Myshkin's and Don Quixote's ideals are without, and consequently more static. Christ behaved as He did, not because of preconceived ideas of man and life, but because His was the path of truth. Throughout His life He was well aware of the limitations of man. Such is not the case with Don Quixote and Myshkin, who want life to fit into their scheme of things and, when they are faced with failure, have to compensate psychologically.

Absolute faith in the *idée fixe* resists the contradictions of reality for some time in the case of Don Quixote and Myshkin. Don Quixote has a supplementary reinforcement—his madness. He lives in a dream world and justifies actual, undeniable fiascoes by fantastic explanations involving giants, enchanters, and so forth, or he simply refuses to recognize them as failures. With such a conviction, he goes from one adventure to another unperturbed. Myshkin's reinforcement is his epileptic condition. The world about him denies his ideal. Nastasya Filipovna, Rogozhin, Ippolit are living contradictions of it, yet his belief survives a long time for, like Don Quixote, he draws strength from his ailment. In crises Don Quixote defends his ideal by fantasy, but he is a Spaniard of the sixteenth century and a madman. Myshkin is a Russian of the nineteenth century and is unable to resort to evil sorcerers to sustain him. He does see his failures, but denies this recognition entrance into his consciousness. A clash between his ideal and reality produces emotional conflicts. Unresolved, they are augmented by others, until a conflict of great intensity produces a stroke. These strokes come at moments critical to his *idée fixe* and are a form of revenge. The world refuses to recognize his ideal, destroys his hopes; therefore, he annihilates the world subjectively. He refuses to let it govern his consciousness. This is well illustrated in Rogozhin's attempted murder of Myshkin. Thus Myshkin's epilepsy parallels Don Quixote's madness.

Dostoyevski obviously had this parallel in mind. His idealist needed a way of compensating for disillusionment, and Cervantes' device of a psychological derangement was the solution. It is important to recall that of all characteristics given to Myshkin in the first draft, epilepsy was the only one retained in the finished portrait. The reversal of the original concept of the hero and its subsequent development was effected when the figures of Christ and Don Quixote entered actively into Dostoyevski's creative processes.

In *The Idiot* the love motif is just as inseparable from the hero's ideal as it is in the *Quixote*, but it is far more complicated. Two women represent two aspects of Myshkin's *idée fixe*. Aglaya is substituted for Dulcinea, and Nastasya Filipovna for abused humanity, whose lot the champion of Good wishes to alleviate. In the *Quixote* this second aspect is developed in a form musicians call "variations on a theme." Don Quixote defends Andrés, Micomicona, the galley slaves, Doña Rodríguez's daughter and many others, in various distinct episodes. In *The Idiot* it is developed in symphonic form—consecutive, unified, following a definite pattern with only two figures, Myshkin and Nastasya Filipovna. His relations with her are founded upon pity, love for suffering man. This love contains in it a fervent desire to help humanity, which he

believes is capable of reaching the heights symbolized by
Aglaya. Much of this attitude is Christlike, but Myshkin's
championship of Nastasya Filipovna Dostoyevski considered don-quixotesque.[19] Definitely, she is not what he
imagines her to be, yet in the face of great contradictions
he clings to his conception of her and defends her against
all odds.

Myshkin loves Nastasya Filipovna and Aglaya fer-
vently, but not passionately. Like Don Quixote, he is
ignorant of woman, except as aspects of his ideal. Physical love would have been just as great a betrayal of his
ideal as it would have been in the case of Don Quixote.
Yevgeni Pavlovich, who represents convention, exclaims,
"And how can one love two at once? With two different
sorts of love?"[20] He cannot understand that Myshkin does
not love the two women at the same time with "different
sorts of loves." He loves his ideal, and *it* he finds in these
two women.

In Myshkin's eyes, Aglaya represents the "elevated
concept of Pure Beauty" and Nastasya Filipovna, human
potentiality for attaining this beauty. Myshkin's trouble
lies in the fact that these women exist in the flesh and,
worse still, they actually love him. Yevgeni Pavlovich
continues, "Do you know what, my poor prince?—the
most likely thing is that you've never loved either of
them." "I don't know, perhaps so," replies Myshkin.[21] He
finally realizes that his conception of love and that of society do not coincide, and that the motives which drew
him into the lists for Nastasya Filipovna are comprehensible to no one. His altruistic gestures of mercy are regarded as an idiot's follies, just as Don Quixote's combats
of mercy were believed to be a lunatic's escapades.

Idealism, firmly fixed as it may be, cannot withstand
the battering of reality indefinitely. In both novels, the
Quixote and *The Idiot*, the ideal finally crashes and tragedy ensues. When Don Quixote is deprived of his mania,
he sinks into apathy. When he was a madman in full

[19] Constance Garnett's translation, pp. 246 ff.
[20] *Ibid.*, p. 588.   [21] *Ibid.*, p. 587.

possession of his dream, life was full; now there is killing emptiness. So long as Myshkin had his concept of beauty, he lived and worked for it, but when Nastasya Filipovna's flight and death wrench it from him, he becomes permanently deranged—equivalent, for him, to death.

Dostoyevski does not have his hero die outright, as does Cervantes, but he borrows Pushkin's denouement. The Poor Knight retired to his castle,

> "In far distant countryside,
> Silent, sad, bereft of reason,
> In solitude he died."

"Bereft of reason," or as an "idiot."

The final relationship between Prince Myshkin and the Poor Knight and their prototype, Don Quixote, is skillfully summed up by the critic Merezhkovski: " 'The castle in the far-off countryside' from which Prince Myshkin came and whither he returned turned out to be for him the Swiss hospital for the mentally diseased; yet, the internal, not external, path—extraordinarily parabolic—which Prince Myshkin and the Poor Knight inscribed in the spiritual sphere is the same one. From the same desert, through the 'world' and struggle with the faithless sons of this 'world'—the 'Saracens'—into a greater desert; from one silence, through belligerent preaching of love for the mysterious 'lady' of his heart . . . into another silence which is even greater—such is this path.

"Both knights, as Aglaya remarks, are somewhat similar to Don Quixote in their tragic fate; but these Don Quixotes are not of the past, but of the future."[22]

[22] D. S. Merezhkovski, *Khristos i Antikhrist v russkoi literature: L. Tolstoi i Dostoyevski* [Christ and Antichrist in Russian literature: Tolstoi and Dostoyevski] (St. P., 1902), II, 248-49.

10 · OSTROVSKI

Considering the entire creative output of A. N. Ostrovski, the great playwright and translator of Cervantes' Interludes,[1] the influence of Cervantes on Ostrovski's own work appears small. Out of forty-eight plays, only one reveals the touch of Cervantes, but so dominant is that influence, and so clearly are its heroes patterned after Don Quixote and Sancho, that it deserves detailed analysis.

The play in question is *Forest*, one of Russia's better dramas of manners.[2] As it opens, Gennadi Neschastlivtsev, a threadbare provincial tragedian, and Arkadi (Arkashka) Schastlivtsev,[3] an equally tattered provincial comedian, meet on a lonely road. Hungry, penniless and homeless, these two grotesque figures engage in a conversation, banal in content but rich in suggestive quality and Cervantian in tone and mood. From it Neschastlivtsev emerges as a morose, pompous individual, lofty in ideas and principles, imperious, impulsive and idealistic in speech and action. Schastlivtsev, like Sancho, is his companion's counterpart. He is simple, good-natured, witty, modest in ambitions, keenly sensitive to the exigencies of life, and he possesses a marvelous ability to use what little he has to the greatest personal advantage. In this short dialogue their mutual relationship is also clearly defined. Neschastlivtsev is condescending and domineering; Schastlivtsev is subservient and tractable. Though socially and professionally they are equals, morally Ne-

[1] Cf. pp. 68-70.
[2] A. N. Ostrovski, *"Les," Polnoye sobranie sochineni* (St. P., 1896), vii, 247-408.
[3] The names Neschastlivtsev and Schastlivtsev mean "Mr. Unlucky" and "Mr. Lucky" respectively.

schastlivtsev is unquestionably the master, and Schastlivtsev the servant.

They are in a dilemma. Neither has money, food or
cigarettes. Neschastlivtsev rises to the occasion by pro-
posing a visit to the near-by estate of his aunt, Madame
Gurmyzhski. But a gentleman cannot travel thus, without baggage, coach or servants. It, therefore, falls to
Schastlivtsev to pose as a valet, to which he reluctantly
but wisely consents. The Gurmyzhski home presents a
disheartening picture of the savage meanness, hatred, intrigue and pettiness of Russian provincial society. Here
the pair spend several days, Neschastlivtsev dreaming
his dreams of art, greatness and good, impervious to
(though conscious of) the vulgar intrusions of reality;
Schastlivtsev trying to resolve the situation sensibly and
profitably.

On the first day of their visit the dreamer is roused for
a moment out of his "trance" by his aunt's complaint of
Bodayev's cheating. Just, passionate wrath erupts from
him in a blasting harangue directed at the crafty peasant,
who is overwhelmed by its force, dignity and conviction.
He repays the full amount to Madame Gurmyzhski, who
offers it to Neschastlivtsev. Needy though he is, he refuses it. He defended her because to do so was a good
deed. To him, as to Don Quixote, a good deed is a source
of joy, and material reward almost insulting. But the
money, so graciously refused, passes into the hands of the
ignominious nonentity Bulanov. Schastlivtsev is dis-
traught and draws his friend's attention to what has happened. His sensible reproach irks and infuriates the idealist in the same delightful fashion that parallel actions by
Sancho provoke his master.

Arkashka, however, has a bit of the scoundrel in him.
Unlike Sancho, he betrays his friend when he sees him
passing up money. He reveals their true position to a
maid who, in turn, informs her mistress. The pair fall into
disgrace and have to leave, but the power of moral superiority is not to be trifled with. Through fear Neschastlivtsev forces his aunt to respect him and his wishes.

Heretofore he ignored the turpitude about him, though he could have caused a great deal of trouble and derived great benefits from it—but digging in a moral cesspool for personal advantage had been contrary to his principles. He descends to it now only because there is another person involved. He induces his aunt to give him the thousand rubles she owes him and which he plans to use for himself and Schastlivtsev. His cousin, however, needs just such a sum for a dowry and her wealthy aunt refuses to give it to her. With one magnificent gesture, Neschastlivtsev presents her with all he has, thus smashing his and Arkashka's dreams of comfort and security.

For Neschastlivtsev, personal desires, necessities and even happiness are secondary to the well-being of others; natural yearnings for comfort and security vanish when comfort entails toleration of moral turpitude. The rejection of these thousand rubles is, therefore, a great, a staggering victory, for in it, as in a similar episode of the *Quixote*, lies the reaffirmation of the essential nobility of man and of the importance of freedom and moral greatness.

Commenting on this play, the critic Mirsky says the characters "are almost as rich in variety and suggestiveness as the great creations of Cervantes. Of all Ostrovski's plays it is the one in which the essential nobility of man is most triumphantly asserted in the moral, though not financial, victory of the Quixotic tragedian."[4]

[4] D. S. Mirsky, *History of Russian Literature* (New York, 1934), p. 311.

PART III

THE PASSING
OF THE EMPIRE

1880-1940

IN THIS period are included the works of pre-Revolutionary Russian writers and those of the *émigrés* who carry on to the present day the traditions of the former era. The writers of the Soviet Union, together with those of Marxist leanings who preceded them, will be discussed in a separate section.

The rise in the 1880's of the Symbolist movement, with its mystically religious *Weltanschauung*, turned many Russian intellectuals from the realism of Cervantes to the mysticism of Calderón. In only a few cases can Cervantes' influence be detected in the work of the symbolists. However, this did not presage the end of Cervantes in Russia. Don Quixote and Sancho Panza passed out of the hands of the *literati* and became the property of the bourgeoisie in much the same way that they did in France, England and Germany. Their images, through universal use, became tarnished and acquired figurative meanings, but this is of minor scholarly interest.

The number of new Cervantes translations that appeared during this period should be noted, as well as the variety of versions of the *Quixote*. On the scholarly side, the wealth of articles on Cervantes by students and writers is significant. The study of Western European literature had developed sufficiently by this time to produce first-rate Russian Hispanists. They not only contributed scholarly research but checked and reviewed the work of their less critical compatriots. The result was that by the end of the nineteenth century the average Russian knew much more about Cervantes than his grandfather did, though Cervantes' influence on the literary leaders had ebbed. An inventory of books and articles shows that he also knew a great deal more about Spain, and thus was in a better position to understand Cervantes.

This intensified awareness of Cervantes' native country is exemplied by the travel account of the writer D. L. Mordovtsev.[1] Embittered and in ill-health, he toured Spain and failed to appreciate it until he reached the Don Quixote region. It might be expected that the Slav would be unresponsive to that austere countryside but, on the contrary, his trip became a Don Quixote pilgrimage, full of reverence and excitement.

Other important travelogues of the period have been left by "S. P-Ski,"[2] V. Nemirovich-Danchenko in *Amidst the Great*,[3] and *Travel Sketches in the Land of the Mantilla and Castanets*, translated by A. N. Bezhetski.[4]

In addition to the publication of such travel impressions as these, periodical literature on Spain becomes so copious that any attempt at enumeration is impossible. Any Russian newspaper of the time contains something on peninsular events. Catalogues of public libraries, another index to popular interests, show a demand for Spanish manuals and books. The Odessa library,[5] for example, has Spanish grammars,[6] a dictionary,[7] translations of

[1] D. L. Mordovtsev, "Po Ispanii, putevie arabeski" [Through Spain, Arabesques], in *Vestnik Yevropy* (1884), I, 73-118, 621-58; II, 233-70.

[2] S. P-ski, "Iz poyezdki v Ispaniyu," *Russkaya Mysl*, 1882, no. 31.

[3] V. Nemirovich-Danchenko, "Sredi velikikh, iz puteshestvia po Ispanii" [Amidst the great, from a journey to Spain], *Russkaya Mysl* (1887), I, 2, pp. 72-84; II, 2, pp. 130-44; IV, 2, pp. 37-50.

[4] R. Foulché-Delbosc, *Bibliografie des Voyages en Espagne et en Portugal*, no. 714.

[5] *Katalog Odesskoi Gorodskoi Publichnoi Biblioteki*, Odessa, 1910.

[6] *Ibid.*, no. 1915, R. Altamira, *Eco de Madrid, Ejemplos prácticos de conversación castellana*. Mit einer deutschen Übersetzung von A. L. Becker (Leipzig, n.d.), no. 2077, *Eine neue Methode, in drei Monaten eine Sprache sprechen, schreiben und lesen zu lernen. Zum selbstunterricht. Spanisch*. (Leipzig, n.d.), no. 2092 Sobrino, *Grammaire espagnole-francais* (Paris, 1897).

[7] *Ibid.*, no. 1959, *Diccionario español-frances*, basado en la parte francesa sobre el gran diccionario de E. Littre y en la parte española sobre el diccionario de la lengua castellana, por F. Corona Bustamante (Paris, 1901).

Ticknor's History of Spanish Literature[8] and of Huber's *History of Contemporary Spanish Literature*,[9] the complete works of Cervantes in various editions,[10] Lope de Vega,[11] and Espronceda[12] and a variety of *Tesoros*.[13]

The addition of Western European literature to university curricula in the seventies yields its harvest now in the books of Shepelevich,[14] Petrov,[15] Bokadarov,[16] Averkyev,[17] and Lazurski.[18] To this material can be added a

[8] *Ibid.*, no. 310, translated under the direction of M. I. Storozhenko, vols. 1-3, Moscow, 1883-1891.

[9] *Ibid.*, no. 101, translated by V. Doppelmayer, Moscow, 1892.

[10] *Ibid.*, no. 2819, *Persiles y Sigismunda* (Brussels, 1618); no. 2820, *El Ingenioso Hidalgo . . .* published D. M. F. de Navarrete (Paris, 1840); no. 2821, *Obras*, vols. 1-4 (Paris, 1840-1841); no. 2822, L. Tieck's translation of the *Quixote*, 5 vols. (Weimar, 1817); no. 2823, L. Viardot's translation of the *Quixote* (Paris, Publication Chez Lahure, no date given); no. 2824, another Viardot edition, of *Don Quixote*, 2 vols. (Paris, 1862); no. 2825, *El ingenioso hidalgo . . .*, 6 vols. (Madrid, 1797); no. 2826, Florian's translation of the *Quixote*, 4 vols. (Paris, 1820); no. 2827, Damas Hinard's translation of *Don Quixote*, 2 vols. (Paris, 1848); no. 2828, L. Viardot's translation of the *Novelas ejemplares* (Paris, 1875).

[11] *Ibid.*, no. 2850, *Chefs d'oeuvres du theatre espagnole*, vol. I (Paris, 1822).

[12] *Ibid.*, no. 3143, J. Espronceda, *Obras poéticas*, ordenadas y anotadas por Hartzenbusch (Paris, 1848).

[13] *Ibid.*, no. 4247, *Tesoro de los romanceros y cancioneros españoles*, recogidos y ordenados por E. de Ochoa (Paris, 1838); no. 4248, *Tesoro del Parnaso español*, . . . recogidas y ordenadas por don M. J. Quintana (Paris, 1838); no. 4249, *Tesoro del Teatro español*, . . . arreglado y dividido en cuatro partes, por E. de Ochoa, vol. III (Calderón de la Barca) (Paris, 1838); no. 4250, *Tesoro de los prosadores españoles* de la formación del romance castellano hasta fines del siglo XVIII, . . . recopilado y ordenado por E. de Ochoa (Paris, 1841); no. 4251, *Tesoro de novelistas españoles antiguos y modernos*, con una introducción y noticias de E. de Ochoa, 3 vols. (Paris, 1847).

[14] Cf. pp. 164 ff.

[15] The best known work by D. K. Petrov is "Ocherki bytovogo teatra Lope de Vegi" [Sketches of Lope de Vega's drama of manners], *Zapiski, Istoriko-filologicheski fakultet. Sanktpeterburgski Universitet*, LX.

[16] N. Bokadarov, *Istoria zapadno-yevropeiskikh literatur*. XVI-XVIII v.v. (Kiev, 1914). I. V. Vladislavlev cites it in *Sistematicheski ukazatel literatury za 1914 god* (Moscow, 1915). It is said to have a chapter on Cervantes and Shakespeare.

[17] D. V. Averkyev, *O drame* (St. P., 1907). In talking about

number of articles on Cervantes, Lope de Vega and Calderón written by Spanish scholars as well as by other
writers. There are also new translations of Spanish works,
such as Calderón's *El alcalde de Zalamea, Amar después
de la muerte, La dama duende, La devoción de la Cruz,
Peor está que estaba, El príncipe constante, El Purgatorio
de San Patricio, La vida es sueño,*[19] Lope de Vega's *Es-
trella de Sevilla,*[20] *El perro del hortelano,*[21] Pedro Alar-
cón's ¡ *Buena pesca!,*[22] Pérez Galdós *Zaragoza,*[23] Eche-
garay's *Gran Galeoto,*[24] *Lazarillo de Tormes,*[25] *Spanish
motives from Santiago,*[26] Palacio Valdés' *La hermana San
Sulpicio,*[27] works of Pardo Bazán, Valle Inclán, Baroja,
Blasco Ibáñez,[28] and articles on contemporary Spanish
literature.[29]

Many plays were translated for performance because
of the great popularity enjoyed by the theater of the

drama the author refers to Cervantes, Lope de Vega, and Calderón (pp. 265-74).

[18] V. F. Lazurski, *Kurs istorii zapadno-yevropeiskoi literatury* [A
course in the history of Western-European literature] (Odessa,
1913). The *Cid* and the *romances* are discussed on pp. 98-114.

[19] L. B. Turkevich, *Calderón en Rusia,* pp. 156-58.

[20] *Zvezda Sevilyi,* translated in verse for the stage by S. A.
Yuryev, Moscow, 1887.

[21] *Sobaka Sadovnika,* translated by Maslov, Moscow, 1891. Another translation by A. N. Bezhetski in 1893.

[22] "Khoroshi lov," translated by M. V. Vatson, published in
Izyaschnaya Literatura, May 1883, pp. 298-309.

[23] "Osada Saragossy," translated from the Spanish by E. Uma-
nets, in supplement to *Istoricheski Vestnik,* 1896.

[24] *Don Kikhot XIX stoletia* was performed in 1891 but without
great success. (*Artist,* 1891, no. 17, p. 129.)

[25] Published in St. Petersburg, 1897, cited by N. I. Storozhenko,
Ocherki istorii zapadno-yevropeiskikh literatur, Moscow, 1910, p.
215.

[26] *Iz ispanskikh motivov. Santiago* (A. E. Burtsev, *Bibliograficheskoe opisanie redkikh i zamechatelnykh knig* (St. P., 1901),
v, 225.

[27] Cited by *Knizhnaya Letopis,* 1913, no. 11778.

[28] *Ibid.,* earlier issues *passim.*

[29] L. Shepelevich, "José de Pereda," *Vestnik Yevropy,* 1905, vol.
236, pp. 319 ff. Dioneo, "Sovremenie ispanskie belletristy" [Con-
temporary Spanish authors], *Russkoye Bogatstvo* (1909), no. 11,
pp. 16-45; L. Shepelevich, "Ocherki iz istorii noveishei ispanskoi
literatury," *Severny Vestnik,* 1897, no. 5, pp. 21-43.

Spanish Golden Age among the Russian symbolists. Calderón's works were the favorites, since they gave producers like Vsevolod Meierhold ample opportunity for imaginative productions. Lope de Vega's plays and Cervantes' Interludes[30] were also included in theatrical programs, some having their Russian premières during this period.

Theater annals of the time list other works that are Spanish in subject, if not in origin: *Isabella, Infanta of Castile,*[31] *The Spanish Nobleman,*[32] *Castile and Florence,*[33] *L'Infante de Zamora,*[34] *Paquita,*[35] *The Pentecost at Toledo,*[36] *The Sevillian Bar,*[37] and the old favorites, *Carmen* and *The Barber of Seville, Spanish Dance*[38] and *Capriccio Espagnole.*

Rimsky-Korsakoff's music, to which the latter ballet was set, is one of the more famous Russian compositions on Spanish themes. It has been used by the Russian Ballet for a very colorful production to which Argentinita gave the final touches and in which she occasionally participated. Another example of Russo-Spanish artistic

[30] Cf. pp. 146-47.
[31] "Izabella, Infanta Kastilskaya," drama in five acts, in poetry, by N. E. Vilde (*Artist*, 1891, no. 14, p. 103).
[32] "Ispansky dvoryanin," by K. A. Tarnovski (*Artist*, 1891, no. 16, p. 138).
[33] *Kapitan korolevskoi gvardii ili Kastilia i Florentsia*, comical operetta in 3 acts and 6 scenes by K. N. Larin, music by A. B. Vilinski, Moscow, 1893 (*Artist*, no. 38, end of the book, no page number).
[34] Translated by Krylov. (*Yezhegodnik Imperatorskikh Teatrov*, sezon 1893-1894, supplement II, p. 18.)
[35] *Paquita*, a ballet in three acts by Fisher and Mosilier, music by Minkus, was performed four times during the season 1897-1898 (*Yezhegodnik Imp. Teatrov*, sezon 1897-1898, p. 33).
[36] *Dukhov Den v Toledo* by K. Kuzmin, presented during the season 1914-1915, in the Moscow State Kamerny Theater [H. Carter, *The New Spirit in the Russian Theater*, 1917-1928] (London, 1929), p. 310.
[37] *Sevilski Kabachok*, presented by Meierhold in St. Petersburg in Dec. 1913; cf. N. Volkov, *Meierhold* II (Moscow-Leningrad, 1929), p. 301.
[38] In Anna Pavlova's repertoire is found the *Danse Espagnole*, music by Rubinstein, and *Spanish Dance* (pas seul), music by Bizet. (Hyden, *Anna Pavlova* (Boston, 1913), pp. 54 and 163 respectively.)

rapprochement, and perhaps the best, is the *Sombrero de tres picos,* for which de Falla wrote the music for Diagheleff, who produced it with his ballet. Other Russian composers with works bearing Spanish titles include C. A. Cui (*Bolero,* op. 17, and *Maisonettes Espagnoles,* op. 40), Tchaikovsky (*Don Juan,* op. 38), and A. P. Borodin (*Serenata alla Spagnola*).

Supplying either literary background or motif, Spain figures in Balmont's *Sin miedo,* Kuzma Prutkov's *Desire to Be a Spaniard*[39] and Bryusov's *Fiery Angel.*[40]

TRANSLATIONS

THE first on the list of translations of the *Quixote* for this period is a revised edition of Karelin's work.[1] Zotov substituted for Karelin's prologues a literal translation from the original, and broke up the chapters according to the Spanish text, giving them corresponding titles. He did not touch the actual text or correct its footnotes. His prologues are no great improvement on Karelin's, for their style is awkward, and the work at times careless.

Russia had had many translations of the *Quixote,* of which two stand out as definitely superior to the rest: Masalski's,[2] as the first attempt at a faithful translation made from the original text; and Karelin's for its stylistic value and completeness. To these can now be added that of Mark Basanin,[3] *The Incomparable Knight Don Quixote of La Mancha.* It was translated from the Spanish, and included an introduction, a biography of Cervantes and notes, and was published in St. Petersburg in 1903. Although it ranks among the best, Basanin's translation is still an inadequate one.

The biography preceding the text, though better than Karelin's, contains inaccuracies. In her foreword, Basanin says that hers is a complete translation, taken from the

[39] *Zhelanie byt ispantsem.*   [40] *Ognenny angel.*
[1] Cf. pp. 66 ff. *Don Kikhot Lamanchski,* translated by V. Karelin, corrected by V. Zotov (St. P., 1893).
[2] Cf. p. 15.
[3] Pseudonym of Lydia Alekseyevna Lasheyeva.

Spanish version corrected by the Madrid Real Academia. It is complete as far as the novel goes, but the introductory poems are omitted. Basanin erroneously thought that the text she had selected was the best, whereas the Fitzmaurice-Kelly edition would have been better. She claims that her work was done from the Spanish, but there is evidence that, like Karelin before her and Tulupov later, Basanin found a French translation exceedingly helpful.

The translation itself is inferior to Karelin's, because, though it is more literal, it lacks gracefulness of style. Obviously aware of this deficiency, Basanin unsuccessfully tried to give the text life and "raciness," resulting in an overembellishment often not in the best of taste.

N. V. Tulupov's translation of the *Quixote*, called simply *Don Quixote of La Mancha*, is exceedingly poor. It was published in Moscow in 1904, in two volumes, with illustrations by Gustave Doré. Tulupov purports to have used the Spanish original as his text, but proper names betray that he had recourse to a French version as well. Not only is the source misrepresented, but the text is badly mutilated by omissions, too great freedom in translation and unnecessary insertions.[4]

M. V. Vatson's *The Ingenious Hidalgo Don Quixote of La Mancha* offers a complete contrast to all preceding Russian translations of the *Quixote*.[5] A deep respect and love for the original and a sense of responsibility to her task characterize the entire work. She uses the 1898 Fitzmaurice-Kelly edition for her text and explains her choice in a preface. Then Vatson includes a good brief biography of Cervantes and a survey of his works, based on such books as Menendez y Pelayo's *Cultura literaria de Miguel de Cervantes y elaboración de "Quijote"* and *El Quijote y los libros de caballerías*, Juan Valera's *Discurso*

---

[4] I. D. Kholodnyak has a justly severe review of Tulupov's translation in *Zhurnal Ministertva Narodnago Prosveschenia*, IX (St. P., 1906), 98-101.

[5] *Ostroumno-izobretatelny idalgo Don Kikhot Lamanchski*, sochinenie Migelya de Servantesa Saavedra, polny perevod s ispanskago M. V. Vatson (St. P., 1907).

para commemorar el tercer centenario de la publicación de El Ingenioso Hidalgo D. Quijote de la Mancha and *La Verdad sobre el Quijote*, the biographies by Shepelevich, Fitzmaurice-Kelly and Watts, as well as other works, like those of Navarro y Ledesma, Cortejón and Diaz de Benjumea.

Vatson's is the first complete and accurate translation of *Don Quixote* into Russian. She does not even shirk the difficult task of translating the introductory poems, a task in which she succeeds rather well. The remainder of the text is handled literally, which is both its main virtue and its greatest defect, for in Vatson's effort at precision and completeness, some of the artistic value and the aroma of the *Quixote* evaporates. Occasionally excessive adherence to the original causes awkwardness in the Russian. Even most of the proverbs are translated literally, dulling much of their original brilliance.

Vatson was aware of her shortcomings, but she had set herself to make a complete and accurate translation, and this she did accomplish with incredible conscientiousness. There are errors, of course, but in comparison with the other translations they are notably few. Her notes are, as a rule, sensible and correct. When she feels that her version fails to convey all the shades of meaning necessary for a good reading, she supplements it with notes elaborating on the connotation of the passage. Proper names are all consistently transcribed from the Spanish, with the exception of Don Quixote, which she retains in the current Russian form.

This translation went through another four editions (1917, 1924, 1929, 1930),[6] until it was supplemented by a new and better translation by Krzhevski and Smirnov in 1929.[7]

There were several other translations of the *Quixote* in this period, apparently complete ones, on which there is little data—an Odessa edition of 1899,[8] those made by

[6] Appendix, nos. 54, 55, 56 and 57.
[7] *Ibid.*, no. 72.   [8] *Ibid.*, no. 37.

L. A. Murakhina,[9] A. S. Panafidina, Chistyakov[10] and
S. M.,[11] as well as one of 1912 mentioned by Ford and
Lansing.[12]

Glivenko's translation of Cervantes' *novela, El celoso
extremeño*, taken from the Spanish, is literal and essentially complete.[13] In some details, however, the translator
occasionally preferred concision to fidelity. Notwithstanding the adulteration of the original resulting from
Glivenko's alterations, he did make an honest attempt to
give Russian readers a fairly smooth and interesting version of the *novela*.

M. V. Vatson's translation of *El celoso extremeño*[14] is
done in the same conscientious manner as her other Cervantes translations. It is literal, and errors are few.

This period produced many new editions and new versions of the so-called "Abbreviated *Don Quixote*." One of
the old ones, the Schmidt-Moskvitinova version,[15] went
through three editions, and the Grech through two.[16] As
for new versions, the Lukovnikov had five editions;[17]
Sytin, six editions;[18] Konovalov, three editions;[19] while
the Konradi,[20] Lyubich-Koshurov,[21] Vatson,[22] Vvoden-
ski,[23] Sinkevich,[24] Borisov-Lavrov[25] and an anonymous
one[26] each had a single edition. Obviously, there was a
sudden rise in demand for the *Quixote* as a tale for children, resulting from wider acquaintance with the book
by the adult reading public. With the number of copies
available for only sixteen of twenty-seven editions, it is
found that at least 117,300 copies of abbreviated versions
were put on sale within fourteen years.

[9] *Ibid.*, no. 38; cf. also no. 39. [10] *Ibid.*, no. 34.
[11] *Ibid.*, no. 62. [12] *Ibid.*, no. 65.
[13] "Revnivets iz Estremadury," *Vestnik Innostrannoi Literatury*
(1892), no. 10.
[14] "Revnivy estremadurets," *Sovremenny Mir* (1916), no. 4.
[15] Appendix, nos. 31-33.
[16] *Ibid.*, no. 16, an edition by the émigrés was published in
Paris, no. 17.
[17] *Ibid.*, nos. 40-41. [18] *Ibid.*, nos. 47-52.
[19] *Ibid.*, nos. 58-60. [20] *Ibid.*, no. 45.
[21] *Ibid.*, no. 61. [22] *Ibid.*, no. 62.
[23] *Ibid.*, no. 63. [24] *Ibid.*, no. 66.
[25] *Ibid.*, no. 67. [26] *Ibid.*, no. 64.

THEATER PRODUCTIONS

THE years which saw the passing of the Empire brought Cervantes' Interludes to the Russian theater-goer. The prominent producers Evreinoff and Meierhold,[1] as well as the Imperial dramatic schools in St. Petersburg and Moscow,[2] were of the opinion that to create a good theater, study should be made of outstanding theatrical periods of the past—not only of the actual plays, but also of the productions, the performance of actors and even the attitude of the audience. In addition, these plays should be performed. Only then could all their wealth of dramatic and histrionic devices and others of proved efficacy be grasped and incorporated into the new Russian theater.[3]

Following out this program, Evreinoff organized two play cycles, one devoted to the medieval theater, produced in 1907-1908, and the other to the Spanish, in 1911-1912. Participating in both were Evreinoff, N. I. Butkovski and N. V. Drizin, with A. A. Sanin as the producer.[4] The settings for the second cycle were based on research in the theater of the Spanish Golden Age, resulting in reproductions of plazas, palaces, the Retiro, and so forth, with costumes copied from the paintings of Velásquez. The pretense was made that the production was given by a group of itinerant players performing, as of old, in the open. For this, halls rather than theaters, and scaffolding rather than stages, were used. Artificialities of the theater such as footlights, curtains, and elaborate scenery were discarded, and the actors performed against the backdrop of a small curtain and on a practically empty stage, thus leaving the actors ample opportunity for communicating the spirit of the play to the spectators' imagina-

[1] N. Volkov, *Meierhold*, II [1908-1917] (Moscow-Leningrad, 1929), 187-88.

[2] Cervantes' interludes and the principal plays of these schools. (Supplement to *Artist*, April 1891, pp. 106-7.)

[3] Ye. A. Znosko-Borovski, *Russki teatr nachala XX veka* [The Russian theater at the beginning of the 20th century] (Prague, 1925), p. 333.

[4] *Ibid.*, p. 335.

tion. And, indeed, the performances did recreate all the contagious fascination of the original plays.[5]

Under such sponsorship, it is not surprising that between 1910-1915 the importance of the Spanish Golden Age drama exceeded even that of Shakespeare in Russia. Of course, it was the full-length plays of Calderón, Tirso de Molina and Lope de Vega that were most frequently produced, yet Cervantes' Interludes, though short, were not neglected. Several productions of these works were recorded by Volkov.[6]

During the summer of 1912 *Los habladores* (sometimes attributed to Cervantes),[7] *La cueva de Salamanca* and *El viejo celoso* were performed. The last two were produced by V. N. Solovyev in the traditions of a "literary side-show" (*literaturny balagan*) without any conventional Spanish settings. For *La cueva de Salamanca*, the set consisted of brownish-red screens upon which were painted arbalists and guns. The actors were placed geometrically around the principal actor in the center.[8]

Volkov describes another set used by Solovyev. Four screens were set upon the stage and three sails were suspended from bamboo poles. The color scheme was a sequence of green, blue, red and yellow. Two barrels stood on the stage and served both as stools and as supports for a large table which was covered with a tablecloth. The actors were dressed in deep crimson, with lavender and light blue trimmings, orange belts and leggings, the actresses in dark lilac with deep crimson belts and cuffs. The designer for this production was A. V. Rykov.[9]

Solovyev produced *La cueva de Salamanca* again in 1915 with his students from Meierhold's Dramatic Studio.[10] In the spring of 1916 the Russian theater joined the rest of the world in commemorating the three-hundredth anniversary of Cervantes' death by performing his Interludes.[11]

[5] *Ibid.*, pp. 340-41.

[6] Volkov, *op. cit.*, p. 263.

[7] *Ibid.*, p. 233.

[8] *Ibid.*, p. 236.

[9] *Ibid.*, p. 374.

[10] *Ibid.*, p. 367.

[11] *Ibid.*, p. 432.

Meanwhile, the Ballet continued billing the two Petipa versions of *Don Quixote*[12] and a reworking of the shorter one, designed by A. A. Gorski.[13] Among the famous dancers who participated in these performances were Cecchetti,[14] Svetlova,[15] Kshesinskaya, Pavlova, Trefilova, Preobrazhenskaya and Legat.[16] The painter Golovin, who shared with Glinka and Rimsky-Korsakoff a love for Spain, did some of his best work in his settings for *Don Quixote*.[17]

Don Quixote was also produced by Anna Pavlova and her group, and many New Yorkers saw her version in 1923. Hyden says of the great ballerina: "She did not religiously follow the exact scheme of the older ballets, and very often a ballet danced by Pavlova under the name of one of the classical favorites, such as 'La Fille

[12] Some of the performances of the long ballet were: once in St. Petersburg during 1881-1882 (*Yezhegodnik Imperatorskikh Teatrov*, no. 7, Sezon 1911-1912, p. xxix); in 1902, on Oct. 13, Nov. 3 and 24, Dec. 6 (*ibid.*, sezon 1902-1903, part ɪɪ, p. 44); in Moscow, 1903, on Jan. 26, Feb. 16, Apr. 20 (*ibid.*, p. 51); in St. Petersburg, 1903, on Sept. 21, Oct. 18, Oct. 26 and in 1904, Jan. 18 and April 25 (*ibid.*, sezon 1903-1904, part ɪɪ, p. 52); in Moscow, 1904, Sept. 5, Oct. 3, Nov. 7 and 28 (*ibid.*, sezon 1904-1905, part ɪɪ, p. 145); in St. Petersburg, 1905, Dec. 4 and 28 and in 1906, Jan. 5, Feb. 11 and Apr. 12 (*ibid.*, sezon 1905-1906, part ɪɪ, pp. 100, 106, 110 and 126 respectively). The short ballet was performed in Moscow, 1890, Oct. 14 and 24 (*ibid.*, season 1890-1891, pp. 8 and 9); in 1891, on Oct. 6 and 16 (*ibid.*, sezon 1891-1892, pp. 5 and 6); in 1892, on Sept. 27, Oct. 7 and Nov. 15 (*ibid.*, sezon 1892-1893, pp. 5, 6, and 10).

[13] It is said to have been performed ten times in St. Petersburg during the season 1901-1902 (Jan. 20, 27, 30, and Feb. 10 are the only dates given), and once in Moscow on Sept. 23, 1901 (*ibid.*, sezon 1901-1902, part ɪɪ, p. 46). No other dates of performances of this ballet have been found but a program for it was published for the St. Petersburg Theaters in 1908, 32 pages long (*Knizhnaya Letopis za 1908*, St. P., 1909, no. 20391) which suggests other performances.

[14] Olga Racster, *The Master of the Russian Ballet: The Memoirs of Cav. Enrico Cecchetti* (London, 1922), p. 188.

[15] Walford Hyden, *Pavlova* (Boston, 1931), p. 25.

[16] N. G. Legat, *Story of the Russian School*, translated by Sir Paul Dukes (London, 1932), p. 85.

[17] W. A. Propert, *The Russian Ballet in Western Europe, 1909-1920* (London, 1921), p. 15.

Mal Gardée,' 'The Fairy Doll' or 'Don Quixote,' and even 'Giselle,' had been very considerably altered to suit her purposes or her caprice. Given the choreography of a traditional ballet, she could not rest until she had introduced variations and generally new music by another composer, making a choreographic and musical patchwork which charmed the audience, but could not fail to annoy those who realized what she had done. All things considered, however, I am inclined to think that she improved every ballet that she revised."[18]

In regard to Pavlova's revised *Don Quixote*, with music by Minkus and choreography by Novikoff after the classical ballet, Hyden writes: "An opportunity was lost of producing a really historic work. The theme, the stage, the dancing, were all adapted for a ballet par excellence, but when I say that the music was utterly undistinguished, I flatter it. The dull, stupid tunes of Minkus, who was nothing more than a 'hack' composer, completely ruined Novikoff's choreography and even Pavlova's Spanish dancing. Music could scarcely be more sickly and maudlin than the stuff used in this ballet to suggest a love episode. It is to be regretted that so much time, money and thought should have been wasted by the revival of a ballet with music which could not have been worse for the purpose. Novikoff was almost driven to distraction by its banality.

"Despite this drawback, the ballet was fairly well received, even in the Latin American countries and Spain. This was because of the interest and humor of the theme. The ballet is in two acts. In the first, Pavlova danced the part of Kitry, an inn-keeper's daughter at Barcelona. Don Quixote, riding on a scraggy nag and accompanied by Sancho Panza on a donkey, comes into the market-place where there is a gay festival. Sancho Panza is tossed in a blanket by the revelers, and there is a fight between Don Quixote and Kitry's lover, Basilio. Basilio feigns to be stabbed, and Kitry expresses her anguish. In Act II Quixote and Sancho, on their journey through the forest,

[18] Hyden, *op. cit.*, pp. 186-87.

149

wearily fall asleep. The Don dreams that he fights with a knight in armor, but is defeated; and as a compensation Dulcinea (Pavlova) invests him with a resplendent Order of Chivalry.

"It will be realized from this description what an opportunity for miming and dancing such a theme gives. Alas, that the opportunity was spoiled by such trivial music! Tscherepnine rescored 'Don Quixote.' . . . All that was possible to do, he did, but a bad tune remains a bad tune, notwithstanding the finest reorchestration."[19]

It is significant that the operatic figure of Don Quixote was created by a Russian, Fyodor Chaliapine. In 1907 Jules Massenet asked the artist whether he would like to play the part of the Sad Knight, to which he gladly consented. Some two years later the score was completed and Chaliapine came to read it. He relates: "Massenet showed me the proofs of his score fresh from the presses and still smelling of printer's ink, which he had just been correcting. Then he sat down at the piano and began to play. From the very beginning the music touched me very deeply. . . . There are many composers, of course, that I could mention who have written more profound music than Jules Massenet. Yet I must confess that I never had been more intensely moved than by his interpretation of the score as he played it to me that day for the first time."[20]

Though Chaliapine had performed a great variety of roles, *Don Quixote* was his first experience with an exalted and noble figure ridiculed by the world. The score and the libretto were so far removed from Cervantes' novel that in creating the hero's role the artist put aside the opera and turned to the original. In his own words: "I read Cervantes carefully, closed my eyes, thought about it, and the external image of Don Quixote ap-

[19] *Ibid.*, pp. 196-98. Pavlova, who had a passion for taking motion pictures, had *Don Quixote, Invitation to the Waltz* and *Fairy Doll* filmed privately in Australia by the company's electrician. *Ibid.*, p. 123.

[20] F. I. Chaliapine, *Pages from My Life* (New York, 1927), p. 287.

peared before me. The book had no pictures, no colors, no precise measurements of the nose, yet the character is so described that I had a picture of him. I could imagine that his eyes were thus and so and that he walked in just this way. It became clear to me that Don Quixote, a man absorbed in himself, should be slow in his movements, and so forth. This gave me the means of acting him, but still this was not the creation of the image. The most important part does not lend itself to verbal or logical explanation. They say, for example, that my make-up for *Don Quixote* is remarkable. Well, to tell you the truth, I worked on it very hard, as I work on every detail of all my roles. Of course, the artist must make the audience believe that the character performed by him is a Spaniard. One must adorn the character with a beard, dress it in armor, and so forth."[21]

This Chaliapine accomplished by make-up, but spiritual traits he achieved by that method which he could not explain. He is said to have put across the footlights to his audience through a very un-Cervantian medium the essence of Don Quixote—his pure love for Dulcinea, his incredible faith, his greatness and his contempt of imprisonment, and finally the tragedy of his soul in the face of Dulcinea's incredulity. This he expressed superbly, subtly transforming the majestic, indomitable figure into a crestfallen human wreck.

"And here he, with his long thin legs, tottering, leaning on Sancho Panza, moves to a chair, groping around for support. His head is bowed and despair oozes out of his fingertips. Meanwhile, Sancho sings an aria denouncing the courtiers. Don Quixote is silent, but it seems that it is he who is singing. There is so much rhythm latent in his convulsive movements, in the pulsation of his wounded body, in the lines of his whole clumsy figure. And finally, as if crucified, he meets his death. Incredible and unforgettable."[22]

This opera had its world première in the Bolshoi Theater in Moscow in 1910.[23] Chaliapine was so pleased with it that he translated the text into Russian for use in his native land.[24] In 1911 it was performed in the Gaîté Theater in Paris. Since then it has had many performances all over the world.[25]

In 1911, six thousand copies of a Russian publication of Wilhelm Kanzel's opera *Don Quixote* were issued.[26] Whether the opera itself was ever produced in Russia cannot be ascertained.

A small edition (110 copies) of a comedy vaudeville sketch entitled "Don Quixote, the Knight of the Sad Visage, and Sancho Panza" appeared in Moscow in 1914. The author is unknown.[27]

In 1934 Chaliapine made a film of *Don Quixote*. It was produced by G. W. Pabst and the scenario was by Paul Morand. Here is a visual record of how well Chaliapine understood the knight of La Mancha and was able to convey his character to the public—despite a bad scenario.[28]

ALLUSIONS

ALLUSIONS to and mention of Cervantes, his works and characters swelled to such proportions during this period that space does not permit proper citation of them.[1] Some

---

Kikhot, F. I. Chaliapine at the Opera Comique), Prague Russian Daily, Dec. 4, 1931.

[23] N. Volkov, *Meierhold*, II, 157.

[24] Another Russian translation of this opera was made by E. M. Matveyeva, St. Petersburg, 1910 (*Knizhnaya Letopis*, May 22, 1910, p. 5).

[25] S. Polyakov-Litovtsev, *op. cit.*

[26] Knizhnaya Letopis, Feb. 5, 1911, no. 2979.

[27] *Ibid.*, June 14, 1914, no. 13100.

[28] This film ran in the Cameo Theater in New York during December 1934.

[1] A. Skabichevski, *Sochinenia* (St. P., 1903), II, pp. 117, 371, 897, and 923. N. P. Dashkevich, "Znachenie mysli i tvorchestva Gogolya" [The meaning of Gogol's thought and works], *Sbornik otdelenia russkago yazyka i slovestnosti Imperatorskoi Akademii Nauk*, 92 (Petrograd, 1914), 53. K. Valishevski, *Syn Velikoi Yekateriny, Imperator Pavel I, yego zhizn, tsarstvovanie i smert (1754-*

comments by Danilevski,[2] Leo Tolstoi,[3] Korolenko[4] and Mikhailovski[5] are cited or discussed elsewhere. Special mention should also be made of some references to Cervantes by P. D. Boborykin (1836-1921), a journalist considered by some to be the dean of Russian letters, and an opponent of Taine. Boborykin writes in his memoirs of his early contact with that great intellectual, S. F. Uvarov, whose stimulating conversations on the beauties of ancient and modern literature stirred his interest in Aeschylus, Sophocles, Euripides, Shakespeare, Dante, Ariosto, Cervantes, Goethe, Heine and others.[6] This interest in world literature was to stay with Boborykin all through his life.

In his work *The Novel in the West*, Boborykin discusses the relationship "between form and content in the aesthetic sense. The entire history of the development of creative art (this also includes the evolution of the novel) shows us . . . that only those ideas and concepts appear in an artistic form that are aesthetic in character. Let us

---

1801) [The son of Catherine the Great, Paul I] (publ. by A. S. Suvorin, n.d.), pp. 449, 478, 479. L. N. Tolstoi, "Chto iskusstvo" [What is Art], in *Pol. Sob. Soch.* (Moscow, 1913), xix, pp. 109-10. N. S. Leskov, letter to P. Schebalski, quoted in *Russkie pisateli o literature*, edited by Balukhaty, Bursov, Bely and Vladykin, ii (Leningrad, 1939). A. Chekhov, *Letters on the Short Story, the Drama and other Literary Topics*, selected and edited by Louis S. Friedlands (New York, 1924), letter to Misha, of July, 1879. A. Blok, *Dnevnik*, pod redaktsiei P. N. Medvedeva (Diary edited by P. N. Medvedev), i [1911-1913] (Leningrad, 1928), p. 54. D. K. Balmont, *Gornie vershiny* [Mountain Tops], i (Moscow, 1904), pp. 174 and 108. I. A. Bunin, "Notre-Dame de la Garde," *Solnechny udar* (Paris, 1925), p. 85; "Antonovskie yabloki" (Antonov apples), *Khudaya trava* (Moscow-Leningrad, 1928), p. 12; *Zhizn Arsenyeva, istoki dnei* [Life of Arsenyev the Well of Days] (Paris, 1930), p. 51. B. Zaitsev, "Zarya" [Dawn], *Sobranie sochineni*, ii (Moscow, 1922), p. 103; "Usadba Laninykh" (Lanin Homestead), in *Sob. Soch.* iii (Moscow, 1923), pp. 44 and 50; "Masha," *ibid.*, p. 180.

2 Cf. pp. 51-52.   3 Cf. p. 112.
4 Cf. pp. 89-91.   5 Cf. Chap. vii, footnote 22.
6 P. D. Boborykin, *Za polveka, moi vospominania* [Half a century, my reminiscences], edited by B. P. Kozmin (Moscow-Leningrad, 1929), p. 114.

take a few examples from the history of world literature, beginning with the moment when the Western European novel attains artistic form in Cervantes' *Don Quixote*. The author's intention of ridiculing the madmen of chivalric literature would have been inadequate for the creation of an aesthetically creative work had this idea of his not also contained that vital material which readily lends itself to imagery. And only thanks to the talent with which this material is handled do we have the world-famous and, in its own way, immortal work."[7]

Boborykin regards *Don Quixote* as one of the earliest and finest examples of the novel. He writes: ". . . over a period of several centuries Cervantes' *Don Quixote* stands as an artistic work of highest merit, and yet, as far as the general current along which the European novel of the seventeenth century flowed is concerned, it has absolutely no significance as a primogenitor. In seventeenth century France, where the novel occupied a prominent place . . . we find the contrary . . . echoes and moods connected with the epoch of the amorous-chivalric novel, whereas the satirical intent of *Don Quixote* was directed mainly against just that kind of literature."[8]

Don Quixote, Boborykin goes on to say, was a work of rebellion against literary tradition. "If we compare the seventeenth and nineteenth centuries, we will find that two hundred years ago writers fatally, as it were, fell under the influence of one model or another. It required the extraordinary talent of a genius to cast off these molds and principles. Earlier . . . Cervantes, setting an example of such emancipation by emerging as a satirist ridiculing the vogue for novels of chivalry, proved by the entire substance of his *Don Quixote* that true artistic creativeness need not go in search of complicated, fantastic subject matter. . . ."[9]

Despite Cervantes' prodigious talent in the medium of

[7] Boborykin, *Yevropeiski roman v XIX stoletii, roman na zapade za dve treti veka* [The European novel in the XIX century, the novel in the West for the last two-thirds of the century] (St. P., 1900), pp. 224-25.

[8] *Ibid.*, pp. 257-58. [9] *Ibid.*, pp. 289-90.

the novel, Boborykin feels that *Don Quixote* "has one of the greatest flaws in form, the intrusion of intercalated episodes, stories, speeches. . . ." This literary device was frequently employed by writers of the period, "not so much from lack of talent, or in a spirit of imitation or submission to tradition and routine, as from a desire on the part of the writer . . . to use his artistic work to discourse on all sorts of questions. . . . This led to a whole series of anti-artistic devices . . . as in *Don Quixote.*"[10] "And from these old traditional techniques," he adds, "many talented persons cannot free themselves in time, even such a genius as was Cervantes in his *Don Quixote.*"[11]

There is a curious passage in Boborykin's writings that should also be mentioned. Holding a brief for the nineteenth century novel, the critic dwells on the greatness of the Renaissance, the intensity and vividness of its life, and he speculates on the absence of outstanding achievement in the novel. There were indications, he writes, "not in Cervantes' *Don Quixote*, which belongs to a later period, that then, too [during the Renaissance], there could have been works portraying in its entirety brilliant forcefulness of characters, picturesqueness of social life, the struggle of the period's passions and temperaments. Something was lacking. It remained for the nineteenth century novel to achieve the point at which artistic portrayal of the most characteristic traits of the epoch and race became completely possible."[12]

[10] *Ibid.*, p. 230. See also p. 228.
[11] *Ibid.*, p. 390.
[12] *Ibid.*, p. 169. Other allusions to Cervantes are to be found in *ibid.*, pp. 93, 95-96; *Za polveka*, p. 224.

12 · CRITICISM

THE articles on Cervantes produced during this transitional period fall into four main groups: criticism by the symbolists, scholarly studies, general essays, and those of the Marxist school. To the first group belong the works of Merezhkovski, Iv. Iv., V. Ivanov, Botkin and Gvozdev; to the second, those of Shepelevich, Petrov, Yevlakhov, Krzhevski and Bickermann. The fourth group, the Marxists, will be discussed in a subsequent chapter. The articles of a general nature that do not lend themselves to specific classification are included at the end of the present chapter.

One of the distinguishing features of Symbolism was a return to the heritage of the past, seeking support for modern ideas in the masterpieces of literary history. For Merezhkovski, a prominent leader of the school, the *Quixote* was one of these "eternal companions," and he devoted an important essay to his interpretation of the novel.[1]

"The Famous Knight Don Quixote" is the title of an essay by Iv. Iv. which offers another example of the symbolists' interest in and re-evaluation of the masterpieces of the past.[2] The critic insists on the importance of the subjective aspect of literary creations. He writes: "The most valuable and lasting are those works in which the hero incarnates the personality of the author and thereby represents his intimate, spiritual aspirations, his thoughts and his relation to contemporary reality. Here lies the source of the attraction of such works for the public—lay

[1] Cf. pp. 182-83.
[2] Iv. Iv., "Servantes, Slavny rytsar Don Kikhot Lamanchski," *Mir Bozhi* (1896), IX, 258-66.

156

and erudite. In every human matter we are primarily interested in the agent, and this interest becomes particularly keen when it concerns an exceptionally gifted creative nature. Consequently, the fusion of personal confessions with phenomena of external reality gives a work its most profound psychological significance and its most lavish realistic content, artistic force of color and lyrical sincerity of tones. The degree of talent and the significance of a work is determined by the harmony between the strong subjective element and the wealth of external reflections. *Don Quixote* is one of these phenomena of art."[3]

Cervantes' novel, Iv. Iv. goes on to say, is a satire on human madness and unreasonableness. At first the heroes impress us as comical, but upon looking closely we feel something else. "Such double impressions are, generally speaking, peculiar to all heroes who are their authors' favorites. You feel and see clearly that the unfortunate knight . . . is often the author's *alter ego*." Many of his monologues are Cervantes' most intimate *professions de foi*.[4] Cervantes himself was an individualist going crosscurrent for the sake of an ideal. He opposed the contemporary taste for books of chivalry and all it represented, when the whole social order was steeped in it. For his don-quixotism Cervantes landed in jail and paid for it with work, yet he never forsook his beliefs. From the first page of the novel to the last, one hears the noblest commandments of higher human culture—and they are uttered by a madman and a simpleton.[5]

Vyacheslav Ivanov (b. 1866), a first-rate poet and scholar, and a power among the symbolists, discusses Don Quixote as one of the great symbols of individualism in his technical article "The Crisis of Individualism," written for the three-hundredth anniversary of the *Quixote*.[6] It is primarily an exercise in logic, using the Sad Knight for illustrative purposes.

[3] *Ibid.*, pp. 260-61.   [4] *Ibid.*, p. 261.   [5] *Ibid.*, pp. 262-66.
[6] Vyacheslav Ivanov, "Krizis individualizma k trekhvekovoi godovschine Don Kikhota," *Voprosy Zhizni* (1905), ix, pp. 47-60.

This study ventures to trace and explain the evolution of individualism—its displacement of the old concept of collectivism, through its flowering and decline, concluding with its own replacement by the new concept of the Superman.[7] Individualism, Ivanov says, owes a great deal to four literary characters who, significantly, appeared at approximately the same time: King Lear, Macbeth, Hamlet and Don Quixote. In them he finds the first expression of the new concept's demands and its tragic fundamental antinomy.[8] To him they are still individualism's first and best spokesmen.[9]

In Ivanov's argument, Hamlet represents the conflict between the old, inherited philosophic postulates and the nascent demands of individualism. It seems to Hamlet that his soul is torn asunder by his painful experience but, if he were to understand himself, he would see that it is not his soul that is riven apart, but the tables with the ciphers of the commandments of old. He struggles with both the old and the new. He is accountable to the shade of his father, and that aspect of his own character which is rooted in the past. He cannot conquer these ghosts and, consequently, he turns upon his true self, which contains the new element—individualism.[10] This new element is rooted in the principle that the motive for personal volition must coincide with the norm of universal will as recognized by the individual. The individual-subjective, rather than the universal-objective, becomes the fundamental basis for thought and action.[11]

The dangers of this individualism are great, Ivanov points out. One may easily get lost; Hamlet vacillates. He does not know whether to step onto this new path of personal freedom, or to follow the one of his ancestors. He chooses the latter and falls as his own victim. But there will be others who will bravely venture on the new path, concludes the writer.[12] "In contrast to Hamlet, Don Quixote seems to incarnate the active pathos of the collective. Like Hamlet, he is the champion of the premises of a

[7] *Ibid., passim.*   [8] *Ibid.*, p. 47.   [9] *Ibid.*, p. 53.
[10] *Ibid.*, p. 49.   [11] *Ibid.*, p. 50.   [12] *Ibid.*, p. 51.

moral world order which lie besmirched and scorned, yet
in combat he is a non-conformist. And again, like Hamlet, he bears *his* tables [of commandments]. Only, he
does not strive to discern new markings upon them. No,
the old ciphers, rejected by the world, are clearly inscribed upon his memory. Apparently it is not a new
attitude that is born with him, but an old one which is
revived. However, in the subconscious depths of his soul,
he too carries the germ of the new spirit—a desire to assert the truth of his own concept of the world in opposi-
tion to reality. If the world is not as it should be—a pos-
tulate of the soul—so much the worse for the world. As
a matter of fact, there is no such world. Don Quixote *does
not* accept it. . . . Enchanters' charms turn the whole uni-
verse into a mere illusion. At first Don Quixote resorts
to magic spells only in the individual incongruities of the
sought and acquired; but gradually the ring of enchant-
ment tightens about his lonely soul . . . but still in the
prison of dark magic this inexhaustible soul thrives. His
Dulcinea exists in truth. What difference does it make if
beauty bears the distorted mask of phantoms? He is condemned to a knighthood of hopeless quests and futile
wanderings; but his knighthood is without fear or reproach.

"Thus, this rebellion against the world, first voiced by
this new Prometheus of 'the Sad Visage,' has left its mark
on the long-suffering shade of the hero from La Mancha.
Hereafter, on the banner of individualism there stands
inscribed that challenge to the objectively-obligatory
truth; that affirmation of 'ennobling illusion' . . . with
which that peculiar gnosiology of Nietzsche still breathes,
'Truth is that which intensifies life; all other truth is
false.' "[13]

Sergei Botkin in his essay "Cervantes" shows how certain national characteristics and trends are reflected in
the novelist's writings. Botkin sees the Spaniards of the
sixteenth and seventeenth centuries as a restless people,
"seeker-adventurers," reaching out for happiness and

[13] *Ibid.*, pp. 51-52.

contentment beyond the present, beyond the real. Some, like the Conquistadores, were mere adventurers; others, the mystics, were idealists. Yet they were all enveloped in this disquiet, differing not in psychological or spiritual powers but in objectives. Cervantes, a typical example of this mood, saw his creations in the same light. His characters, those of his *novelas* as well as those of the *Quixote*, are ever wandering, ever searching for something—love (*Las dos doncellas*), knowledge (*Coloquio de los perros*), material well-being (*Celoso extremeño*)—and the main motive of Cervantes' heroes is a quest for adventure and personal freedom. Just as all the activity of the period was motivated by this restlessness, so are Cervantes' works.[14]

According to Botkin, Cervantes believed that even the basest of men has a drop of good in him, and the reverse —that the best of men has a drop of evil. The portrayal of this aspect of human nature the novelist greatly enjoyed. This predilection, however, does not belong to Cervantes alone, but is shared by his generation as a whole. Taking Murillo as an example, he points out that this painter, ethically and aesthetically so similar to Cervantes, reflected this interest in his depiction of the more charming side of the Spanish ragamuffins.[15]

Then Botkin discusses Cervantes' interest in the common people and his naturalism. He stresses Cervantes' preference for hideously ugly individuals, saying that in this the novelist is a typical baroque painter like Pacheco, El Greco, Velásquez and Zurbarán.[16] All in all, Botkin's is a very good essay, showing intimate knowledge of Cervantes, his works and his period. The Symbolist approach that colors its first part adds to, rather than detracts from, its interest.

Echoes of Symbolism are heard in Gvozdev's article on "Cervantes and the Tragedy of Heroism," which deals

[14] S. Botkin, "Servantes," *Vestnik Yevropy* (1916), CCXCIX, 77-98; cf. pp. 77-89.
[15] *Ibid.*, p. 91. [16] *Ibid.*, p. 96.

with *Numancia*.[17] The critic considers this play to be one of the most important monuments of early Spanish drama. In it the author's poetic vision, hardened in battle and the suffering of captivity, creates "moving images of superhuman torments, resurrects in an idealized form the highest volitional aspirations, and paints the birth of heroic emotions from excruciating attacks of despair. Powerful elevation of national feeling, unconditional submission of the individual to higher patriotic duty, manliness in the face of death, faith in eternal fame—all these fundamental themes of tragedy are doubtlessly the enlightened echo of Cervantes' own attitude towards the heroes and victims of the war, and the artistic incarnation of those ideals which Cervantes considered the historic fate of his people."[18] Then Gvozdev relates the stories of Numancia, historical and Cervantian, and demonstrates the latter's virtues and failings. This is done competently, untainted by subjective criticism, and could be classed with the products of Cervantes scholarship.

L. Shepelevich was undoubtedly one of the most important Cervantes scholars produced by Russia. He ranks as the first, the most prolific and the most inspiring. (Among his pupils are found such men as A. Beletski.[19]) Shepelevich was born in 1863, studied at the University of Moscow under N. I. Storozhenko, then went to Germany where he mastered the scholarly techniques so sorely needed in Russia. Thereupon, he returned to his homeland and eventually became professor of Western European literatures at Kharkov University, where he remained until his early death in 1909. His publications deal mainly with Cervantes, although he worked in other fields in Spanish literature.[20]

One of his earliest articles, which remained unfinished, deals with the dramatic works of Cervantes. Feeling that this aspect of Cervantes' genius had not been given due

---

[17] A. Gvozdev, "Servantes i tragedia geroizma," *Severnia Zapiski* (1916), v, pp. xxii-xxviii, cf. p. xxiii.

[18] *Ibid.*, p. xxiii.   [19] Cf. pp. 212-14.   [20] Cf. p. 140.

attention, Shepelevich undertook to acquaint his compatriots with it. He quotes a good portion of the prologue to the dramas, stressing the valuable information that it contains. Then he analyzes the plays, classifying them into three groups: those based on the author's experiences, those owing their genesis to literary influences, and those which may be called comedies of manner. In this article Shepelevich concentrates on the first group, which includes *El trato de Argel, Los baños de Argel, El gallardo español* and *La gran Sultana.*[21] He summarizes the plots, checks the subject matter against existing authorities, and comments on the plays' relative merits, points of interest and weaknesses. He then turns to the various phases of Eastern life which they portray, and concludes: "They are a brilliant picture not only of Christian life, but also of the life led by other groups living in Algiers, and marvelously illustrate and amplify historical accounts. Though weak as dramas . . . they are rich in the epical and lyrical, and acquaint us with the five-year captivity of the great novelist. The work of a keen observer and psychologist as well as a convinced and humane moralist is evident in every line."

Shepelevich's next work, *Avellaneda's "Don Quixote" and the Question of Its Author,*[22] has not been available to the present writer.

In his article *"Don Quixote* and the Novels of Chivalry," Shepelevich deals with the question of whether or not *Don Quixote* is a parody of the chivalric novels, possibly of *Amadís de Gaula.*[23] He concedes that Cervantes' main purpose in writing *Don Quixote* was to discredit the genre. He then enumerates the social and cultural reasons prompting this move and explains the indignant reaction of the upper class to the *Quixote.* Before discussing the

[21] L. Shepelevich, "Dramaticheskia proizvedenia Servantesa," *Zhurnal Ministerstva Narodnago Prosveschenia,* July, 1899, pp. 277-300.

[22] Shepelevich, *Don Kikhot Avelyanedy i vopros ob avtore etogo romana,* Kharkov, 1899.

[23] Shepelevich, "Don Kikhot i rytsarski roman," *Obrazovanie,* 1902, nos. 5-9, pp. 79-90.

question of parody he examines the fundamental character traits of the hero: Don Quixote goes mad at fifty and
decides to resurrect chivalry by his own example. Thus
fantasy has to become his reality. One might expect, says
Shepelevich, that Cervantes would make his hero a *reductio ad absurdum* of some more popular fictitious
knight.

"But the author preferred another more artistic
method. His hero acquires the general conditions of
knight-errantry, is permeated with the ideas that motivated the better exponents of that group, and enters the
lists in the name of these ideas. The content of the exploits, however, is completely new, and only the form
into which they are poured is old. The substance of life
has changed. The conditions under which knight-errants
fought and triumphed have receded into eternity."[24] With
uncanny mastery, Cervantes contrasts the real conditions
among which Don Quixote lives with his dreams. From
this contrast springs anachronism and the source of comedy. Shepelevich rejects the theory that *Don Quixote* is
a parody on the novels of chivalry. Their influence is obvious in the plot, made up as it is of individual episodes,
in separate psychological moments of the work and in
some of Don Quixote's ideas, but the general tone of the
work is realistic and foreign to the novels of chivalry.
Neither the plan nor the composition bears any resemblance to the works it satirizes.[25]

In the same year, 1902, Shepelevich published a bibliography of Russian translations of the *Quixote* (abbreviated versions are omitted) with brief comments on their
value, and a list of critical articles written on the subject
by his compatriots.[26] This article, as well as the preceding
ones, were apparently amplified and incorporated into
his great treatise on Cervantes.

It was particularly disappointing to the present writer

[24] *Ibid.*, p. 86.   [25] *Ibid.*, p. 90.
[26] Shepelevich, "Russkaya literatura o Servantese," *Yubileiny
sbornik v chest N. I. Storozhenka, izdany yego uchenikami i pochi-
tateliami*, Moscow, 1902, pp. 161-65.

not to have been able to locate a copy of this major work of Shepelevich, *Cervantes' "Don Quixote": The Life of Cervantes and His Works*.[27] It is a two-volume treatise, the second volume of which (1903) was reviewed by D. Petrov,[28] another prominent Russian Hispanist. The essential points of Petrov's excellent review are as follows.

The contents of Shepelevich's work are distributed in the following manner: Chapter I (pp. 1-8) discusses the editions of the *Quixote* and stresses the merits of the one by Fitzmaurice-Kelly (1898). Chapter II (pp. 9-41) defines a novel of chivalry, explains its worth from the standpoint of customs and manners (*bytovuyu*) and its effect on Spanish customs of the sixteenth and seventeeth centuries. This is followed by an analysis of *Amadís de Gaula* and *Don Quixote's* relation to it. Chapter III (pp. 42-67) deals with the influences of Boiardo, Ariosto and some of the Spanish picaresque novels on *Don Quixote*. Chapter IV (pp. 68-102) is a discussion of Avellaneda's *Don Quixote* and a commentary on the imitations of the *Quixote* in later Spanish literature. Chapter V (pp. 103-20) contains a critical evaluation of Russian literature on *Don Quixote* and the important Russian translations. Chapter VI is devoted to the historical, social, literary and philosophical significance of the *Quixote*, its autobiographical elements, the self-sufficiency of the novel and the features that link it to Cervantes' other works. The main portion of the book is followed by two appendices, one of which contains remarks on the Russian bibliography of Cervantes, and the other, notes on Shepelevich's own investigations.

According to Petrov, the merits of the work include: (1) Its appearance. (2) The author undertook to study his subject from all different angles and moments, and

[27] Shepelevich, "Don Kikhot Servantesa, Zhizn Servantesa i yego proizvedenia," 2 vols. (St. P., 1901-1903).

[28] D. Petrov reviews this work in *Zhurnal Ministerstva Narodago Prosveschenia* (March, 1904), pp. 163-79. Petrov did for Lope de Vega what Shepelevich did for Cervantes.

although not all of his arguments may meet with universal approval, their intentions were good. (3) His chapters on *Amadís* and Avellaneda's spurious *Quixote* offer a mine of new information to many a reader. (4) Chapter v is valuable in that it points out the shortcomings of Karelin's translation and introductory articles. Its comments on Merezhkovski's article, Petrov finds, are unusually astute, as well as Shepelevich's own interpretation of Don Quixote's and Sancho's psychology. "Shepelevich points to the wealth of psychological details which prevent one from regarding the heroes of the novel as abstract symbols and the novel as a work written *ad hoc*."[29] (5) Although chapter vi has no startling originality or depth, it is interesting. (6) The book's most valuable asset is the ardent love of the author for his subject, which pervades the entire work.

As for its shortcomings: In the first place, Petrov feels that a more detailed résumé of the *Quixote* would have been desirable. Then there are some vague or unsubstantiated statements, e.g., on the effect of the *Quixote* on the minds of Cervantes' contemporaries; on the parallel between the *Quixote* and the picaresque novel; on the many similarities in content and form between *Don Quixote* and other works of world literature (Dante, Milton, Rabelais, Shakespeare).

Petrov criticizes Shepelevich's chapter on the novels of chivalry, on chivalric customs and *Don Quixote* (chapter ii), maintaining that the arguments contained therein are not convincing and often contradictory. The reviewer agrees with Shepelevich's presentation of Cervantes' Spain, showing that certain chivalric customs and features were still in existence in that country during the sixteenth and seventeenth centuries, but he considers Shepelevich's subsequent statements contradictory— "The conditions under which knight errants fought and triumphed have receded into eternity," and "the external world surrounding Don Quixote and the world of novels of chivalry offer no analogy." Petrov feels that either the

[29] *Ibid.*, p. 166.

165

chivalric customs were in vogue or passé, but not both.[30] If certain features were still in existence, then there was no anachronism, and Don Quixote's delusions would provide no source of comedy. Don Quixote and his squire may have seemed a bit out of date, Petrov continues, but they were not strange to the social mind of the time. In the Spain of the sixteenth and seventeenth centuries, chivalry was not an anachronism, for the fire of adventure still burned in the hearts of the people, as is evident in contemporary works.[31]

Petrov agrees with Shepelevich that Cervantes' intention was to ridicule the novels of chivalry, lauding his observation that Cervantes did not choose the short cut to his purpose, a *reductio ad absurdum* of some popular chivalric hero. "He chose a different path, logically connected with his literary methods, the path of strictly realistic creation permeated with the high ideals of Christian and national culture. In this way he achieved two purposes: the direct—ridicule of the novels of chivalry—and the indirect—the creation of two positive, universal types. This is correct, but Shepelevich follows this up with a contradiction. . . . In the first place, maintaining that one cannot regard *Don Quixote* as a parody on any particular novel of chivalry, he sets *Amadís de Gaula* on the same level with other novels of its kind. Cervantes did not consider *Amadís* an absurd and false chivalric novel, therefore he had no reason to ridicule it."[32]

Secondly, Shepelevich claims that in the general scheme of the novel there is nothing similar to the novels of chivalry, that the similarity is evident only in individual episodes and moments. This Petrov rightly refutes:

[30] In his article on the subject, which apparently was the basis for this chapter, Shepelevich also discusses the existence of certain superficial features of chivalry during Cervantes' time and then later makes the statements cited by Petrov. He makes it clear, in the article, at least, that this chivalry was very different from that of old, from that which Don Quixote wished to restore, and that is the reason for the anachronism. The customs, the outer shell, may be there, but the core is gone.
[31] Petrov, *ibid.*, p. 169.   [32] *Ibid.*, p. 171.

"In spite of the differences between *Don Quixote* and *Amadís*, the plan of their adventures (centered about the hero) are very much alike. Cervantes decided to ridicule novels of chivalry and the first thing that occurred to him was to build his parody on the same plan. Despite the amount of new material in the *Quixote*—its wealth of psychological observation—it is still constructed along the old plan wherein the hero's adventures do not grow out of his character, but are drawn into the arena of action for the purpose of revealing the hero's character. Don Quixote's adventures are endlessly varied, alive and amusing, but the scheme is an old one. Spanish literary history and Cervantes' own aims led Cervantes to the novels of chivalry for the scheme and plan of *Don Quixote*."[33] Petrov finds another inconsistency in Shepelevich's work in the juxtaposition of his statement claiming that Don Quixote's exploits are inimitable and original creations of the author's imagination, and an unusually well-chosen list of parallels between *Don Quixote* and *Amadís de Gaula*.[34]

Petrov then points to the flaws in Shepelevich's presentation of the relation between Boiardo's and Ariosto's poems and *Don Quixote*. He questions Shepelevich's omission of Pulci's poem *Il Morgante Maggiore*, since both *Don Quixote* and Pulci's work ridicule an outmoded form of literature. Turning to Shepelevich's discussion of Boiardo's and Ariosto's poems, Petrov thinks that an analysis of the poems, with special attention to their fundamental points, would have clarified borrowings and similarities. As things stand, he finds Shepelevich's argument weak, enabling the reader easily to deduce the contrary.[35]

Here Petrov proceeds to show the differences between *Don Quixote* and the aforementioned poems. They differ both in development and in content. *Don Quixote* is concerned with the adventures of two persons who are also the center of the action. In Boiardo's and Ariosto's poems the episodes are more important than the characters and

[33] *Ibid.*, p. 172.   [34] *Ibid.*   [35] *Ibid.*, p. 173.

the intrigue is divided into so many threads that at times it is hard for the reader to keep track of their interrelation. Cervantes may have received the original impulse for his work from these poems, Petrov admits, but the plan of his novel has little in common with the Italian works. Another difference between the works lies in the role played by love. Boiardo's and Ariosto's heroes love with an ardor and sincerity more akin to that of Amadís than of Don Quixote, who only dreams of love. There is also a difference in attitude to the ideals of chivalric life. For Cervantes the principles of chivalry were definitely something sacred, something above laughter. The deeply religious aspect of knighthood so dear to Don Quixote and Cervantes was not understood by the Italian knights and their bards. It was the more glamorous aspects of chivalry that appealed to the Italians of the fifteenth and sixteenth centuries; consequently, the three Italian poets in question often laugh not only at the brute force of knights but even at their honesty and modesty.[36]

Petrov then compares Ariosto and his milieu to Cervantes and his group. The former was a poet, an epicure and a courtier, while Cervantes was but a poor unlucky hidalgo who had gone through the hard school of life. Backgrounds so vastly different could not help but put a different coloring on the works of these writers.[37]

Returning to Shepelevich, Petrov says that his attempts to show wherein Cervantes was indebted to Ariosto are inconclusive and contradictory. Shepelevich suggests that irony manifests itself differently in the works of Cervantes and Ariosto. This remark Petrov develops independently. Cervantes' irony does not touch the essence of knighthood, while that of the Italian poet at times actually penetrates it. Cervantes' irony is objective, while the Italian's is subjective. The foundations of *Don Quixote* are realistic, while those of the Italian poem are fantastic. "It is this erroneous interpretation of the surroundings that makes *Don Quixote* comical. It is not in the contrast, not in the fact that Don Quixote does not see the differ-

[36] *Ibid.*, p. 174.   [37] *Ibid.*, p. 175.

ence between the social life of the days of chivalry and
his own, but in the fact that he accepts *a* for *b*, because
he is mad. And it is from this madness that we must begin
an interpretation of the novel. In its humor it may approach the grotesque, but here Cervantes is not in bad
company—Rabelais, Scarron and others."[38]

Shepelevich's chapter on Cervantes and the picaresque
novel Petrov finds good in its suggestion of Cervantes' indebtedness to Mateo Alemán and in its stress on the importance of realism in Spain prior to Cervantes. The critic
regrets, however, that Shepelevich did not develop the
relation between the picaresque novels and *Don Quixote*.
He merely mentions that the picaresque novel and *Don
Quixote* are united by the sober realism of their composition, inimitable popular humor, lack of pathos and
tragic circumstances, natural manner of exposition, and
by the irony of the authors. Petrov, of course, contradicts
Shepelevich's statement that there is no pathos in *Don
Quixote*. "We still cannot find a satisfactory answer to
the reason for the death of this kind old man."[39] And he
concludes: "The picaresque novels and *Don Quixote* are
different in the *Weltanschauung* lying at their base. Don
Quixote . . . always serves the high ideals of love for his
neighbor, of his country and religion, whereas a *pícaro*
serves only his stomach. Aside from these 'knights of the
stomach,' Spain of the sixteenth and seventeenth centuries was able to create two types having both universal
significance as well as brilliant national coloring—Don
Quixote and Sancho Panza. They are a hidalgo, a knight
at his best, and a Spanish peasant, who although he is
bound to the soil is able to rise to high ideals. The Spanish peasant and the nobleman, the servant and the master
—here is the explanation of the supposed allegory of the
novel. Cervantes did not plan any antitheses or contrasts,
he merely portrayed in poetry what lived together in life.
Regarded from the historico-cultural point of view, this
juxtaposition contains the novel's greatest significance."[40]

[38] *Ibid.*, p. 177.   [39] *Ibid.*, p. 178.   [40] *Ibid.*, p. 179.

Shepelevich's article "The Three Hundredth Anniversary of Cervantes' *Don Quixote*"[41] is essentially a summary of his book. The approach is the historico-literary one, and most of the material in the essay has either been discussed or mentioned above, with the exception of the following point. Shepelevich shows Cervantes as the painter of his time, his country[42] and his people, and then turns to a discussion of Don Quixote and Sancho. "The Lamanchan knight's character does not have the unity presupposed by the symbolist interpretations. In the early chapters he is a madman, but as the tale progresses Don Quixote develops and grows, revealing more and more often the noble qualities of his soul and a mature mind. At times you can even reproach him with cowardice, thus making any generalization of intrepidity impossible. His personality is so rich and varied that it does not lend itself to a narrow one-sided interpretation."[43]

Shepelevich believes that if one cannot consider Don Quixote as an unadulterated idealist, neither can one regard Sancho as his antithesis—the representative of the bourgeois attitude towards life. Fascinating as such a contrast would have been, Cervantes did not exploit it. Sancho is not opposite from, but similar to, his master. Conceived as a *gracioso*, he develops into a wise man, retaining at the same time kindness and honesty. Spiritually, Sancho has a far more complicated life than Don Quixote. In fact, at times he is baffling. He has a highly developed instinct of self-preservation, and yet he subjects himself to open dangers. He is sane, and yet he follows a madman. Although he is covetous, he is at the same time very carefree and thoughtless. He is at once credulous and skeptical. His character has a wealth of such inconsistencies.[44]

Sancho's spiritual life is very interesting. At the beginning of the novel he is naïve and credulous, but in

[41] Shepelevich, "Trekhsotletie 'Don Kikhota' Servantesa," *Vestnik Yevropy* (1905), vol. 233, pp. 328-40.
[42] *Ibid.*, pp. 335-37.   [43] *Ibid.*, p. 338.
[44] *Ibid.*, p. 339.

chapter xv he becomes skeptical and follows his master because of curiosity and a fairly well-developed imagination. Like a true Spaniard, he is responsive to Don Quixote's brilliant eloquence, as a result of which he gradually acquires his master's *Weltanschauung* and his style of talking. The covetous impulses in him are overshadowed by his deep attachment and devotion to Don Quixote. "Both master and servant are illuminated by that light of human kindness, and it is this kindness, humaneness and mutual attachment that binds them more tightly than could any contrast in character. Therefore we have to renounce Turgenev's and Heine's interpretations," says Shepelevich.[45]

It matters little to him whether Cervantes copied Don Quixote from one man or another. "It remains that his creative talent produced a new and original combination. The significance of a literary work is determined not only by the sum of the new creative elements, or materials, but also by the sum of those mental efforts consumed in its comprehension, the sum of those noble and elevated emotions which it arouses, and by the sum of enthusiasm that it evokes. Here lies the invaluable contribution of Cervantes."[46] This may be the evaluation that Petrov liked so well in Shepelevich's book.[47]

The great scholar was also very active in acquainting his compatriots with new works on Cervantes appearing abroad. He reviewed Pérez Pastor's *Documentos cervantinos*,[48] the Fitzmaurice-Kelly and Ormsby edition of the *Quixote*,[49] Icaza's *Novelas Ejemplares de Cervantes*, Abaurre y Mesa's *Historia de varios sucesos ocurridos en la aldea después de la muerte del ingenioso hidalgo Don Quixote de la Mancha*, Cotarelo y Mori's *Estudio de historia literaria de España*, Rodríguez Marín's *El Loaysa de "El celoso extremeño,"*[50] Asensio's *Cervantes y sus obras*,

[45] *Ibid.*, pp. 338-39.   [46] *Ibid.*, p. 340.
[47] Cf. p. 165.
[48] *Zhurnal Ministerstva Narodnago Prosveschenia* (1898), no. 2, pp. 324-27.
[49] *Ibid.* (1899), no. 12, pp. 303-08.
[50] *Ibid.* (1902), no. 6, pp. 414-18.

Mainez' *Cervantes y su época*, Cortejón's *La Coartada*,[51] Cortejón's new edition of the *Quixote*, Rius' bibliography, Cejador y Frauca's *Lengua de Cervantes*, Cotarelo y Mori's *Resumen cronológico de la vida de Miguel de Cervantes Saavedra*, Unamuno's *Vida de Don Quijote y Sancho según Miguel de Cervantes Saavedra . . .* ,[52] Morel Fatio's *Etudes sur l'Espagne* and Groussac's *Une Enigme littéraire, le Don Quichotte d'Avellaneda*.[53]

A well-informed Hispanist, Shepelevich gives credit and praise where it is due, but has no patience with stupid pretension to originality. For instance, Yevlakhov's article "For the Three Hundredth Anniversary of *Don Quixote*,"[54] which purports to be a critical survey of the interpretations advanced by Storozhenko, Turgenev, Shepelevich and Ticknor, is an inept rehashing of other people's works (drawn second-hand, at that), and more than deserves Shepelevich's scathing review.[55]

Boris Krzhevski in his article "Cervantes and His *Novelas ejemplares*"[56] deals briefly with the themes of the *novelas*, their ideological content, purpose, value and technique. He considers Cervantes' contribution to the genre, contemporary criticism of his innovation, the influence of the form on later writers like Kleist, Tieck, Hoffman and others, and the influence of the content on subsequent Spanish dramatists. Krzhevski's expert handling of the material reveals a high quality of Spanish scholarship.

Joseph Bickermann's (b. 1867) long work, *Don Quixote and Faust: the Heroes and the Works* is of course well known to Cervantes' students. It has long been available

[51] *Ibid.* (1904), no. 6, pp. 464-70.
[52] *Ibid.* (1905), no. 8, pp. 460-64.
[53] *Ibid.* (1904), pp. 214-17.
[54] A. Yevlakhov, "K trekhsotletiyu Don Kikhota" [For the 300 anniversary of Don Quixote] in *Mir Bozhi* (1905), no. 5, pp. 47-69.
[55] L. Shepelevich, "Po povodu statyi Yevlakhova" [Concerning Yevlakhov's article], *Obrazovanie* (1905), no. 7, pp. 299-300.
[56] B. Krzhevski, "Servantes i yego novelli," *Severnia Zapiski*, 1916, no. 5, pp. xxix-xxxix. Krzhevski later translated the *Novelas, Don Quixote* and *El rufián viudo*. (Cf. pp. 192-95.)

to all in Spanish[57] and German[58] translations and through reviews of such experts as Américo Castro.[59] Bickermann's work can be characterized as scholarly in preparation and interpretative in execution.

Among the essays on Cervantes that belong neither in the Symbolist group nor with those of primarily scholarly interest is V. Fisher's "Cervantes and *Don Quixote*," a short journal article for the general public.[60] It opens with a brief biography of Cervantes, and goes on to a discussion of Cervantes and his masterpiece. Cervantes was a realist, Fisher maintains. He knew reality, while his hero denies it from the very first page. For this rejection Cervantes subjected Don Quixote to all kinds of misfortunes out of which both the hero and reality emerged unchanged. At first Cervantes laughed at the knight, but gradually he developed an affection for him, and instead of regarding him as a half-witted adventurer, he saw him as a man of high ideals. The critic dwells on the literary theories expounded in *Don Quixote* and Cervantes' aesthetic reaction to the spurious second part of his novel, and concludes with a word about Carrasco's attempt to bring Don Quixote back to reality.

Dioneo in his essay "Miguel Cervantes"[61] discusses briefly Cervantes' life and works and his cultural background, and then turns to his major work. Dioneo entertains the contradictory theory that *Don Quixote*, though as formless as life itself, follows the pattern of life formulated by Petrarch and Pascal. The novel begins with absolute faith in illusion, then demonstrates how this faith changes into belief that life is a comedy, and terminates, as life does, with disillusionment. The critic traces

[57] J. Bickermann, *Don Quijote y Fausto, los heroes y las obras* (Barcelona, 1932), translated by P. Felix Garciá.

[58] Joseph Bickermann, *Don Quijote und Faust, Die Helden und die Werke*, Berlin, 1929.

[59] *Revista de Filología Española*, XVII (1930), 292-93.

[60] V. Fisher, "Servantes i Don Kikhot," in *Russkaya Mysl* (1916), no. 5, pp. 1-10.

[61] Dioneo, "Miguel Servantes (1816-1916)," *Russkia Zapiski*, 1916, v, 64-89.

173

through the novel the author-hero relationship. Like
Fisher, Dioneo says that at first Cervantes does not understand his heroes fully and sees in them only the potential for comedy, but, as they live together, Cervantes
comes to fathom their characters and significance. Don
Quixote becomes the defender of an ideal. In him,
thought and action are one. While the average man is
accustomed to the separation of thought from action, to
modifying his dreams to fit reality, Don Quixote does the
reverse. He imposes his ideal upon reality, resulting in an
apparent madness of action. *Don Quixote* brings to us a
world of illusion. It may, as Dioneo remarks, be foolish
to believe in illusion, but why should we not? When illusion goes, death is soon to come.[62] The second part of
the novel, Dioneo contends, carries to all Spanish literature a message of tolerance, respect for thought and
word, and resistance to the blackguard clergy who had
ruined Spain. Interesting though Dioneo's article is, it
contains several inaccuracies, such as the mention of a
second part to *Galatea*, and the statement that in Cervantes' time the vogue for novels of chivalry was a thing
of the past.

N. N. Evreinoff (b. 1879), the prominent producer and
dramatist who contributed so largely to the revival of the
plays of the Spanish Golden Age in twentieth century
Russia,[63] evolved a provocative theory of art. In his book
The Theater in Life he devotes a section to *Don Quixote*,
in relation to what he termed "the theater for oneself."[64]
His theoretical considerations are based on the concept
of an inherent sense of theater in man (*teatralnost*), a
fundamental instinct which exists quite apart from the
actual theater and determines man's thoughts and habits.

Like Heine, Evreinoff believes that the pen of a genius
is always wiser than the genius himself, for it covers
much wider ground. We are not interested, he says, in

[62] *Ibid.*, p. 88.   [63] Cf. p. 146.
[64] N. Evreinoff, *The Theater in Life*, edited and translated by A.
I. Nazaroff, with an introduction by O. M. Saylor (New York,
1927).

Cervantes' avowed aim of dealing a death blow to the novels of chivalry. "The thing that appeals to us most in the book is the sincere and enthusiastic protest against the aggressive reality which triumphs over our earthly lives. For it is exactly this protest that shines forth through Don Quixote's 'fabulous' exploits."[65] He achieves it by creating a "theater for himself."

Evreinoff points to the conversation between Sancho and Don Quixote wherein the squire tells his master that knights all had reasons for their sufferings, while Don Quixote has none. The knight answers, "I certainly have not. . . . *The thing that really matters is to lose one's mind for no reason at all!*" Here, the writer feels, lies the real explanation of Don Quixotism.[66] "The 'theater for oneself' to which Don Quixote has dared to surrender is the most logical, the most uncompromising, and the most complete expression of man's will to the theater. If you are fascinated by a fairy-tale, you naturally wish to see it materialized; if you remember with delight the golden years of your childhood, you naturally wish to see some of its vivifying gold on the years of your maturity as well. . . ."[67] "Yet it is true," Evreinoff says, "that one cannot learn to understand Don Quixote; Don Quixote can be only *felt*, and in order to feel him one must have in one's soul something of Don-Quixotism."[68] "Don Quixote, however, is such a limit of our own Don-Quixotism, such a *reductio ad absurdum* of our own will to the theater, such an acute form of theatricalization that we instinctively shrink in horror from him."[69]

Then Evreinoff projects Robinson Crusoe, whom he calls "Don Quixote in disguise," against the same backdrop, shows how he, like the knight, creates a theater for himself, and then points out a shade of difference between the two characters. Robinson Crusoe is very fond of his "theater for himself," but "he can also laugh and ironize over this theater." "Don Quixote has fallen asleep once and for ever to the realities of our life. Robinson is

[65] *Ibid.*, pp. 84-85.   [66] *Ibid.*, pp. 86-89.   [67] *Ibid.*, p. 92.
[68] *Ibid.*, p. 89.   [69] *Ibid.*, p. 93.

asleep and awake at the same time: there is Robinson,
the fantastic dreamer and theatricalizer, and Robinson, a
sound realist. Which of them vanquishes the other in the
last account? Certainly Robinson, the Don Quixote."[70]

For bibliographical completeness, mention should be
made of the following works: P. Vainberg's essay "Cervantes" (1892) is a glorifying, enthusiastic and often inaccurate biography of the novelist. He draws indiscrimi-
nately upon apocryphal tales that had grown up around
Cervantes, and produces a figure of flawless nobility,
patriotism and martyrdom more appropriate for readers
of "Superman" than of *Mir Bozhi*.[71] A. D. Alferov's *Ten
Lectures on Literature* (1895) which is said to have a
chapter on Cervantes,[72] a translation of Louis Viardot's
Life and Works of Cervantes,[73] E. During's *Great Men in
Literature* (1897)[74] and O. Peterson's *Cervantes, His Life
and His Works* (1901),[75] have not been available.

In 1905 a short note on Cervantes appeared in the journal *Niva*,[76] occasioned by the three-hundredth anniversary of the *Quixote*. It is introductory in nature, since it
was intended to arouse public interest in Cervantes. The
same year saw the publication of N. I. Konorov's article
"Don Quixote as a Complete Pathological Personality."[77]
This was followed by A. Altayev's *Miguel Cervantes*
(1907),[78] the chapter on Cervantes in D. V. Averkyev's

[70] *Ibid.*, p. 95.
[71] P. Vainberg, "Servantes," in *Mir Bozhi* (1892), no. 10, pp.
44-61.
[72] Cited by *Literaturnaya Entsiklopedia*, III (Moscow-Leningrad, 1930), 385.
[73] In *Slavny Don Kikhot Servantesa* translated by S. M. (Moscow, 1895), vol. I.
[74] E. During, *Velikie lyudi v literature* (St. P., 1897), pp. 35-
46; cited by "Literaturnaya Entsiklopedia," III, 385.
[75] O. Peterson, *Servantes, yego zhizn i proizvedenia*, St. P.,
1901; cited by "Katalog Odesskoi Gorodskoi Publichnoi Biblioteki," III, 69.
[76] "Rytsar pechalnago obraza," *Niva*, 1905, no. 18, pp. 349-51.
[77] N. I. Konorov, "Don Kikhot, kak tselnaya patologicheskaya
lichnost," *Vestnik psikhologii, kriminalnoi antropologii i gipnotizma*
(1905), IV.
[78] Al. Altayev is the pseudonym of Margarita Vladimirovna

book *On the Drama* (1907),[79] a biography of the Spanish novelist in Tsomakion's *The Lives of Remarkable People*,[80] a study of Cervantes and Shakespeare by N. Bokardov in *The History of Western European Literature of the Sixteenth and Seventeenth Centuries* (1914),[81] and L. Chizhikov's and N. Bakhtin's *Bibliography of Cervantes* (1914).[82]

Yamschikova (born 1872), author of historical sketches and stories for children. Her biography of Cervantes was published in St. Petersburg.

[79] D. V. Averkyev, *O drame*, 1907.

[80] Tsomakion, *Zhizn zamechatelnykh lyudei*, mentioned by N. Storozhenko in *Ocherki istorii zapadno-yevropeiskoi literatury*, p. 215.

[81] N. Bokardov, *Istoria zapadno-yevropeiskoi literatury XVI-XVII vekov*, Kiev, 1914.

[82] *Literaturnaya Entsiklopedia*, III, 385.

13 · SOLOGUB AND MEREZHKOVSKI

THE Symbolist movement in Russia was very complex, taking on various guises, such as the religious mysticism of Solovyev, the realistic mysticism of Blok, the satanism of Sologub and others. From the point of view of the present study, it is significant that the three authors just mentioned had one thing in common with Don Quixote. They were united "symbolically" among themselves and with Don Quixote by their devotion to a mysterious, intangible lady. Don Quixote had Dulcinea, Solovyev— Sofia, Blok—Neznakomka or Prekrasnaya Dama (The Unknown or Lovely Lady), and Sologub—Dulcinea. It is also interesting that whereas in other periods it was Cervantes' heroes who entered into the creative processes of the Russian writers, in this period of effeminate decadence Dulcinea eclipses Don Quixote and Sancho.

The very ephemeral nature of Symbolism makes it difficult to get at concrete examples of Cervantes' influence. It is certain, however, that F. Sologub (b. 1863) conceived an early and lasting admiration for *Don Quixote*. The preface to his famous novel *The Little Demon*[1] was modeled directly after the concluding pages of the first part of the *Quixote*. "I once thought," writes Sologub, "that Peredonov's career was finished, and that he would never come out of the psychiatric ward to which he was committed after he killed Volodin. Yet recently news began to reach me that his mental disorders were temporary, and did not prevent his regaining his freedom. . . ." The writer then continues to relate what rumor sup-

[1] F. Sologub, "Melki Bes," *Sobranie sochineni* (6th ed., St. P., n.d.), VI, 3-4.

posedly has brought to his attention concerning Peredonov's life after the end of the novel. "I even read in one
paper that I was planning to write a second part of *The
Little Demon*." This touch clearly recalls Cervantes.

A more subtle expression of the effect produced by
Cervantes on Sologub is found in the fact that the symbolist drew on the tale of Don Quixote's transformation
of Aldonza into Dulcinea to express his own credo. Dulcinea is for him the symbol of Beauty for whom man
searches. She haunts man, consoling and cajoling him,
pleading for him to recognize and crown her as Dulcinea.
Yet he, the blind slave of the world of Evil, which is characterized by diversity, desire and vulgarity, cannot sever
earthly fetters, look within himself and become the master of the world of Good, a world of unity, calm and
beauty. Such being the case, he is not aware of Dulcinea,
who stands beside him unrecognized and uncrowned. He
searches for her in the earthly realm and what he mis-
takes for Dulcinea turns out to be a common Aldonza.

One aspect of this theme appears in the drama *The
Triumph of Death*. It is introduced by a prologue in
which Aldonza enters, carrying two pails, one containing
the water of life, the other the water of death. She grieves
over the fact that people refuse to acknowledge the value
of the waters—the creation of a new life—but her lament
is interrupted by the entrance of the King, who recog-
nizes her. "You are the peasant girl, Aldonza," he says,
"the same one who makes the street boys laugh because
some madman has called you by the sweet name of Dulcinea, the dear enchantress, the most lovely of all maidens
upon the earth. You have learned to enchant and to
weave spells, serpent-eyed one, and yet you have not
found yourself a bridegroom." She replies, "I am waiting
for a king and a poet who will crown me. They will
crown beauty, and depose ugliness. They will reject the
commonplace, and will strive to achieve the unattain-
able."[2] But no one does acclaim her. Even the poet to

[2] The English translation quoted here is by John Cuornos, in
Drama, vi (1916), 347-84; cf. p. 349.

whom she says, "You have come here, in the depth of time . . . in order to sing in praise of me, the loveliest of earthly maidens, the enchantress, Dulcinea, who in this dark land is called improperly Aldonza,"[3] treats her lightly. She bewitches the five characters of the prologue into watching an eternal drama, in which Beauty conquers Ugliness by love in death. "Again the spectacle will remain a spectacle, and not become a mystery," says Aldonza.

"Again the true beauty of this world, of the enchantress Dulcinea in the form of the serpent-eyed Aldonza, shall remain uncrowned, unsung, unloved. Great is my weariness, and great my sadness. But I will not give up my design. Tireless, I will strive in order that beauty shall be crowned, and ugliness deposed. Unwearyingly I shall appear in various forms to the poet, the lover, and the king. Sing my praises—I will say—fall in love with me, crown me. Come to me, follow me. Only I am alive in life and in death, only within me is life, only to me the ultimate triumph. I will now take the form of the slave Malgista, and I will send my daughter to a great deed, to the fulfilment of my eternal design. To her virginal freshness I will add my eternal witchery. Whether the triumph be life's or the triumph be death's, the triumph shall be mine."[4]

The plot for the ensuing play was drawn from the tale of Queen Bertha, the Long-legged. Bertha, the symbol of Ugliness, is wed to King Khlodoveg. Upon the instigation of Malgista, her daughter Algista, the symbol of Beauty, usurps Bertha's place, and the true Queen is banished. Algista gives the King ten years of idyllic happiness and a healthy youngster. Bertha, however, returns to accuse the impostor, who accepts the challenge. Algista and her child are whipped to death, but at night their ghosts rise and Algista appeals to the King's love. She begs that he reject ugly Bertha, but he refuses. She returns to death, but the King, Bertha and their entourage turn to stone.

[3] *Ibid.*, p. 352.   [4] *Ibid.*, pp. 354-55.

Algista triumphs in death, since "Love and Death are one."[5]

The Hostages of Life, another of Sologub's works, presents the eternal discord between thought and reality, art and life, Dulcineas and Aldonzas. Man is ever pursuing what he believes to be Dulcinea, who in fact is nothing but Aldonza, while the real Dulcinea, the dream (*mechta*), so strange, unselfish and beautiful, stands beside him unrecognized.

The creative basis of life is represented in the play by Mikhail, and earthly life by Katya. They are passionately in love with each other, but circumstances demand a postponement of their union. Katya marries Sukhov, the symbol of uncreativeness and hoarding. Mikhail is left to make his career, but the emptiness in his life is filled by the lunar, ecstatic, lovely Lilith (Dulcinea), the idealistic basis of life. She loves Mikhail for his creativeness and comes to console him in his loneliness. Demanding nothing, she remains with him as long as he needs her. The tragedy lies at the end of the play when Katya and Mikhail are reunited and remain life's hostages. They think that Lilith, "that sad, wide-eyed creature, went away, went away to him who dreams," and do not see the curtain in the rear of the stage rise. There illuminated are seven steps, on the top of which stands Lilith in black raiment, her head crowned with a golden diadem. Unseen, unrecognized, uncrowned by them, she stands. "I am tired," she says. "I am deathly tired. Many centuries have passed over me. I beckon man, and then, having completed my mission, I go away. Dulcinea still remains uncrowned, and the path ahead is so long."[6]

This use which Sologub makes of Dulcinea seems, perhaps, the most curious manifestation of Cervantes' influence in Russia. Here, ironically enough, a symbolist, a man of dream and fantasy comparable to the writers of chivalric lore, employs material from the *Quixote,* of

[5] *Ibid.,* p. 382.
[6] Sologub, "Zalozhniki Zhizni," *Literaturno khudozhest vennie almanakhi,* xviii (St. P., 1912), 11-108; cf. p. 108.

which the avowed purpose was to kill the books of chivalry.

Considering the vast literary output of D. S. Merezhkovski (b. 1866), the influence of Cervantes on his works was slight. He wrote a three-page descriptive poem entitled "Don Quixote" which he concludes with these words: "Both love and faith are sacred, and by this faith are moved all great madmen, all prophets and poets."[7]

Cervantes' influence is evident in a minor character of Merezhkovski's *Peter and Alexis*. "The Quixote of astronomy" is the nickname given to Pastor Gluck in the work, a kind, clever and peculiar man, engaged in writing commentaries on Newton's *Commentaries of the Apocalypse*, an endeavor truly worthy of his namesake. This involved task leads the poor old man into confusing metaphysical debates with himself, reminiscent of those of Don Quixote on the contents of the novels of chivalry. When a friend points out that Newton was in his dotage at the time he wrote the *Commentaries*, Gluck replies, "Your Excellency, I would rather be mad with Newton, than reasonable with the rest of us bipeds!"[8]

Merezhkovski's essay "Eternal Companions: Cervantes" is an important contribution to Russian Cervantes criticism. As a symbolist, his approach to literature is, of course, subjective. He believes that with time a universal work acquires a value and significance far exceeding that consciously given to it by the author, the extent of this significance depending on the reader's perception.[9] The *Quixote* Merezhkovski regards as a satire on a defect of man—the inactivity of his brain—and Don Quixote himself as a ridicule of the deficiencies of medieval culture.[10] Don Quixote is to the critic a symbol of medievalism.

[7] D. S. Merezhkovski, "Don Kikhot," in *Polnoye sobranie sochineni*, xv (Moscow, 1912), 86-88.

[8] Merezhkovski, *Peter and Alexis* (sole authorized translation published by G. P. Putnam and Sons, New York-London, 1906).

[9] Merezhkovski, "Vechnie sputniki, Servantes," [Eternal companions: Cervantes], *Polnoye sobranie sochineni*, xvii (Moscow, 1914), 101-35; the date of the article is 1889.

[10] *Ibid.*, p. 118.

This he finds expressed in the knight's blind faith in place of critical examination, in his imitative qualities instead of originality, in his subjection to higher authority rather than independent thought, in his pessimistic outlook on the future fate of man, in his love of simplicity, in his idealization of simple folk and scorn for civilization.[11]

Then the symbolist offers a typical Merezhkovskian antithesis. Don Quixote is the representative of the cold, barren North, Sancho of the warm, sunny South, with its humor and kindliness, its effusiveness and understanding of the vagrant life of the gipsies. Sancho lacks the severity characteristic of Northern peoples.[12] His temperament is too carefree to let his religion become fanatical. It does not have those deep mystical roots which are found in the concentrated religiousness of the Northerners. Sancho's *Weltanschauung* is completely expressed in his proverbs, which comprise his greatest wealth.[13] Sancho and Don Quixote represent the attraction of opposites, and live together in complete understanding and love. Don Quixote changes everything into a dream or fantasy, the squire into a joke. The heroes are comical and are the dupes of pranksters, but the satire falls on their tormentors, who spend their life in idleness and seek recreation in this low form of diversion.[14]

As proof of Cervantes' relation to Symbolism, Merezhkovski points to his religious instincts, as they are manifested by the dearth of nature description in the *Quixote*. He accounts for this in that "Cervantes was a faithful son of the Roman Catholic Church. His devoutness was confined to definite organic forms of orthodox dogma and not a drop of this religious feeling was wasted on nature."[15] Thus Cervantes becomes in the eyes of Merezhkovski a great religious writer and a father of contemporary mystical Symbolism!

11 *Ibid.*, p. 111.   12 *Ibid.*, p. 118.   13 *Ibid.*, pp. 122-23.
14 *Ibid.*, pp. 128-33.   15 *Ibid.*, p. 108.

PART IV

THE MARXISTS
AND THE SOVIET
(1903-1940)

14 · BACKGROUND

The year 1917 ushered a new political era into Russia. The ideology and aspirations of the Soviet regime produced a very definite effect on all forms of literature. Creative writing took on a new morality, new ideas and a new life. Marxist criticism, which had been developing since 1890, now dominated the scene, to the exclusion of almost all other types. The Formalist school, however, did rise in protest against the Marxists' excessive didacticism, and paid exaggerated attention to style at the expense of ideas. Foreign as well as Russian "bourgeois" literary works were re-edited in handsome volumes with greater precision and more accurate annotation than ever had been produced by the Russian "bourgeoisie." Letters and archives of famous Russian authors and drafts of their works were retrieved from oblivion and offered to the public, shedding new light on long-familiar masterpieces.

As has been shown, Russia had long had cultural, economic and diplomatic relations with Spain, but never before had Spain been as close to the whole Russian people as it was during the years of its Civil War. Previous to the Spanish revolution in the 1930's, Russian travelers such as Leon Trotsky,[1] the scientist N. I. Vavilov[2] and Ilya Ehrenburg, the journalist,[3] visited the country and wrote accounts of their impressions. To these can be added some of a different nature: *Documents of the*

[1] L. Trotsky, "Delo bylo v Ispanii" [It happened in Spain] *Krasnaya Nov*, July, 1922, pp. 123-43, and Jan. 1926, pp. 127-59.
[2] N. I. Vavilov, "Moyo puteshestvie v Ispaniyu" [My trip to Spain], *Novy Miv* (1937), ii, 225-53.
[3] Ilya Ehrenburg, *Ispania* (Moscow, 1932), p. 69.

Spanish Revolution (1873-74), edited by E. Adamov,[4] *Documents of the Hispano-British Conflict* (1898-99), edited by F. V. Kelyin,[5] and L. M. Bernar's *Spain in Flames*,[6] dealing with the events of 1931. These are isolated works, appearing as a result of the authors' interest and reaching the few who cared to read them, but after 1936 the picture is different.

A passionate enthusiasm for the Loyalists surged up in the Russians. Russian periodicals were flooded with news of Spanish events, often collected by correspondents in Spain, such as Ehrenburg and M. I. Koltsov. The most interesting expression of this interest is to be found in the number of propaganda books issued—letters of Spanish soldiers to the Russian proletariat, and volumes of pictures of the Civil War.[7] Just one example of this type of literature is *The Peoples of USSR to the Spanish People*.[8]

[4] E. Adamov, "Ispanskaya revolyutsia (1873-1874). Dokumenty," *Krasny Arkhiv* (1931), XLIX, 3-54.
[5] F. V. Kelyin, "Ispansko-britanski konflikt, 1898-1899 godov. Dokumenty," *Krasny Arkhiv* (1933), LX, 3-59.
[6] L. M. Bernar, *Ispania v ogne* (Moscow, 1934).
[7] P. R. Gorozhankina, *Rabochi klass Ispanii i gody revolyutsii* [Spain's working class and the years of the revolution], edited by L. Geller (Moscow, 1936). I Erenburg, *Ispania* (Moscow-Leningrad, n.d.). Vol. I is devoted to showing the horrors of pre-revolutionary Spain and the beginning of the conflict; vol. II to the period between July and December 1936. The book is mainly pictorial. E. Varga, *Ispania v revolyutsii* [Spain in Revolution] (1936). *No pasarán*, a 139-page pictorial survey of the Civil War, published in 1937. *Grazhdanskaya voina v Ispanii, politicheskie karikatury i risunki sovietskikh khudozhnikov* [Civil War in Spain, political caricatures and pictures by Soviet artists] (Moscow, 1937), album collected by E. M. Vesenin and L. M. Kublanovski. It includes cartoons by V. Yefimov and Kukrynski. B. Y. Friedlands, *Fashistskie interventy v Ispanii* [Fascist intervention in Spain], caricatures edited by B. F. Malkin. *Fashistskie vandaly v Ispanii*, statyi i fotodokumenty [Fascist vandals in Spain, articles and photodocuments], edited by T. I. Sorokin and A. V. Fevralski (Moscow, 1938). M. Y. Koltsov, "Ispanski Dnevnik" [Spanish diary], *Novy Mir* (1938), book IV, pp. 5-125, continued in subsequent volumes; also "Ispanski Dnevnik" *Khudezhestvennaya literatura* (1938), vol. I. A. Kantarovich, "Batalion Chapayev," translated by R. Rait, *Literaturny Sovremennik* (1938), no. 12, pp. 100-33, excerpts from book of that name published in Madrid, 1938. It is a series of letters from soldiers at the front.
[8] *Narody SSSR Ispanskomu narodu* (Moscow, 1937).

It has a fiery foreword by Stalin, excerpts from speeches by N. M. Shvernik ("Hands off the Spanish People"), E. Bystrov ("You Are Not Alone, We Are with You") and A. Fersman ("The Eyes of the Workers Are on Heroic Spain"), propaganda poems, pictures of women packing clothes and food to be sent to Spain, of the meeting held in the Red Square on August 3, 1936, devoted to Spain, of Spanish ruins, and so forth. The whole tone of the book can be summed up as saying, "We are behind you in your struggle for the freedom of your people from the Fascist yoke."

The theater also reflects this preoccupation. Repertoires contain, besides the traditional *Spanish Caprice*, *Don Quixote*, *Carmencita* or Calderón's dramas, works such as *Hail, Spain!*, a romantic drama in two parts with an epilogue,[9] and a translation of G. Mdivani's *Alcázar*, a heroic drama in four acts dealing with the great siege.[10]

Russia had no Spanish-Russian dictionary until 1930. In that year a good one of 30,000 words, compiled by Ignatov and Kelyin, was published. In 1931 it was followed by a larger one.[11] Both were very adequate, containing all that one would need for reading contemporary literature. But, in 1937, a dictionary appeared of which the editors wrote:

"The tremendous interest in USSR in the Spanish language and literature, especially in connection with the heroic struggle of the Spanish people for its independence against Fascism, prompted the Lexicographical Publications to put through a special second edition of the Spanish-Russian dictionary of 1930.

"The present dictionary has as its aim to make it possible for the public to read the Spanish newspapers and contemporary Spanish literature. In this edition South American, specialized and archaic words are omitted. . . . As for abbreviations, we have at the end of the book the

[9] A. N. Afinogenov, *Salyut, Ispania* (Moscow, 1936).

[10] G. Mdivani, *Alkazar*, translated by V. Radysh (Moscow, 1937).

[11] *Ispansko-Russki Slovar*, compiled by S. S. Ignatov, and F. V. Kelyin, 40,000 words, with peculiarities of the Spanish language of Central and South America included (Moscow, 1931).

political and war terminology used in the Spanish Republican press. Also at the end is a short summary of Spanish grammar and a list of Spanish cities.

"Along with this edition the editors are preparing a third edition, enlarged and revised."[12]

Academic work in Spanish literature, interrupted for a decade by the Civil War in Russia and the following readjustment period, was resumed by the specialists, producing such works as Vygodski's *Literature of Spain and Spanish America*,[13] Koulle's *The Present Status of Spanish Literature*,[14] Armesto's *The Problems of Revolutionary Literature in Spain*,[15] Vygodski's *Spanish Literature of Our Day*,[16] V. Uzin's and D. Vygodski's article on Spanish literature and art in the *Large Soviet Encyclopedia*,[17] sections on Spain in Lunacharski's *History of Western European Literature*.[18] Such scholars as these pooled their training in the Spanish publications of the Russian publishing house "Academia."[19] The results were good new translations of *Lazarillo de Tormes*,[20] *Don Quixote*,[21] *Spanish and Portuguese Poets, Victims of the Inquisition*,[22] Calderón's dramas,[23] *La Vida del Buscón*,[24]

---

[12] *Ispansko-Russki Slovar*, compiled by S. S. Ignatov and F. V. Kelyin, assisted by K. A. Martsishevski, about 30,000 words, second revised edition (Moscow, 1937). Cf. note from the editors.

[13] D. Vygodski, *Literatura Ispanii i ispanskoi Ameriki* (Leningrad, 1929).

[14] P. Koulle, "Segodnya ispanskoi literatury," *Vestnik inostrannoi literatury* (Moscow, 1929), no. 5.

[15] F. F. Armesto, "Zadachi revolyutsionnoi literatury Ispanii," *Literatura mirovoi revolyutsii* (Moscow, 1932), no. 3.

[16] D. Vygodski, "Ispanskaya literatura nashikh dnei," *Literaturny kritik* (Moscow, 1934), nos. 7-8.

[17] *Bolshaya Sovietskaya Entsiklopedia*, xxix (Moscow, 1935), 535-46.

[18] A. Lunacharski, *Istoria zapadno yevropeiskoi literatury v eyo vazhneishikh momentakh* (Moscow, 1924), 144-80.

[19] Cf. pp. 191-92 for further information on the Academia.

[20] *Zhizn Lasarilio s Tormesa i yego bedy i neschastya*, translation, articles, and notes by K. N. Derzhavin. Illustrations by S. B. Yudovin (Moscow-Leningrad, 1931).

[21] Cf. p. 192.

[22] *Ispanskie i portugalskie poety-zhertvy inkvizitsii*, collection

Guerras civiles de Granada,[25] Cervantes' *Novelas ejemplares*,[26] Tirso de Molina's plays,[27] *Marcos de Obregón*[28] and the plays of Lope de Vega.[29] From the Portuguese was translated one of Uriel d'Acosta's works.[30] A work on Spain made outside the auspices of the "Academia" is Volski's *Pizarro*.[31]

TRANSLATIONS

IN RECENT years the Russian book market has received a lavish as well as attractive array of books, brought out at the instance of the "Academia" of the Soviet Union. Since its establishment in the late twenties, this publishing group has worked untiringly, producing new editions and translations of literature, art and music. In every case the new work surpasses anything previously done in Russia.

In 1933 Stalin gave his compatriots a slogan—"Mastery of technique"—and it was taken up by the editors of the "Academia," who expounded their interpretation of it at the seventeenth meeting of the VKP: "World literature in its finest works is the treasure box in which humanity in

made, translation, comments and notes by Valentin Parnakh (Moscow-Leningrad, 1934).

[23] Kalderon, *Dramy*, edited by M. N. Rozanov (Moscow-Leningrad, 1935).

[24] Kevedo, *Zhizn Buskona*, translation, article and notes by S. S. Ignatov (Moscow-Leningrad, 1936).

[25] Peres de Ita, *Grazhdanskaya voina v Grenade*, translation and commentaries by A. E. Sipovich, edited by M. N. Rozanov. Article by M. V. Sergiyevski (Moscow-Leningrad, 1936).

[26] Cf. pp. 194-95.

[27] Tirso de Molina, *Teatr*, translated by V. A. Pyast and T. L. Schepkin-Kupernik. Edited by F. V. Kelyin.

[28] Espinel, *Obregon*, translation, article and commentaries by S. S. Ignatov, Moscow-Leningrad.

[29] Lope de Vega, *Teatr*, translation, article and notes by S. S. Ignatov. The manuscript was complete in 1938 but not published at the time.

[30] Uriel d'Acosta, *O smertnosti dushi, primer chelovecheskoi zhizni*, translated by S. S. Ignatov and A. Denisov, introductory article, editing and notes by I. K. Luppol (Moscow-Leningrad, 1934).

[31] S. Volski, *Pizarro* (Moscow, 1935).

the course of class struggle has accumulated great wealth. In the light of Stalin's slogan, the purpose of the 'Academia' is to take possession of this treasure, to re-work its contents critically, to make it accessible to the builders of the socialistic society, and to utilize it for the formation of the new man in a classless society. Of course, no publishing house of the old world could have ap-proached literature with such aims."[1]

Existing translations of foreign classics were judged to be unsuitable, and work was commenced on making new, "adequate, accurate, as well as artistic"[2] versions of them. "But a good translation alone is not enough," the "Academia" said. "We would also like to give an ex-planation of its [the original's] significance in the history of human thought, its role in the course of social struggle, its value, which makes us take this monument from the shelf of history and introduce it into the current of con-temporary ideological struggle."[3] This is now being un-dertaken through the cooperation of the older Hispanists and the new "Marxist investigators."

The work on the new edition of Don Quixote[4] was done mainly by Boris Krzhevski, the author of the article "Cervantes and His Novelas ejemplares."[5] His task was the interpretation of the text, and A. A. Smirnov's was the artistic rendition. These Hispanists had already, in their earlier work, carried on the tradition of Shepelevich and Petrov in the field of Spanish studies. The poetry in the new translation was done by Lozinski and Kuzmin. Smir-nov outlined the translators' aims and methods in a short article, "On the Russian Translations of Don Quixote,"

[1] *Izdatelstvo "Academia" k XVII syezdu VKP*, zadachi, perechen izdani, plan [The editorial organization "Academia," for the xvııth meeting of the VKP, problems, list of publications, plan], Moscow-Leningrad, 1934, pp. 5-6.

[2] *Ibid.*, p. 6. [3] *Ibid.*, p. 9.

[4] *Khitroumny idalgo Don Kikhot Lamanchski*, perevod pod redaktsiei s vstup. statyami B. A. Krzhevskogo, i A. A. Smirnova, vvedenie P. I. Novitskogo (Moscow-Leningrad, 1929). The text we used here for comparative purposes is the third edition (Mos-cow-Leningrad, 1934-1935).

[5] Cf. p. 172, also 194-95.

which precedes the novel. They wanted, he explains, to fill the gap between Karelin's artistic rendition and Vatson's accurate, literal translation of the work. "This aim is by no means an easy one," Smirnov writes, "when one considers the peculiarities of Spanish phraseology, which is so far removed from the Russian, as well as the great internal variety of Cervantes' style."[6]

As far as the actual language of the text is concerned, Krzhevski and Smirnov sought for the golden mean between the archaic and the modern (favoring the latter slightly, since their purpose was to create a live, artistic text just as easily comprehensible to modern readers as it was to Cervantes' contemporaries). Above all, however, their efforts were directed towards the concreteness, plasticity and dynamics of words, expressions or images, so vital a trait of Cervantes' style.[7]

On the whole, this text is superior to that of Karelin and Vatson. When possible, proverbs and *dichos* are rendered by well-chosen parallels conveying the flavor of the *Quixote* to Russian readers. Furthermore, allusions obscure to the Russian public are annotated. These annotations are concise and mainly derived from Rodríguez Marín's of 1915-1916. Most of them are correct, with the exception of obvious typographical errors in figures and spelling. Nevertheless, these, as well as some more serious misinterpretations of the text, should have been corrected by the time they reached a third edition, but they have not been. Preceding the translation are several articles interpreting the novel from the Marxist point of view, which will be discussed in the subsequent chapter on Marxist criticism.[8]

No other new translations of the novel were made during this period. Vatson's *The Ingenious Knight Don Quixote of La Mancha* had several new editions; one in 1924, edited by Lunacharski, and another in 1929.[9] The latter has not been available for study, but Smirnov comments

---

[6] A. A. Smirnov, *O perevodakh Don Kikhota, ibid.*, p. lxxxviii.
[7] *Ibid.*, pp. lxxxix and xc.   [8] Cf. pp. 206-12.
[9] Appendix, nos. 55 and 56 respectively.

on it in his survey of Russian translations: "Quite recently the publishing house 'Molodaya Gvardia' put out a new edition of *Don Quixote*. The translator's name does not appear on the title page, but editor's notes tell us that it was done on Vatson's translation. And, true enough, her version is fully reworked here, giving it lightness and smoothness. What was the net result? On the one hand, the main value of M. V. Vatson's work, its accuracy, disappeared, and on the other, the limited literary value thus acquired by the text turned out to be characteristic of the Russian editor, but not of the Spanish original. What a mean favor to Cervantes!"[10] This version went into a second edition in 1930.[11]

The first complete translation of the *Novelas ejemplares* appeared in 1934, made by Boris Krzhevski, the co-translator of the Soviet edition of the *Quixote*.[12] He used the texts of Schevill-Bonilla, Rodríguez Marín, the latter's special edition of the *Rinconete y Cortadillo* (Madrid, 1905), Foulché-Delbosc's and Alonso Cortes' editions of *El Licenciado Vidriera* (1899 and 1916 respectively), Amezúa y Mayo's *Casamiento engañoso* (Madrid, 1912), and Wolf's *La tía fingida* (Berlin, 1818). The *Novelas* are printed in the sequence of the 1613 edition and, in addition, the *Tía fingida* is included. Some of the *Novelas* had appeared individually at various times in Russia during the nineteenth century, but in translations that were inadequate for one reason or another. Krzhevski's two volumes are the work of a competent Hispanist and a master of the Russian language.

The translation itself is literal, the proverbs are given Russian equivalents, the texture of the original language is preserved as much as possible, and still the reader does not feel that he is reading a translation. There are, however, occasional slips which a Hispanist like Krzhevski should never have made. There are notes at the end of

[10] A. Smirnov, *O perevodakh Don Kikhota*, p. lxxxvii.

[11] Appendix, no. 57.

[12] *Nazidatelnie novelly*, perevod i primechania B. A. Krzhevski (Moscow-Leningrad, 1934), I, 66.

each volume, taken mainly from Rodríguez Marín, which fully explain many of the textual allusions. They have not the flaws found in the notes to the *Quixote* translation of the "Academia."

Two individual *novela* translations preceded this collection of Krezhevski's. They are *Rinconete y Cortadillo* and *El Licenciado Vidriera*.[13] Through issued in large editions, neither has been available to the present writer.

This period also offers new editions of Ostrovski's translations of *El viejo celoso*, *La cueva de Salamanca* (1919)[14] and *El rufián viudo* (1923). A new translation of the last Interlude was made by B. A. Krzhevski in 1923.[15]

As for abbreviated versions of the *Quixote*, a new edition of the Sytin one appeared, and an abbreviated and revised edition of the complete Basanin translation.[16] To these were added the versions appearing in Friche's *Spanish Literature of the Sixteenth and Seventeenth Centuries*, and those by N. Sher, M. Leontyeva and A. Deich.[17]

THEATER PRODUCTIONS

THE most interesting adaptations of *Don Quixote* for the theater during the Soviet period are plays by A. V. Lunacharski (1875-1933) and G. Chulkov (1879-1939). Lunacharski's *The Liberated Don Quixote*[1] employs Cervantian material to depict the Russian social revolution and the attitude of the "intelligentsia" towards it, and to defend the new government's conduct. For Lunacharski, Don Quixote serves as a symbol of the intelligentsia.

The play opens with Don Quixote's liberation of three captives and his arrival at the Duke's palace. Here, as in

[13] Appendix, nos. 93 and 94.
[14] In the same year appeared Ostrovski's translation of the anonymous *entremés* attributed sometimes to Cervantes, *Los Habladores*.
[15] Appendix, nos. 107, 108, 109 and 110.
[16] *Ibid.*, no. 52.
[17] *Ibid.*, nos. 68, 69, 70 and 71 respectively.
[1] A. V. Lunacharski, *Osvobozhdenny Don Kikhot* (Moscow, 1922), nine scenes and an epilogue.

the novel, the heroic dreamer is forced to play the clown. These courtiers, symbols of the old regime, are a vicious lot, who derive sadistic pleasure from their diversion. Don Quixote, lacking sane discrimination, bears his humiliation with dignity until he is caught under Mirabella's window. As in the novel, the vixen has tied his hand to the window and left him dangling there. Fortunately, another character frees him just before the Duke and his friends arrive to enjoy the sorry spectacle. Their false accusations break the spell of illusion and, now sane, the hero challenges the Duke. The knight is overpowered and the Duke imprisons him, but his incarceration does not last long. The captives whom Don Quixote had freed have incited a successful revolution and liberate their benefactor. Their methods of force, however, are just as distasteful to the knight as were those of the nobles. He becomes their open foe, meddles in their affairs and injudiciously frees the perverted nobleman Murcio, who organizes an infinitely more cruel counterrevolution. The revolutionaries bring this to Don Quixote's attention and urge him to leave. They justify temporary ruthlessness and subordination of popular will by showing that it is a means of exterminating the more inhuman atrocities of the old rulers. Distracted and resigned, Don Quixote withdraws, accompanied by Sancho.

This didactic play retains the idealistic, critical aspect of the knight, his name, a few of the episodes of the novel and the outer shell of Sancho and the ducal company. Dulcinea and other characters, complications and ideas important in the original are omitted.

G. Chulkov's play *Don Quixote* sets out "to reveal both the abstract dreaminess of Don Quixote and the equally abstract rationalism of Carrasco."[2] The play deals with Don Quixote's visit with the Duke and Duchess and hinges on the contrast between their empty uncharitableness and the knight's dream of human equality and the eradication of evil. Don Quixote says, "Injustice! Here

[2] G. Chulkov, *Don Kikhot*, tragicomedy in four acts (Moscow, 1935), p. 12.

lies the ulcer of this world. One man is rich, another starving and poor; one lives in honor, another in disgrace; power have the fools and slavery the rest. Let some astrologer reveal the mystery of Don Quixote's life. I know not what is dream, what reality. What is fame, what shame."[3] In another place, referring to himself, he says, "To distinguish truth from falsehood is not a simple matter for one who ponders on the mystery of life."[4] The Duke puts Don Quixote through most of the stunts found in the same episode of the novel, and in all of them he is not a bellicose adventurer, but a tender, noble dreamer-philosopher—the real Don Quixote in his lyrical and melancholy moments. Chulkov's depiction of his struggles, floundering as Don Quixote does amid the fantastic, is a spectacle at once great and pathetic.

As the play continues, Don Quixote is overpowered by the masquerading rationalist Carrasco and leaves the castle. He and Sancho spend the night in the forest where the squire sleeps and the master paces restlessly. His soliloquy reveals a profound anguish and awareness of the Duke's prank. At daybreak the ducal party cages him and returns him to the castle to pay restitution to Altisidora. Sancho uncovers the hoax and in one second a hilarious practical joke turns into tragedy. Don Quixote lies on the ground dead, while Altisidora, who has really fallen in love with her victim, cries hysterically, "I don't believe it! No. He is not dead—he is asleep."[5]

Though drawing copiously on the *Quixote*, this play is by no means a mere dramatization of the novel. Chulkov takes the characters, sets the scene in the castle of the Duke and Duchess, and telescopes various other episodes from the novel—André's flogging, the galley slaves and the encounter with Sanson Carrasco—to help develop his idea. The Cervantian sociological and critical implications of the novel are suppressed, and everything is focused on the ethical aspect of the hero.

There are also several outright theatrical imitations of

[3] *Ibid.*, p. 22.   [4] *Ibid.*, p. 31.   [5] *Ibid.*, p. 110.

Don Quixote belonging to this period: Ada Chumachenko's *Don Quixote of La Mancha*, a play for children,[6]
and Brushtein's comedy *Don Quixote.*[7] No new Cervantian ballets were designed, and the classic Petipa versions
still held the interest of Leningrad and Moscow audi-
ences, as is indicated by their performance during the
hectic years of 1917-1923[8] and again in 1933-1934.[9]

[6] Ada Chumachenko, "Don Kikhot Lamanchski" (po Servantesu), *Detski Teatr* (Leningrad, 1926), pp. 171-231.
[7] A. and B. Brushtein, "Don Kikhot" (po Servantesu), comedy in
three acts (Moscow, 1928).
[8] H. Carter, *The New Spirit in the Russian Theater, 1917-1928*
(London, 1929); cf. appendices, pp. 312-14.
[9] *Knizhnaya Letopis*, Jan. 1934, no. 2, no. 699.

15 · CRITICISM

Marxism pervaded the intellectual atmosphere of Russia at the end of the nineteenth century. It found its political expression in the crescendo of the October Revolution, its economic and social realization in state socialism. *Das Kapital* was the inspiration and the bible for this far-reaching upheaval. The changing environment had its effect on Russian literary criticism. An outgrowth of the sociological school of criticism, Marxism paid particular attention to Cervantes. Marx had liked Cervantes, and what Marx liked and said was intellectual law.

Marxist criticism had its antecedents in the works of Kogan and Friche. As the early work of Kogan shows, its methods at first were vague, but with time they became defined into the following scheme: first, analysis of the economic structure of a given society; second, explanation of its social conditions and class divisions; and third, deduction of the resultant social psychology. This system in its mature form lies at the base of articles on Cervantes by Friche, Lunacharski, Novitski, Beletski and Kelyin.

In dealing with immortal works, particularly in making new editions of them, the Marxists enlisted the aid of scholars in the field, and their contributions reveal a greater interest in the works themselves than in the fashionable critical approach. An example of this compromise between scholarship and Marxism is furnished by the post-Revolution criticism of Krzhevski.

It has been of utmost importance to Russian critics throughout this period that Cervantes was one of Karl Marx's favorite authors and that both Marx and Engels in controversies with their opponents often used images

199

from *Don Quixote*. Similar use of them has not been re-stricted to men of letters—*vide*, for example, a conversa-tion of Stalin's with Emil Ludwig,[1] and newspaper arti-cles like one in *Pravda* directed against German Fascism and one against Secretary Morgenthau.[2]

The first article on Cervantes by a Marxist is "The Tragedy of Idealism" by P. S. Kogan (1872-1932). Der-javin, a Marxist of recent years, sums it up as an analysis "of the social sources of Don Quixote, the representative of the lesser *hidalguía* of the sixteenth century, whose atavistic feudal spirit clashed violently with the social and psychological conditions of the transitory period in Spanish history."[3] Actually, the issue is not as clear cut as all that. Kogan himself says that "the whole novel is the history of the ideal existence and the story of its clash with the most varied of life's phenomena."[4] The source of this idealism he finds in Cervantes' own life, which shows that idealism can be strong enough to resist the relentless persecution of fate. It was only when Cervantes found himself in a Spanish prison (where he began *Don Quix-ote*) that he apparently lost all ability to contemplate life through the smoke-screen of his idealism. He checked the flight of his aspirations and decided to examine reality and its intransigent laws.[5]

Kogan explains that the first part of *Don Quixote* deals with everyday reality, and in it simple human interests are intertwined with the cruelty of life. Here Don Quix-ote appears as a man who regards bravery and purity as adequate excuse for action. This in itself offers the first cause for "the tragedy of idealism." People misunder-stand him because life is complicated enough without

[1] I. Stalin, "Beseda s nemetskim pisatelem Emilem Lyudvigom," *Bolshevik*, April 30, 1932, no. 8, p. 34.

[2] An article in *Izvestia*, cited by *New York Times*, October 1, 1936.

[3] C. Derjavin, "Crítica cervantina en Rusia," *BAH*, xciv (1929), 215-38.

[4] P. S. Kogan, "Tragedia idealizma," *Russkaya Mysl*, 1895, no. 8, p. 93.

[5] *Ibid.*

their bothering about the motives of a nature as complex as his. This misunderstanding is harmless for the time being, since people are amused by the unaccountable so long as it does not affect them personally. We feel sorry for him, and yet we realize that he is dangerous rather than beneficial to a world in which people do not have time to indulge in dreams, in which, upon occasion, they exploit such idealism for their own selfish ends.[6]

Ten years elapse between the publication of the first and second parts of the novel. In the meantime, Kogan goes on, the environment in which the hero first appeared is supplanted by a higher social setting. The original role of the hero changes likewise. No longer is he a sorry, wandering madman, misunderstood and ridiculed by the common people. Now he emerges as an honest, wise preacher, an accuser in whose fantastic ravings notes of truth, goodness and enlightenment (the voice of the author) sound more and more distinctly. The epithet "mad" is applied to him with less frequency. The reader's laughter, provoked by Don Quixote in the first part, turns to sympathy and respect. Now Don Quixote is head and shoulders above his surroundings. Though the picture changes, however, the basic conflict remains. But, asks the critic, consider the moments of ineffable bliss that are given to him and no one else. Here lies the secret of Cervantes' love for his own sufferings.[7] Kogan concludes: "One can see happiness in the quick attainment of the highest degree selected by society as the measure for happiness. People who have selected this criterion will never understand Don Quixote. They will always be sorry for him, will always call him unfortunate. But he who can appreciate the meaning of spiritual freedom, he who can understand the blessings of moral satisfaction, will also understand Don Quixote's speech about freedom."[8]

Kogan's chapter on Cervantes in his *Sketches of the History of Western European Literatures* (1903)[9] is not

---

[6] *Ibid.*, pp. 97-98.   [7] *Ibid.*, pp. 98-100.
[8] *Ibid.*, p. 100.
[9] Kogan, *Ocherki po istorii zapadno-yevropeiskikh literatur*, 3rd

interpretative, but informative and pedagogical. Kogan summarizes Brandes', Morley's, Shakhov's, Storozhenko's and Veselovski's works, and then methodically surveys the more important intellectual, social and political currents of European literature. He dwells on the background of the Renaissance and its French, Italian, German and Spanish representatives. For the latter he chooses Cervantes, and discusses the Spaniard's life, personality, and the purpose of his great novel. He indicates the popularity of the novels of chivalry at the time, the reasons for the fad, and the struggle to suppress them. Cervantes won the battle, he says, by depicting not only a madman, but also a very remarkable man, a deep thinker with an exalted soul, full of honor and lofty aspirations. Thus he was better able to show the destructive effects of the novels of chivalry. Kogan then summarizes the interpretations of the more famous critics, such as Turgenev and Heine, and concludes with his own characterization of Don Quixote: (1) The knight valued life only in so far as it gave him an opportunity to realize his ideal. (2) From the human point of view, if Don Quixote is not always mad, he *is* always reasonable. (3) He is happy, and nothing can make him change his mind. (4) He is an idealist standing outside of life, despising its benefits; therefore, he feels independent. Sancho's transformation shows how idealism, even in a comical form, does not vanish without a trace.

Another early critic of the Marxist school, V. Friche (1870-1929), discusses in "Shakespeare and Cervantes" (1916)[10] the way in which social and political conditions are expressed in the attitude and works of these two authors. Theirs, he says, was the period of the nobles' decadence. Shakespeare rose from the middle class and spent many years near the court, while Cervantes, a member of

---

edition (Moscow, 1908), vol. i, pp. 84-102, are devoted to Cervantes. There is a review of the first edition by V. Friche, *Obrazovanie* (1903), x, 124-26.

[10] V. M. Friche, "Shekspir i Servantes," *Sovremenny Mir*, 1916, iv, 110-23.

the disintegrating group, spent most of his life among the common people. These facts played an important role in their writings. Shakespeare's works show that he hated the class of his origin, loved the court, which he portrayed with remarkable vividness, and sided with the aristocracy in its struggle against the bourgeoisie.[11] Cervantes, on the other hand, rarely dealt with the middle class, but when he did (*Coloquio de los perros*) he betrayed no feeling of antagonism.[12] He was a proud member of the *hidalguía,* and he liked to depict aristocrats uniting with persons of humbler origin (*La Gitanilla, La ilustre fregona*).[13] He did not know the court, and his pictures of it are pale in color, while his knowledge of the Spanish people was based on long and intimate acquaintance, producing brilliant canvases of their life. It was from these common people that Don Quixote and Sancho Panza came.[14]

Don Quixote, writes Friche, is not only a man from the country, but he is also a hidalgo, all of which brings him closer to Cervantes. The novelist ridicules the knight, but this ridicule reveals great sympathy. As the plot progresses, the hero's noble qualities eclipse the ridiculous side of his nature, and at the end he emerges with a halo of martyrdom. This figure rouses in the reader laughter through tears.[15]

Falstaff is for Friche a blood relation of Don Quixote. He, too, is of the decadent nobility, proud of his origin. He lives in the past and detests the present. Like Don Quixote, since he is maladjusted to the new conditions that demand work, he leads a parasitic life. In addition, Friche feels that this poor fellow was mistreated by his author. Not belonging to Falstaff's class, Shakespeare looked down upon the charming sot; he trampled on him, and drowned him in the mire.[16]

As Cervantes' attitude towards Don Quixote has a duality, so it has also towards his squire. As a son of the

[11] *Ibid.*, p. 116.
[12] *Ibid.*, p. 115.
[13] *Ibid.*, p. 112.
[14] *Ibid.*, pp. 113 and 116.
[15] *Ibid.*, pp. 112-13.
[16] *Ibid.*

city and also of feudalism, he endows Sancho with some qualities of the baser order, such as materialism and shrewdness, while, as a member of declassed nobility, he no longer looks down upon him. As the plot develops, Sancho grows spiritually and becomes increasingly wise until he stands as an exemplary governor. "The old order," says Friche, "based on the rule of the 'tops' and the submission of the 'bottoms,' is turned topsy-turvy."[17]

Friche also touches upon the effect the destruction of the Spanish Armada and Spanish colonial expansion had on the writings of Shakespeare and Cervantes.[18]

The distinguished modern critic A. V. Lunacharski (1875-1933) in his *History of Western European Literature* (1924) has a section on Don Quixote, whom he considers an ideal hero. After an introductory survey of Spanish history and a concise biography of Cervantes, he offers his explanation for the *Quixote's* longevity, its greatness, and for the appeal of its characters: "The reason lies in the fact that Cervantes knew how to deal with Don Quixote. It is true that he was interring feudalism, but he was doing it in no ordinary fashion. While he was laughing at this feudalism, he was mourning its finest qualities. . . ."[19]

Lunacharski then recalls the original Christian, idealistic qualities of the early knights, whose exploits were for the good of their "neighbors." This conception of knighthood fell into decay and became falsified. "And Cervantes, who was himself a noble individual, was himself a Don Quixote, who considered that man must sacrifice himself for his 'neighbor,' was the best representative of the current bourgeoisie in its protest and in its struggle to wrench itself from the claws of falsehood. . . . Cervantes worshiped that old ideal. . . . He would have liked to have had the world as Don Quixote envisaged it. Unfortunately, it was not such. . . ." One feels, says Lunacharski, that Cervantes saw before him a bleak picture.

[17] *Ibid.*, p. 121.   [18] *Ibid.*, p. 123.
[19] A. Lunacharski, *Istoria zapadno-yevropeiskoi literatury*, Moscow, 1924, part I, p. 177.

"The ideal is dead. Dead is genuine kindness. Dead is sacrifice. In your world . . . an ideal knight is funny. . . . Understand, you scoundrels, that this comical Don Quixote is a thousand times better than you, that he is a martyr, that he is kind." For men like Don Quixote, there was no place in that world or in any succeeding one. Only now, the critic believes, can the question of the ideal and reality be resolved. "Only we communists are in a position where the highest ideals of mankind do not become Don Quixotism, but a reality. . . ."[20]

He then devotes a page to Sancho, and finds that Cervantes was somewhat disrespectful to the squire. Essentially, he says, there is nothing amusing about Sancho, and yet we laugh at him. The reason for this lies in the contrast between the knight and his squire. One would expect such an ill-matched couple to quarrel, but they do not, because Sancho with his healthy peasant heart feels Don Quixote's greatness, and because he is Don Quixote's co-crusader.[21]

Lunacharski concludes that the *Quixote* carries an appeal to the future: "Don Quixote is perishing. Don Quixote is comical, Sancho is comical, but they are inherently better than anyone else. Apparently, in all of Spain there is not another decent man, and these two are perishing because the time for them has not come. . . . Centuries will pass and Don Quixote and Sancho Panza will continue to suffocate in this world . . . until socialism becomes a reality. Then many ardent Utopists, Don Quixotes, will find use for their heroic romanticism . . . and, not becoming fantastic knights because of it, they will be really practical individuals. The more they believe in their ideal, the more practical idealists will they become, the more dependable, more powerful co-crusaders of our common cause. Often a man of the true Sancho Panza type . . . responds to the call of the revolution . . . and performs his tasks well. Times are such that in our midst

[20] *Ibid.*, pp. 177-78.
[21] *Ibid.*, p. 179.

both Don Quixotes and Sancho Panzas are highly desirable and become the actual fighters for the future."[22]

An essay on *Don Quixote* was written by Lunacharski in 1924 for an abbreviated version of the novel.[23] This edition has not been available to the present writer.

P. I. Novitski's article "Cervantes' *Don Quixote*" starts with the premise that "every cultural scheme creates its own artistic forms and genres which are in accordance with the peculiarities of the ruling class."[24] The Renaissance marks the end of feudalism and the birth of the new bourgeois "intelligentsia." The latter's self-confidence, pride in its historical mission, creative flair and feeling for the real and the natural create a new genre. Consequently, beside the old aristocratic genre—the novels of chivalry—appear the germs of the bourgeois genre—satirical parodies, *fabliaux*, moralizing *novelas* and political pamphlets. The survival of the fittest leaves the satirico-social (*satiricheski-bytovii*) naturalistic novels.[25]

According to Novitski, *Don Quixote* represents the struggle of this new genre for supremacy. Its flaws (occasional mechanical weaknesses) are signs of its vital connection with the epoch, since they show that the genre was in a state of flux. *Don Quixote* is at once the child of the struggle between literary forms and the victor. Expressing new social and cultural forms, it begins the literary history of the naturalistic novel.[26]

Don Quixote's thematic conception is the discredit of the books of chivalry, but it has a deeper significance for the Marxist critic. "*Don Quixote* is a forceful pamphlet against aristocratic culture, a revelation of the historical limitations and internal contradiction of the epoch that bore it," writes Novitski.[27] The novel shows, on the one

[22] *Ibid.*, p. 180.
[23] A. V. Lunacharski, *Posleslovie k sokraschennomu izdaniyu Don Kikhota* (Moscow, 1924), 243-252.
[24] P. I. Novitski, "Don Kikhot Servantesa," *Khotroumny idalgo Don Kikhot Lamancheski*, p. ix.
[25] *Ibid.*, p. xii. [26] *Ibid.*, pp. xii-xvi.
[27] *Ibid.*, pp. xvii-xviii.

hand, the mad wanderings and fantastic flights of the im-
poverished *hidalguía,* which had severed ties with reality
and lived in a world of phantoms, and on the other hand,
the untainted reality of life—the animalistic and stupid
existence of the peasantry, the businesslike bustle of the
merchants, the covetousness of the innkeepers and the
cynicism and cruelty of the higher nobles. And, by virtue
of artistic generalization, Cervantes raised the ideo-psy-
chological experiment of his period to great artistic
heights, thereby endowing the ideological content of his
images with symbolical values. *Don Quixote* is not only a
pamphlet on the Spanish nobility of the sixteenth century, but a representation of the fates of centuries and
centuries of human culture as well.[28]

Novitski believes that the history of art includes not
only the history of the work and its creators, but also that
of the responses to it. They indicate the service a work of
art renders to the cultural interests of new classes and
eras. Accordingly, he considers the interpretations of
Don Quixote by Heine (which he likes) and Turgenev,[29]
and offers his own: Don Quixote's ideals were of the
past; they dealt with ghosts and had no social basis.
Therefore, the results of his efforts have negative value
and his misapplied enthusiasm appears false and comical. One can argue and win only in the name of the future, he says. Ideals must not be phantasmagoria, but
dreams of the future, having justification in reality and a
possibility of realization. Critics who praise the knight
forget to consider the direction and aims of Don Quixote.
Humaneness was not always his motivation. Like many
aristocrats, he was often guided by the formal code of
chivalry.[30]

Novitski concludes his essay by indicating the meaning
of *Don Quixote* to the Soviets: *Don Quixote* shows that
one cannot correct the present by the way of fancy and
chimeras, as the knight sought to do, but by practical
idealism. One must give genius, enthusiasm and talent a

[28] *Ibid.,* pp. xvi-xix.   [29] *Ibid.,* pp. xix-xxvi.
[30] *Ibid.,* pp. xxvi-xxxiv.

reason and an aim lying with the living, with the future, and not among the shades of the past. The past is irrevocable, as Cervantes demonstrates.[31]

As has been mentioned above, the "Academia," in preparing and prefacing new editions of foreign classics, often found itself short of trained editors. In such cases, older scholars were called in to do the task in cooperation with "Marxist-investigators." Novitski is obviously the "Marxist-investigator" of the "Academia" translation of *Don Quixote*. In the article by him which precedes the translation,[32] he tries to fit the novel into a fixed scheme of critical philosophy, crushing Don Quixote into a mold. Furthermore, Novitski cannot seem to make up his mind about certain points. On the one hand, he says that *Don Quixote* is a forceful pamphlet against the noble-aristocratic culture and, on the other, that "it was not a pamphlet against the Spanish nobility that Cervantes wrote in his novel. . . . At the beginning of the essay, he dwells on the conflicting currents of the sixteenth century, and then follows this with the statement that the unity of *Don Quixote* comes from the unity of the period."

Boris A. Krzhevski, whose earlier work has been discussed under "The Passing of the Empire," carried over into the Soviet regime the traditions of Western Hispanic scholarship. He and Smirnov have served as a link between the great Shepelevich and the new generation of Russian Hispanists. The article which he contributed to the "Academia" translation, "*Don Quixote*: The Background of Spanish Literature of the Sixteenth and Seventeenth Centuries," presents a marked contrast to Novitski's essay.[33] It is the work of a Cervantes scholar who loves and knows *Don Quixote* well and is at the same time aware of, but not hypnotized by, Marxian critical methods. It deals with Cervantes' life, literary influences reflected in *Don Quixote* and the general appreciation the novel received prior to and after Friedrich Schlegel. The

[31] *Ibid.*, pp. xxxvi-xxxvii.   [32] Cf. pp. 192-93.
[33] B. A. Krzhevski, "Don Kikhot na fone ispanskoi literatury xvi-xvii st.," *Khitroumny idalgo Don Kikhot Lamanchski*, pp. xli-lxxix.

quality of his scholarship is good and the sources reliable. Of particular interest is its second section, which is devoted to chivalric, pastoral and picaresque novels, their history, interrelation and influence on *Don Quixote*.

The history of the novels of chivalry, Krzhevski points out, falls into three periods: the first (1250-1400) was permeated with the idea of feudal service and platonic love; the second (1400-1480) was characterized by gallant love and a spirit of adventure; in the third (1480-1605), the ideology of knighthood was reorganized and applied to decadent feudalism. These three stages, with their praise of independent adventure and love, their graceful forms of life and the traditional veneer of knighthood, answered the cravings and ideals of the aristocratic circles educated by the Italian school of the sixteenth century, living under absolute monarchy. *Amadís de Gaula*, a brilliant, fascinating and well-written encyclopedia of Renaissance culture, was its finest expression and the source of numerous imitations of increasingly inferior caliber. Cervantes criticized the *Amadís'* extravagance and lack of truthfulness, but he appreciated the pliability of the form as such, which gave talent a broad field for action. And if, in addition to Cervantes' declared approbation of certain phases of the genre, the vestiges of feudal ideology present in *Don Quixote* and Cervantes' *Persiles y Sigismunda* are considered, it becomes evident that it was the content of the decadent chivalric novel and not the genre proper that disgusted Cervantes. After all, says the critic, a substantial portion of his own creative efforts was devoted to this genre—negatively in *Don Quixote* and positively in *Persiles y Sigismunda*.[34]

Turning to the pastoral novel, Krzhevski suggests that it corresponds to the counter-Reformation policies of the Catholic Church, which sought to curb the sexual freedom popularized by Renaissance literature. The pastoral novel adopts a platonic, idealized form of love. "Using the scheme of 'the impeded wedding' that lies at the base

[34] *Ibid.*, pp. l-lv.

of the novels of chivalry, the pastoral novel presents only the sentimental adventures, analyzes the diverse 'cases' of love, thereby creating a sort of *ars amandi*." Since reality offered no social milieu suitable for this type of composition, it adopts the artificial one of the shepherds. Essentially, however, the pastoral novel does not reject reality; it merely considers one aspect of it, the sentimentally erotic.[35]

The picaresque novel, Krzhevski continues, employs the biographical scheme of the novels of chivalry and preserves its episodic structure of adventures, with accent on craftiness and deception rather than on sentimental or chivalric love. Like the novels of chivalry, it is also an encyclopedia, not of feudal culture, however, but of practical wisdom.[36]

Don Quixote he finds a remarkable blending of the chivalric and picaresque novel. The form common to both is also used in *Don Quixote*. The heroes typical of the genres are also found in *Don Quixote* in the knight-pícaro combination. These, however, are not only combined externally, but blended psychologically. Their strange friendship leads ultimately to the modification of the extreme characteristics of each, showing the interaction of the picaresque and chivalresque. It is thus that Cervantes takes traditional forms and gives them new life.[37]

"Almost everyone concedes that Cervantes parodied *Amadís de Gaula*," says Krzhevski, and he points to the obvious episodic similarities between the two novels. Like its model, *Don Quixote* is didactic in character and an encyclopedia of feudal-aristocratic life, written in the spirit of humanistic education of Cervantes' time and calculating on the familiarity of its readers with this atmosphere.[38]

The influence of the picaresque novel on *Don Quixote* is even more potent. It is directly responsible for Cer-

[35] *Ibid.*, pp. lv-lvi.
[36] *Ibid.*, pp. lvi-lviii.
[37] *Ibid.*, pp. lviii-lx.
[38] *Ibid.*, pp. lx-lxi.

vantes' choice of Spain of the sixteenth century and not a fantastic kingdom as the backdrop for his novel. His choice, at the same time, is conditioned by the novels of chivalry, which required that the heroes wander over hill and dale. Therefore, Cervantes' realistic pictures of Spain are drawn from the provinces. They are not synthetic accounts of social ills, but actual replicas of Spain as Cervantes knew it, and as such clearly fix a definite period in the development of Spanish society.[39] Thus, by drawing attention to the darker sides of reality, Cervantes conveys his social message. There is still another aspect to his social propaganda—*casticismo [narodnost]*, which is apparent in his sympathetic portrayal of Sancho. The squire is not a good-for-nothing peasant, but a man endowed by nature with a good heart and common sense. When one considers that Sancho is performing the role of the *pícaro*, says Krzhevski, the reason for his creator's novel attitude towards him becomes self-evident.[40]

Cervantes' indebtedness to the pastoral genre is apparent in episodes of purely pastoral character, and in those in which the general scheme of the genre prevails despite the courtly urban figures participating. The artistic similarity of the latter to the former is shown in their sentimental nature, in the analytical character of the interpretations of the "cases" in question and in their cold, rhetorical style, which is so different from the delightfully realistic language of the novel proper. This element appears in chapters XII-XIV of part I, and again from chapter XXIII to XLV, where it weaves in and out of the main line of the tale. The explanation for the presence of this foreign element lies not only in the type of love innervating Don Quixote, but in the prevailing literary tastes of the epoch.[41]

Krzhevski touches upon one other element that went into the composition of *Don Quixote*—the dramatic. The heroes themselves and their dialogue have great dramatic

[39] *Ibid.*, pp. lxi-lxiii.   [40] *Ibid.*, p. lxiv.
[41] *Ibid.*, pp. lxiv-lxix.

value, indicating the author's own dramatic sensitivity, as well as the influence of Lope de Rueda.[42]

Thus, by combining in one novel all the basic genres and styles of the period, Krzhevski concludes, Cervantes sought to impress his readers with the wide range of his talent and at the same time to achieve variety and avoid monotony in the development of the novel.[43]

Completing the introductory material to the "Academia" edition of *Don Quixote* is Smirnov's short article on the Russian translations of the novel.[44] He deals with the general value of Karelin's, Basanin's and Vatson's versions, and cites a few examples of the type of errors they make. He then explains the methods employed in the "Academia" translation by Krzhevski and himself.

In the second volume of *The Literary Encyclopedia* there is a short article on *Don Quixote* by I. Nusinov,[45] which tries to sum up the various readings of the character of Don Quixote and to set up the Marxist interpretation of the literary figure.

A. Beletski, a prominent Soviet critic, professor at Kharkov University, regards *Don Quixote* as playing a part in the class struggle of the sixteenth and seventeenth centuries.[46] Before beginning an exposition of his own interpretation of the novel's significance, he reviews important attitudes towards the book held by preceding critics, and attacks their weaknesses. He then reviews the class struggle of Cervantes' time on the basis of historical facts, stressing the fall of the nobility and bureaucracy. He observes that, despite its internal weakness, Spain still remained the vanguard of the Catholic reaction, the bulwark of the counter-Reformation, as well as of the feudalistic-monarchical counter-revolution. In literature he

---

[42] *Ibid.*, lxx-lxxii.   [43] *Ibid.*, p. lxvii.

[44] A. A. Smirnov, "O perevodakh Don Kikhota," *Khitroumny idalgo Don Kikhot Lamanchski*, pp. lxxxiii-xci.

[45] I. Nusinov, *Don Kikhot* in "Literaturnaya Entsiklopedia," vol. II, Moscow-Leningrad, 1929.

[46] This article was intended as an introduction to a new edition of M. O. Ivanov's Ukrainian translation of *Don Quixote*. The present writer was fortunate in being able to read it in manuscript form.

finds this reflected in the baroque style, the aim of which was to touch up the failing Catholicism by aesthetic means on the one hand, and on the other to spirit the reader away from reality into the realm of dreams of the useless heroism of the past.

Beletski then discusses Cervantes as a man of the Renaissance, first cautioning his readers against certain popular misconceptions about Cervantes—for example, his professed lack of education, which is nothing more than a satirical jab of the Renaissance man at the man of the Baroque; his attitude towards the Moriscos, which is actually a veiled indictment of government policy in the matter; the idea that Cervantes was a typical "son of his time," a reactionary Catholic and a monarchist. Beletski strips Cervantes of the mantle so attractive to many biographers. His captivity, the critic says, was sheer bad luck. He was a soldier because that was the only occupation open to him. He never did suffer for his faith. He had ample opportunity in the *Quixote* to champion Catholicism, but he did not do so. Cervantes was a true son of the Renaissance, a man permeated with the ideas of the bourgeoisie of his period—its interest in man and his life, its interest in art as an imitation of nature, and in the pursuit of truthfulness. These ideas are all expressed by Cervantes' characters and by the main motif of the book— the condemnation of the novels of chivalry, the products of the diseased feudal Catholic reaction.

Critics have claimed that Cervantes laughed chivalry off the face of the earth by creating the most charming of knights. This is not so, Beletski maintains. Don Quixote is not a charming man, but a sick one, and Cervantes did not love him, but condemned him. Alonso Quixano, not comprehending the interests of his class—those of bourgeois development—styled himself "Don Quixote," invoking the phantoms of the past, a malady peculiar not only to him, but to all Spanish politics of the time. Cervantes considers Don Quixote's exploits mad, not great. Don Quixote's blindness to the fact that evil does not consist of isolated abuses drains the strength from his best intention, that of combating evil. While bringing consolation to no one, this madness is socially dangerous because of its contagious nature. It infects Sancho, who also turns into a romantic, with but a shade of difference. While Don Quixote seeks fame, Sancho seeks material return. Don Quixote is content with having a book written about him; Sancho longs for his island. He even has ideas of someday becoming like his master. All this represents in Sancho the same struggle between sanity and insanity that exists in the knight. The only difference is that the peasant recovers earlier than the hidalgo.

The first part of the novel is purely negative, says Beletski, but in the second part certain positive elements emerge. It ceases to be pure condemnation and presents the writer's constructive ideals. The hero's personality changes, but not in the manner described by other critics. The knight realizes his error. The climax comes in the swine episode, where the knight, having been trampled upon by the herd, comments, "This disgrace was sent to me as punishment for my sin." This sin, for Cervantes, was romanticism. Were Don Quixote a youth, such flights of fancy would have been understandable, but in an experienced man such behavior is socially dangerous, since it is directed to the restoration of the past. Sancho's remark after his return from the "island" sums up the main idea of the book: "We had better come down to earth and walk upon it with our own two feet."

The secret of the novel's long life, concludes Beletski, lies in the fact that it holds a definite place in the class struggle of Cervantes' time. It is all the more remarkable because its images lend themselves by their flexibility to the portrayal of this issue. For this, too, it is still the whip for all irrational dreamers.

F. V. Kelyin's introduction to the *Novelas ejemplares*[47] is unsuccessful in that it suffers from being overambitious. In forty-seven pages the critic attempts to discuss

---

[47] F. V. Kelyin, *"Nazidatelnie novelly" Servantesa*, in volume I of the "Academia" edition (Moscow-Leningrad, 1934), pp. 7-47.

the influence of the *Novelas* in England, France, Germany and Russia, the reasons for their success, the history of the *novela* in Spain, the dating of the *Novelas ejemplares*, Spanish history, the revolutionary significance of the *Quixote* and many other topics. And yet, he touches but lightly upon what would be most essential in an introduction to the *Novelas ejemplares*—an explanation of their title. He merely suggests that four of the *Novelas* are the illustrative material of the *Quixote*, its examples. This is, of course, very feeble and naïve, whereas a discussion of the title written from the Marxist angle would have been interesting, to say the least. What little discussion of the *Novelas* Kelyin includes is directly quoted from Marx.

When Kelyin says that the *Novelas* are a counterpart, that is, illustrative material, of the *Quixote*, he means this: In *Don Quixote* Cervantes fights against a decadent class of society—the *hidalguía*. In the *Novelas ejemplares* he turns upon the *picardía*. Four of the *Novelas* represent four stages of this literary crusade. *Rinconete y Cortadillo* contains a statement of his case and introduces his "battle" with the class; *El Licenciado Vidriera* bears in it the indictment; *La ilustre fregona*, a parody of the picaresque novel, represents in part the actual combat; and, finally, *El Coloquio de los perros* is the artistic and ideological summation and resolution of Cervantes' views on society.

Kelyin's article, despite its wealth of material and information, suffers from too many quotations, unnecessarily long digressions and blank statements. On the whole, it conveys the impression of lengthy research and hasty composition.

C. Derjavin's bibliographical article,[48] written in Spanish, though not complete, is valuable in that it informs the non-Russian world of the numerous Russian translations of *Don Quixote* and of many Russian articles dealing with Cervantes that have been little known.

---

[48] C. Derjavin, *Crítica cervantina en Rusia.*

In his short book *Don Quixote,*[49] Derjavin had originally planned to trace the route taken by Cervantes' novel, leading from the rocky and dusty roads of old Castile into the highways of world literature but, in so doing, he became absorbed in an analysis of the period. The result is, instead, a disquisition on the manner in which *Don Quixote* represents the internal discord of Spanish life in Cervantes' time.

Derjavin advances the theory that *Don Quixote* is a composite picture of the period, presenting Spain's greatness and decline: it reveals the social and economic dislocation that plunged the nation from world supremacy into the abyss of poverty, from which she sought liberation through bureaucratic despotism and religious fanaticism.[50] Developing this idea, the critic discusses the social, political and economic background of the novel, showing how Spain's national economy was ruined by authority's artificial curtailment of normal social development. A paradox of external grandeur and internal decay resulted, which "found expression in the mysticism of Santa Teresa, Luis de León, in the morose pathetics of Calderón, in the skeptical grotesques of Velásquez' canvases, in the annihilating aestheticism of Góngora's poetry, in the cynical realism of the picaresque novel and in the madness of the knight Don Quixote."[51]

The *hidalguía* was aware of this crisis, Derjavin contends, for it was affected by the fall of Spanish might much more quickly and more acutely than the other important classes in contemporary society. Cervantes, a representative of the *hidalguía*, created in *Don Quixote* one of the first novels of social criticism in European literature. In it he not only painted a broadly objective picture of his time, but also subjected it to a merciless anatomical dissection.[52]

"Exposing in Don Quixote the ideological essence of his class, Cervantes—in defiance of the cruelty and heartlessness of the morals of the sixteenth and seventeenth

[49] C. Derjavin, *Servantes i Don Kikhot* (Leningrad, 1933).
[50] *Ibid.*, p. 7.   [51] *Ibid.*, p. 32.   [52] *Ibid.*, p. 33.

centuries—raised his voice in defense of the *déclassée hidalguía* . . . which he idealized as the depository of national prestige, magnanimity and social justice. The cruelest indictment of the epoch and his class go hand in hand with his ideological glorification [of the *hidalguía*]—the only and the final weapon of class self-defense in conditions of social downfall and inevitable destruction of the petty bourgeoisie."[53]

To Derjavin, the basic theme of the novel is discord. At first, it is found in the conflict between Don Quixote's fantasy and the objective world around him; later, in that between the knight and the existing social reality. The first is a preparation for the second, both creating, by means of class self-criticism, a justification of the *hidalguía* in a specific setting. The method of development chosen by Cervantes is the theme of madness, through which the reader is made to feel the knight's helplessness and tragedy—a subtle form of social protest. This theme is supplemented by Don Quixote's delusions of grandeur, a veiled social criticism of precisely such a complex as was gripping the Spanish nation. But madness is the font of Don Quixote's wisdom and, in the end, madness passes and wisdom remains. "In the finale," says the critic, "lies the highest illusion, the prison into which fell not the knight from La Mancha, but Cervantes himself. It is the illusion of the possibility of the ideological rehabilitation of his own class, the illusion that there was a chance for the decaying *hidalguía* to recover from its social ills. This disease seemed to the author the result of subjective rather than historical and objective reasons."[54] What Cervantes believed was one thing, but what his own anatomical analysis proved conclusively was the impossibility of such a recovery.

In his discussion of the aesthetic sources of the novel, Derjavin accepts the contention that *Don Quixote* is a refutation of the novels of chivalry and other books of the same type. This intention, he finds, produced the literary

[53] *Ibid.*, p. 72.   [54] *Ibid.*, p. 73.

217

scheme of the novel, which proceeds at first as a parody of the traditional chivalric romance. The parody, however, does not include knighthood *per se*, which was deeply esteemed by Cervantes. He mocks only that illusory artificiality which, through these books, was creating a national psychosis.[55] Later, the parody becomes saturated with its own significance, breaks off from the model and unfolds as a grandiose canvas of a satirico-realistic epic.[56] "The hero grows correspondingly, emerging now not only as a madman from La Mancha, but as an apostle of human morality, tolerance and social justice."[57]

Derjavin also comments on the picaresque sources of *Don Quixote*, and makes the following observation: "The authors of the picaresque novel liquidated their class, the *hidalguía*, by diluting its ideology in the ideology of the *déclassé* elements of society and by an exposé of its historical and social incompetence. Cervantes emerges as the defender of this class, which is the bearer of high moral and philosophical ideals, the bearer of the finest heritage of ancient knighthood, now open to ridicule and extermination."[58] Cervantes' canvas is not as gloomy as those of the picaresque novelists because, as he criticizes, he glorifies and extols his own *hidalguía*.[59]

Because of its very brevity, Derjavin's pamphlet cannot be thorough. Too frequently he is forced to digress to explain some peculiarity of Spanish life to clarify his point. His paragraphs on the concepts of the *hidalgo viejo*, *honra*, *fama*, the importance of pride, the preponderance of money both as a commodity and a literary theme, and other such aspects of the life of the period may be tedious to some readers, but they assist in an understanding of his argument. The section which surveys briefly some of the more significant contributions to Cervantes criticism, such as those of Schlegel, Heine, Byron and Turgenev, adds to popular information, and from it one can acquire quickly an impressive veneer of Cer-

[55] *Ibid.*, p. 37. [56] *Ibid.*, p. 36. [57] *Ibid.*, p. 38.
[58] *Ibid.*, p. 41. [59] *Ibid.*, p. 40.

vantes "scholarship." The disturbing factor in the work is its organization or, rather, its lack of it, which leads to unnecessary repetitions and digressions. This, of course, is not a fault peculiar to Derjavin. As for the basic concepts, one can easily quarrel with them but, as Derjavin says, "The historical significance of Cervantes' novel lies in the fact that it affects the feeling and thought of its readers"[60] and he himself offers one more example of how varied are the manifestations of that effect.

Only the Formalists, whose critical techniques developed along the lines of pure aesthetics, diverged from the Marxist approach to Cervantes during this period. One of the earlier exponents of the school is A. G. Hornfeld (b. 1867), whose writings are largely concerned with the poetics of art in its formal-aesthetic aspect. His criticism often replies to, or one might say refutes, an artistic judgment of which he disapproves. Such a refutation is found in his article on Don Quixote and Hamlet, in which he analyzes Turgenev's speech.[61]

Victor Shklovski (1893-) may be called the principal theoretician of formalism. He deals with *Don Quixote* in the opening sections of his work *The Development of a Subject*.[62] Rejecting all extraliterary elements—ideological, sociological, psychological, biographical, and so forth—he approaches the novel as nothing more than an interplay of devices for making reality strange [*ostrannenie*]. He regards Don Quixote as such a device, a thread upon which episodes and speeches are strung which in turn give the subject or theme a new guise, a strange and novel appearance. At first, he says, Cervantes planned a series of adventures for which nothing could have offered a better motivation than the follies of a silly old man. But as the story advanced, Cervantes, using the knight as a mouthpiece for his own views, sensed the effectiveness of a contrast between foolishness and wisdom. He then proceeded consciously to exploit this dual-

[60] *Ibid.*, p. 54.   [61] Cf. pp. 112-13.
[62] V. Shklovski, *Razvertyvanie syuzheta* (Petrograd, 1921).

ity for his artistic aims, making Don Quixote a "thread" on which are strung speeches on fame, linguistics, arms and literature, speeches of which the actual motivations were but slight.[63] "It is curious," he remarks, "that as Don Quixote becomes wiser and wiser, an analogous change occurs in Sancho. The point in the matter is that Sancho is the thread carrying folkloric wisdom, whereas Don Quixote carries book learning."[64]

Shklovski points out several differences between the two parts of the *Quixote*. In the first place, part II is far more like a mosaic in structure than part I, because it contains a greater number of small interpolated episodes and anecdotes—the incidents in the visit of Don Quixote and Sancho at the Duke's palace. Second, it contains a new element: the mystification and duping of the heroes by the other characters. Third, Don Quixote becomes aware of himself. His indignation at the apocryphal *Don Quixote* is that of a man, and not of a fictitious character.[65]

The formalist critic also discusses the interpolated *novelas* of the *Quixote* (the episodes of Marcella, Leandro, Cardenio-Lucinda, Dorotea-Don Fernando, and that of the Captive), their division into types (*novelas* of customs and those of pastoral character), and Cervantes' methods of linking them together in the book (by means of the narrator, any form of interruption by the principal characters of the main or of the secondary plot, or joint participation in the action by the characters of both the primary and secondary plots), and the various means he uses to introduce them into the story.[66]

As might be expected, a refutation of this analysis was quick to come from the rival school. P. N. Medvedev, an exponent of the Marxist method, discusses Shklovski's work in his book *The Formal Method in Literature*.[67] He accuses the formalist of disregarding the organic element

---

[63] *Ibid.*, pp. 23-25.   [64] *Ibid.*, p. 25.
[65] *Ibid.*, pp. 50-53.   [66] *Ibid.*, pp. 34-60.
[67] P. N. Medvedev, *Formalny metod v literaturovedenii. Kriticheskoye vvedenie v sotsiologicheskuyu poetiku*, "Priboi," (1928).

of the novelistic genre. Unity, he says, is not the result of external devices, but of internal coordination. Otherwise, the work would be a mere collection of *novelas*. He then turns to Shklovski's concept of Don Quixote's function and remarks that a hero can be the unifying element only when he is also the thematic one. As for Shklovski's hypothesis that Cervantes needed the knight's folly to motivate his adventures, Medvedev feels that Don Quixote is valuable *per se*, as are all essential, constructive elements of the work. With Sancho as contrast, this pair realizes the basic thematic concept of the novel . . . and all episodes, speeches, *novelas*, evolving therefrom are subordinate in importance.[68]

"The whole first part of Shklovski's work," Medvedev writes, "is devoted to an analysis of the motivations of Don Quixote's speeches. . . . If these were included in the novel, it was not for motivation, but, according to Shklovski, the motivations were included to introduce the speeches. Evidently the whole creative energy of the author was spent on the creation of the speeches and not on the motivations." The Soviet critic concludes, "Shklovski never considered what the essential significance of their content [that of the speeches] in the novel is."[69] And, indeed, Shklovski's study is an ingenious exercise in aesthetics, but it seems somewhat paradoxical and certainly a *tour de force*.

[68] *Ibid.*, pp. 183-87. [69] *Ibid.*, p. 190.

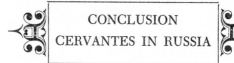

CONCLUSION
CERVANTES IN RUSSIA

THE purpose of this final chapter is not recapitulation, but the setting down of some general points of interest about Cervantes' reception in Russia that have emerged from the foregoing study.

Perhaps the first noteworthy aspect of that reception is the astounding number of Russian translations of Cervantes' works that have appeared since the inauguration of Russian concern with Spanish literature during the reign of Catherine the Great. The general popularity of Cervantes' masterpiece, *Don Quixote*, is attested to by the fact that thirty-four more or less complete editions of the novel have been produced during the years 1769-1940. From the first youthful and inadequate attempts of Osipov and Zhukovski (it is interesting to note that Cervantes' work appealed to both men at a very early stage in their careers), the excellence of these translations has increased steadily, to the mature and scholarly work of the Krzhevski-Smirnov version sponsored by the Soviet "Academia." Moreover, very sizable modern editions of others of Cervantes' works—for example, *Rinconete y Cortadillo* and *El Licenciado Vidriera*—indicate that Soviet interest in Cervantes is not confined to his great novel.

Equally significant is the number of the abbreviated versions of *Don Quixote*, begun by A. N. Grech in the mid-nineteenth century. There is record of the appearance of thirty-nine of these children's editions, in issues ranging from 2,000 to 10,000 copies. Such literary treatment, which indicates enormous popularity among the people of a country, is usually reserved for native masterpieces. No doubt it was the element of fantasy and high adventure, involving heroic battles and the rescue of the distressed, which caught the fancy of the Russian child. The only other foreign work that has received comparable attention in Russia is *Robinson Crusoe*, and Defoe's book has never been accorded the same respect among the *literati* that *Don Quixote* has enjoyed.

Clearly Cervantes has loomed large on the literary scene in Russia, but wherein lies his appeal to the Russian taste? *Don Quixote* made an indelible impression upon many Russian readers in their childhood. Some, like Karamzin and Pushkin, revealed in their writings the vividness of this early contact. Others did not encounter the work until they were adults, but the wealth of allusions to Cervantes' characters, the analytical treatment they received by writers of all schools of Russian thought, from the Romantic to the Marxist, and the influence they exerted on such disparate geniuses as Gogol, Turgenev, Dostoyevski and Sologub, evidence the fascination they held for the Russian mind.

As for Don Quixote himself, it is the symbolic aspect of the Knight of the Sad Visage that attracted the Russian reader. Although occasional critics, Avseyenko chief among them, dealt with the aesthetic value of Don Quixote's role in the novel, it was the conception of him as a symbol of the eloquent but impractical dreamer in man that predominated in Russian criticism. The dauntless idealist, ill-suited to the realities of life, the victim of its ironies—this was the figure that awoke a response. Perhaps the Russians found in Don Quixote's nobility and beauty of character a justification of their own inherent impracticality and the idealism that was frustrated by the relentless reality of an autocratic regime. There was considerable tendency, certainly, as in the case of Karamzin and Grigoryev, to self-identification with Don Quixote among the intelligentsia. Significantly, from Odoyevski's Segeliel to the wonderfully conceived Prince Myshkin, the figure of the crusader in conflict with society recurs again and again, under Cervantes influence, in Russian literature.

On the other hand, the character of Sancho Panza held surprisingly little appeal for the Russians. In English and French literature, *Don Quixote's* influence has frequently been manifested in juxtaposed pairs of characters, exemplifying the master-servant relationship of Don Quixote and his squire. Perhaps the only clear-cut Russian example of this relationship is to be found in Ostrovski's drama *The Forest*, and there the social inequality between Neschastlivtsev and Schastlivtsev is only assumed, although the moral superiority of the former is genuine. There is another echo of this device in a minor work, Sollogub's *Tarantas*, but on the whole it appears so rarely as to seem significant.

The best explanation of Sancho's lack of success seems to lie in the fact that his prototype was simply not to be encountered in Russian society in the nineteenth century. The muzhik of Imperial Russia was not a very intelligent, lively servant, full of popular wisdom. Centuries of serfdom had to a great extent immobilized his spirit of independence and adventure. To understand Sancho, the French writer had only to observe the peasant of his own country, with all his delightful idiosyncrasies; the Russian author had no such assistance. When he created a typical Russian servant, the result was a Selifan and Petrushka, in the case of Gogol, Turgenev's Khor, Yermolai and Kalinich, or Leskov's Tula artisans. One exception might be made: in an episode between the hero and the coachman Anton in Pushkin's *Dubrovski*, Anton reveals the same common sense and store of proverbial wisdom that characterizes Sancho.

In general, a relationship such as existed between Don Quixote and Sancho Panza was not readily conceivable to the Russian novelist. Psychologically, he was unable to bridge the gap between master and servant, despite his efforts. Tolstoi's experiments at Yasnaya Polyana, for example, sincere as they were, aways savored of "patronizing," and the true peasant regarded them with animosity. To create a fully rounded character, an artist must, of course, understand the material which goes into its composition. Complete understanding of Sancho was not possible in nineteenth-century Russia, neither on the writers' part, nor on that of the majority of the readers of Cervantes. He failed, therefore, to enter into the Russian creative imagination to the extent that Don Quixote did.

Still less response did the character of Dulcinea awake, until the emergence of the Symbolist movement at the end of the century. Then, as has been seen, Dulcinea was identified as a symbol of the Beauty for which man searches, and she eclipsed her fellow-characters. This preoccupation was confined, however, to the Symbolists, and with the coming of the Soviet period, it is Don Quixote once more on whom the attention of the Russian critics is largely fastened.

In the course of the re-evaluation and re-interpretation of the masterpieces of world literature that have been undertaken, so ingeniously at times, by the Marxist school, Don Quixote emerges as a symbol of the disintegrating nobility, knighthood, or even bourgeoisie, while the book as a whole is seen to reflect the class struggle in Spain of the sixteenth and seventeenth centuries and the decay of capitalism and monarchy. Cervantes' penetrating and critical depiction of various social and economic institutions of his time has supplied much grist for the Marxist mill.

In this connection one might observe that it is surprising the Marxists have not exploited a further issue implicit in *Don Quixote*—that of the church. Cervantes never took anything for granted, least of all anything so intimately connected with the life of Renaissance Spain. To criticize the church of his country openly would scarcely have been wise for him, but he was a master of discreet innuendo. There is material in his novel which might be cut to the pattern of anti-religious propaganda. It is true that the Marxists have held no special brief against the Roman Catholic Church *per se*. They have been primarily concerned with the Orthodox Church, and the Roman Church, if anything, represents in Russian eyes a persecuted minority. Yet it is curious that the opportunity to demonstrate that Cervantes was a critic of an institution whose position in sixteenth century Spain was comparable to the Church-State affiliation in Czarist Russia has not, as yet, been grasped.

In the twentieth century, *Don Quixote* and Cervantes' *novelas* and Interludes have become better known throughout Russia than ever before. His characters are now a part of the language, a property of the people as a whole, through the wide dissemination of his works. But, since the passing of the Symbolists, there has been little evidence of his direct influence on the work of Russian writers, and the present century has not as yet produced a new Russian portrait of Don Quixote. The mood for one was wanting in the atmosphere of the First World War, the Revolution and the establishment of the new order. The concern was first with naturalism in literature, and the subsequent reaction to it has involved the creation of a new hero, a national patriot who is a practical builder. The Second World War further defined the features of this literary hero. He is a Russian of lofty aims (steeped in Soviet ideology), which of necessity are not subject to the slightest doubt; he does not stand the remotest chance of disillusionment.

In this post-war period when, presumably, the Soviet world is still in a state of instability, both psychologically and physically, literature offers an escapist reassurance by presenting this hero of unchallengeable ideas in an environment that in the end inevitably yields to him. However, when life is restored to normalcy and the urge for national and racial self-justification and affirmation bows to the importance of personal, human values, artists may venture to create a different hero. Then, among the new canvases, we may again discern the familiar features of the Knight of the Sad Visage, reproduced in new colors, in a new technique and frame, but spiritually— eternally—the same.

APPENDIX

A BIBLIOGRAPHY
OF THE RUSSIAN TRANSLATIONS
OF CERVANTES' WORKS

The abbreviations for the books, bibliographies, journals, etc., cited are as follows:

BAH—*Boletín de la Real Academia de la Historia*, Madrid.

B—Bonsoms y Sicart, Isidro, *Catáleg de la Collecció Cervántica*, in 3 vols., Barcelona; vols. II, 1919, and III, 1925, are cited.

T—Dmitrovski, N. V., *Katalog Knig Russkago Otdelenia Turkestanskoi Publichnoi Biblioteki*, St. Petersburg, n.d.

EFR—*Entsiklopedicheski Slovar*, published by Brockhaus i Efron, in 41 vols., St. Petersburg-Moscow; vol. XXIX, 1900, is cited.

F—Fitzmaurice-Kelly, James, *The Life of Miguel de Cervantes Saavedra*, London, 1892.

FL—Ford, J. D. M. and Lansing, R., *Cervantes, a tentative bibliography of his works and of the bibliographical and critical material concerning him*, Cambridge, Mass., 1931.

OPB—*Katalog Odesskoi Gorodskoi Publichnoi Biblioteki*, in 5 vols., Odessa; vol. II, 1903, is cited.

KL—*Knizhnaya Letopis, Gosudarstvennaya Knizhnaya Palata*, St. Petersburg-Moscow, issued weekly after 1908.

IB—Mezhkov, V. I., *Russkaya Istoricheskaya Biblioteka za 1865-1867*, in 8 vols., St. Petersburg; vol. IV, 1884, is cited.

MB—Mezhkov, V. I., *Sistematichski Katalog Russkim Knigam prodayuschimsya v knizhnom magazine Bazunova za 1869-1874*, St. Petersburg, n.d.

MG—Mezhkov, V. I., *Tretie Pribavlenie k Sistematiches-koi Rospisi Knigam prodayuschimsya v knizhnykh magazinakh Ivana Ilyicha Glazunova, sostavleno za vremya s 1873 po Ianvar 1881 goda*, St. Petersburg, 1882.

NG—Mezhkov, V. I., *Pyatoe Pribavlenie k Sistematiche-skoi Rospisi Knigam prodayuschimsya v knizhnykh magazinakh Ivana Ilyicha Glazunova, sostavleno za 1883-1887 vkl.*, St. Petersburg, 1889.

RR—Río y Rico, Don Miguel Martín del, *Catálogo bib-liográfico de la Sección de Cervantes de la Biblioteca Nacional*, Madrid, 1930.

R—Rius y de Llosellas, Leopoldo, *Bibliografía crítica de las Obras de Miguel de Cervantes Saavedra*, in 3 vols.; vol. I, 1895, is cited.

TPD—Sinyukhaev, G. T., *Trudy i Dni Ostrovskogo*, pp. 303-409, in "Ostrovski—Novie materialy, pisma, trudy, i dni: statyi," edited by M. D. Belayev, Moscow-Petro-grad, 1924.

BS—*Sistematicheski i Khronologicheski Katalog Biblio-teki Bibliofila i Bibliografa Ya. F. Berezina-Shiryaeva*, in 2 vols., St. Petersburg; vol. I, 1900, is cited.

SO—Sopikov, V. S., *Opyt Rossiiskoi Bibliografii, redak-tsia, primechania, dopolnenia i ukazatel V. N. Rogo-zhina*, in 5 vols., St. Petersburg, 1904-1906.

ST—Storozhenko, N. I., *Ocherk Istorii Zapadno-Yevro-peiskikh Literatur*, Moscow, 1910, p. 215.

SB—Suñé Benages, Juan, y Suñé Fonbuena, Juan, *Biblio-grafía crítica de Ediciones del Quijote impresas desde 1605 hasta 1917*, Barcelona, 1921.

SF—Suñé Benages, Juan, y Suñé Fonbuena, Juan, *Biblio-grafía crítica de Ediciones del Quijote impresas desde 1605 hasta 1917 continuada hasta 1937 por el primero de los citados autores*, edited by J. D. M. Ford and C. T. Keller, Cambridge, Mass., 1939.

MK—*Tsennie i Redkie Russkie Izdania*, no. 70, Antik-varny Katalog, no. 14, Mezhdunarodnaya Kniga, Mos-cow, 1932.

EG—*Yezhegodnik Gosudarstvennoi Tsentralnoi Knizhnoi Palaty*, Moscow-Leningrad; Kniga v 1928, 1930, and Kniga v 1929, 1931, are cited.

BIBLIOGRAPHY

DON QUIJOTE

1. *Istoria o slavnom Lamankhskom rytsare Don Kishote*, St. Petersburg, 1769, translated from the French version of Filleau de St. Martin by N. Osipov. The British Museum has two volumes bound together in one book. Volume I, containing 162 pages, begins directly with the first chapter of the text, omitting Filleau de St. Martin's "Avertissement" and "Table de Chapitres." It includes parts I and II of the French text, and volume II, containing 250 pages, has parts III and IV. (R #815, FL p. 82, F p. 351, and SB #878.)

2. *Neslykhanny chudodei, ili udivitelnia i neobychainia priklyuchenia knrabrago i znamenitago stranstvuyuschago rytsarya Don Kishota*, sochinenie Mikhaila Servanta, perevel s frantsuzskago N.O. (Translated from the French by N.O.), St. Petersburg, 1791, 2 vols. This is probably a revision of the 1769 edition. (R #816, FL p. 82, F p. 351, SB #879, SO III #6835.) *Russki biograficheski slovar* (St. P., 1905), p. 391, cites an edition of 1796 bearing the same title. Since there is no other evidence of such an issue, and since the edition of 1812 is a second one it can be assumed that there has been an error in the date of publication.

3. *Neslykhanny chudodei ili udivitelnia i neobychainia priklyuchenia khrabrago i znamenitago stranstvuyuschago rytsarya Don Kishota*, sochinenie Mikhaila Servanta, perevel s frantsuzskago N.O., Moscow, 1812, second edition, 2 vols. (SO III #6836, R #818, FL p. 82, F p. 351, SB #881.)

4. *Don Kishot La Mankhski*, sochinenie Servanta, perevedeno s frantsuzskago Florianova perevoda V. Zhukovskim v tipografii Platonayeketova (Translated from Florian's French translation by V. Zhukovski), Moscow, 1804, 6 vols.; vol. I has 274 pages. Rius says, "Hay la traducción rusa del prólogo de Florian, y de la 'Vida de Cervantes' y 'Noticias acerca las obras de Cervantes,' por el mismo Florian. Luego viene el prólogo de Cervantes y el texto que alcanza al capítulo XVII inclusivo. Vi este primer tomo de la traducción de Joukovski en la Biblioteca Real de Bruselas . . . Buen papel e impresión regular. Algunas láminas, copia malísima de la edición de Didoy, de Paris, l'an VII que es la que

sirvío de modelo a la presente." (Cf. R #817, FL p. 82, F p. 351, SB #880.)
5. *Don Kishot Lamankhski*, sochinenie Mikhaila Servantesa, perevel s frantsuzskago perevoda g. Floriana Vasili Zhukovski, izd. vtoroe, 6 ch. s figurami (translated from the French translation of Florian by V. Zhukovski, 2nd edition, 6 parts with illustrations), Moscow, 1815; vol. i—250 pp., 3 illustrations and the title page with portraits of Florian and Cervantes; vol. ii—208 pp. and 4 illust.; vol. iii—246 pp., 3 illust.; vol. iv—241 pp. and 5 illust.; vol. v—224 pp., 3 illust.; vol. vi—201 pp. and 2 illust. It contains a translation of Florian's prologue, life of Cervantes, and notes on Cervantes' works. The text of the *Quixote* begins on page 61 of vol. i. The first three volumes are devoted to part i and the remaining three to part ii, and are all to be found in the Madrid Biblioteca Nacional and the Library of Congress. Bonsoms says that it is also to be had at the Paris Bibliothèque Nationale. Zhukovski in a letter to A. I. Turgenev says that for this edition he "mended a bit" his version. (SO v, #12890, R #819, FL p. 82, F p. 351, RR #641, SB #882, B ii #453.)
6. An 1820 edition of Zhukovski's translation, *Don Kikhot Lamankhski*, is cited by F p. 351.
7. *Don Kikhot La Mankhski*, sochinenie Servantesa perevel s frantsuzskago C. de Chaplet, St. Petersburg, 1831, 6 vols., 16 mo. (BS vol. i, p. 168.)
8. *Don Kishot La Mankhski*, 6 vols., St. Petersburg, 1831, 16 mo. (F p. 351, R #820, FL p. 82, SB #883). This is probably the same as #7.
9. *Don Kishot* . . . (s.l.) 1837, Rius says, "Traducción de Chaplet, tomada del francés, según cita de Masalski." This is also probably a reference to the edition listed as #7. (R #821, FL p. 82, SB #884, B #821.)
10. *Don Kikhot Lamanchski*, sochinenie Servantesa, perevedeno s ispanskago Konstantinom Masalskim, v tipografii izdatelya A. Plyushara (translated from the Spanish by Constantin Masalski), St. Petersburg, 1838, 2 vols. It has a preface on the life and works of Cervantes, the prologue to the work, and the text of both parts of the novel. It is the first Russian translation of

the *Quixote* made directly from the Spanish text. (R #822, FL p. 82, F p. 351, SB #885, MB #11335.)

11. *Don Kikhot Lamanchski*, roman Mikelya Servantesa, perevedenny s ispanskago Konstantinom Masalskim, v tipografii Konstantina Zhernakova, St. Petersburg, 1848, 2 vols. Second edition. Bonsoms describes the first volume as devoting pp. i-lxvi to the life of Cervantes and a study of his works, pp. i-xii to the prologue to part I of the *Quixote*, and pp. 5-362 to the text which contains 27 chapters. At the end is the table of contents. It is illustrated by Tony Johannot. (MB #11335, R #823, FL p. 83, F p. 351, SB #886, B II #671.)

12. *Don Kikhot Lamanchski* Servantesa, razskaz dlya detei, perevod s frantsuzskago A. Grecha, Izdanie vtoroye (*Don Quixote*, a story for children, translated), St. Petersburg, 1860. No information about the first edition of this translation is available. This is a revised edition, and in spite of its inadequacies (cf. review in "Russkoye Slovo," St. Petersburg, Mar. 1860, p. 150) it became the most popular abbreviated version in Russia. (MB #2511, R #824, FL p. 82, F p. 351, B #821.)

13. *Don Kikhot Lamanchski*, razskaz dlya detei, perevod s frantsuzskago A. Grecha, Izdanie tretie ispravlennoye (third edition, revised), izdanie Mavrikia Osipovicha Volfa, St. Petersburg-Moscow, 1868, 257 pp. Rius says, "Esta abreviación del 'Quijote' es un extracto del arreglo francés del abate Lejeune, y por consecuencia, comprende trozos de la continuación de Saint-Martin. Hay algunas de las láminas de Demoraine. Bella impresión y buen papel." (R #827, FL p. 83, F p. 351, SB #889.)

14. *Don Kikhot Lamanchski*, razskaz dlya detei, perevod s frantsuzskago A. Grecha, s 6 khromolitografirovannymi kartinami, chetvertoye ispravlennoye izdanie (story for children, translation from French by A. Grech, with 6 lithographic pictures, fourth revised edition) izdanie knigoprodavtsa-tipografa M. O. Volfa. It was passed by the censorship Oct. 8, 1880, has 194 pp. plus ii, and the text is divided into 20 chapters. (R #830, FL p. 83, F p. 351, RR #643, SB #892.)

15. *Don Kikhot Lamanchski*, razskaz dlya detei, perevod A. Grecha, izdanie M. O. Volfa, St. Petersburg-Moscow, 204 pages. No date or edition number are given. Copies of the book are in the Bibliothèque Nationale in Paris and in C. T. Keller's private collection in Boston, Mass.

16. *Don Kikhot Lamanchski*, razskaz dlya detei, perevod A. Grecha, s 78 illyustratsyami Gustava Doré, tretie izdanie, izdanie M. O. Volfa (story for children, translated by A. Grech, with 78 illustrations by Gustave Doré, third edition, published by Volf), St. Petersburg-Moscow, passed by the censorship Feb. 8, 1902, 262 pp. From Río y Rico's description of the book it seems to be the same as those above; therefore, the reason for its being the third edition cannot be explained. (RR #646, BS #899, SF #1207.)

17. *Don Kikhot Lamanchski*, Miguel de Servantes, perevod A. Grecha, illyustratsii Gustava Doré. It is advertised in a catalogue of the T-vo Obyedinennykh Izdatelei in Paris. Neither the place nor date of publication are given, but the latter is about 1932. The title page has a picture of Don Quixote on his horse and Sancho on the donkey.

18. *Don Kikhot Lamanchski*, sochinenie Miguelya Servantesa Saavedry, perevod s ispanskago V. Karelina, v pechatni V. Golovina, St. Petersburg, 1866 (translated from the Spanish by V. Karelin), 2 vols.; the first has 514 pp. and the second 559 pp. The text is complete, with the exception of the dedications and prologues. (R #825, FL p. 83, F p. 352, SB #887, MB #11334, B II #821.)

19. *Don Kikhot Lamanchski*, sochinenie Miguelya Servantesa Saavedry, v dvukh chastyakh, perevod s ispanskago V. Karelina, izdanie vtoroye, izdanie N. A. Schigina (in two parts, translated from the Spanish by V. Karelin, second edition, published by N. A. Schigin), St. Petersburg, 1873. Pages v-xxiv are devoted to Karelin's article on "Cervantes and His Book 'Don Quixote.'" The text of the novel covers pages 1-661. It has full page and smaller illustrations by Roux. There were 2,000 copies printed and one is in the Library of Congress and another in the British Museum. In spite of

what Karelin says, the translation was actually made from the French. (R #828, FL p. 83, F p. 352, RR #642, SB #890, B ɪɪ #944.)

20. *Don Kikhot Lamanchski,* sochinenie Miguelya Servantesa Saavedry, perevod s ispanskago V. Karelina, s prilozheniem kriticheskago etyuda perevodchika "Don Kikhotizm i Demonizm," 2 toma s portretom avtora i 630 risunkami, izdanie (N. A. Schigina) tretie, illyustrirovannoye (translated from the Spanish by V. Karelin, with the translator's critical study "Don Quixotism and Demonism," two volumes with a portrait of the author and 630 pictures, third illustrated edition by N. A. Schigin), St. Petersburg, 1881. Vol. ɪ has xxiv and 528 pp. and vol. ɪɪ has 654 pp. (T #4815, FL p. 83, F p. 352, R #828.)

21. *Don Kikhot Lamanchski,* sochinenie Miguelya Servantesa Saavedry, s portretom Servantesa i 372 risunkami, perevod s ispanskago V. Karelina, ispravlenny i dopolnenny V. Zotovym, s prilozheniem kriticheskago etyuda V. Karelina "Don Kikhotizm i Demonizm," izdanie chetvertoye illyustrirovannoye (N. A. Schigina), (with a portrait of Cervantes and 372 illustrations, translated from the Spanish by V. Karelin, revised and augmented by V. Zotov, with Karelin's critical study "Don Quixotism and Demonism," fourth illustrated edition of N. A. Schigin), St. Petersburg, 1893. Pages v-xxiv devoted to Karelin's article "Cervantes and His Book 'Don Quixote,'" which appeared in previous editions. Pages xxv-xxxii contain Cervantes' prologue to part ɪ translated from the Spanish by Zotov, and therefore better than Karelin's. The text of 491 pages remained unchanged, except that Zotov broke up the chapters to correspond to the original. The chapter headings were substituted for translations taken from the original text. There are also three pages of table of contents. Vol. ɪɪ has Cervantes' prologue done by Zotov on pp. v-viii, Karelin's translation of the second part of the *Quixote,* 544 pp., the article "Don Quixotism and Demonism" as a supplement to the novel, pp. 5-68, and a table of contents, pp. i-iv. The illustrations are by Tony Johannot. The dedications and preliminary verses of part ɪ are omitted. The British Museum has a copy

of this edition. (R #834, FL p. 83, SB #896, B III #1361.)

22. *Don Kikhot Lamanchski* (Don Quijote), sochinenie Miguelya Servantesa Saavedry, s portretom Servantesa i 372 risunkami, perevod s ispanskago V. Karelina, ispravlenny i dopolnenny V. Zotovym, s prilozheniem kriticheskago etyuda V. Karelina "Don Kikhotizm i Demonizm," izdanie chetvertoye illyustrirovannoye (P. Soikina), St. Petersburg, passed by the censorship Oct. 18, 1895. Except for the publisher this edition is exactly the same as #21 in content, size, and number of pages. It appeared two years after #21 and is still marked the "fourth edition." (RR #644, SB #897, FL p. 83.)

23. *Don Kikhot Lamanchski* (Don Quijote), sochinenie Miguelya Servantesa Saavedry, s portretom Servantesa i 362 risunkami, perevod s ispanskago V. Karelina, ispravlnny i dopolnenny V. Zotovym, izdanie pyatoye illyustrirovannoye, izdanie V. I. Gubinskago (fifth illustrated edition, published by V. I. Gubinski), St. Petersburg, 1901. SF describes it in the following manner: "T. I: xxxi págs. prel. que contienen: Retrato de Cervantes, portada, leyéndose en su verso la censura firmada en S. Petersburgo a 31 de Marzo, 1900, y el pie de imprenta. Viene después un estudio biográfico de Cervantes, prólogo del mismo y tabla, a la que siguen 463 págs., una portadilla y el texto de los 52 capítulos de la primera parte. T. II: vii pág. prel. que abarcan anteportada, frontispicio, portada y prólogo de Cervantes. Siguen luego 516 págs. conteniendo una portadilla, lámina y texto de la segunda parte y tabla. Edición adornada con 362 dibujos del celebrado artista Tony Johannot." (SF #1206, RR #645.)

24. *Don Kikhot Lamanchski*, sochinenie Miguelya Servantesa, v dvukh chastyakh (in two parts), s portretom i biografiei avtora, polny perevod s ispanskago V. Karelina, ispravlenny i dopolnenny V. Zotovym, izdanie shestoye V. I. Gubinskago (sixth edition, published by V. I. Gubinski), St. Petersburg, 1910, 707 and iii pages with 700 illustrations. 4,000 copies issued. (KL Nov. 20, 1910 #25713.)

25. *Don Kikhot dlya detei*, Servantesa, izdanie N. Lvova

(*Don Quixote* for children, novel by Cervantes, edited by N. Lvov), v pechatni V. Golovina, St. Petersburg, 1867. Rius says, "En 8 de 2 hojas prel. y 275 págs. Es un texto abreviado para los niños, y dividido en 28 capítulos. Lleva algunos grabados de Bertall. (R #826, FL p. 83, F p. 352, SB #888, B II #833, MB #2512.)

26. *Don Kikhot Lamanchski* M. Servantesa, peredelanny dlya detei Frantsom Gofmanom, perevod s nemetskago N. K. Gernet, izdanie Berndta, s kartinami (M. Cervantes' *Don Quixote de la Mancha* revamped for children by Franz Hofmann, translated from the German by N. K. Gernet, published by Berndt, with pictures), Odessa, 1874, 3,000 copies issued. (MG #3145, R #829, FL p. 83, F p. 352, SB #891, B III #1223.)

27. *Don Kikhot Lamanchski*, M. Servantesa, peredelanny dlya detei Frantsom Gofmanom, perevod s nemetskago N. K. Gernet, vtoroye izdanie Berndta (Berndt's second edition), s kartinami, Odessa, 1882. A copy of this edition is in the British Museum. It has 287 pp. of text which is divided into 24 chaps. It is a concise narration of the various episodes of the *Quixote* with the exception of the intercalated novelettes. Like the previous edition, it has colored illustrations. (R #831, FL p. 83.)

28. *Don Kikhot Servantesa.* In A. Filonov's "Russkaya khrestomatia dlya vysshikh klassov srednikh uchebnykh zavedeny," St. Petersburg, 1875, fifth revised edition, vol. I, sec. 8, is found the titles of *Don Quixote* by Cervantes, *Ivanhoe* by Walter Scott, *Dombey and Son*, etc. It cannot be definitely said what the nature of this version is, but from the title of the book it is assumed that this is an abbreviated version of the *Quixote*. (IB #44119.)

29. *Don Kikhot Lamanchski, rytsar pechalnago obraza i rytsar lvov*, peredelano po Servantesu dlya russkago yunoshestva, O. I. Shmidt-Moskvitinovoi, s 6 khromolitografirovannymi risunkami A. Devriena (*Don Quixote de la Mancha*, knight of the sad visage and knight of the lions, arranged according to Cervantes for the Russian youth by O. I. Shmidt-Moskvitinova, with 6 chromolith. Illustrations by A. Devrient), 64 pp., 3,012 copies issued. Since it was reviewed in "Zhenskoye

Obrazovanie" in 1883, the date of publication must be about 1883. The place of publ. St. Petersburg. (NG #2416, R #832, FL p. 83, F p. 352, SB #895.)

30. *Don Kikhot Lamanchski, rytsar pechalnago obraza i rytsar lvov*, peredelano po Servantesu dlya russkago yunoshestva, O. I. Shmidt-Moskvitinovoi, s 6 khromo-litografirovannymi risunkami A. Devriena, vtoroye iz-danie (second edition), St. Petersburg, passed by the censorship Dec. 9, 1885, date of publ. 1886 (B III #1300 and 2395).
   Detail concerning the third edition is not available.
31. *Don Kikhot Lamanchski, rytsar pechalnago obraza i rytsar lvov*, peredelala po Servantesa dlya russkago yunoshestva O. I. Rogova, s 6 khromolitografirovan-nymi risunkami A. Devriena, chetvertoye ispravlen-noye izdanie (fourth revised edition), St. Petersburg, passed the censorship Aug. 9, 1904, 64 pp. Rogova and Shmidt-Moskvitinova are the same person. SF says that this version has 20 chapters based on both parts of the *Quixote*. (SF #1210, RR #649.)
32. *Don Kikhot Lamanchski, rytsar pechalnago obraza i rytsar lvov*, peredelala po Servantesu dlya russkago yunoshestva O. I. Rogova, izdanie pyatoye ispravlen-noye (fifth revised edition), St. Petersburg, 1911, 67 pp. and 6 illustrations, 3,200 copies issued. (KL Jan. 14, 1912, #1282.)
33. *Istoria znamenitago Don Kikhota Lamanchskago* Ser-vantesa, s 64 risunkami, perevedena pod redaktsieyu M. Chistyakova, izdanie vtoroye Gubinskago (with 64 illustrations, translated under the editorship of M. Chistyakov, second edition, published by Gubinski), St. Petersburg, 1883, 354 pp., 3,000 copies issued. (NG #11736, R #833, FL p. 83, F p. 352, SB #894.)
   Information concerning the first, third, and fourth editions is not available.
34. *Istoria znamenitago Don Kikhota Lamanchskago* Ser-vantesa, perevedena pod redaktsieyu M. B. Chistya-kova, izdanie pyatoye Gubinskago (fifth edition), St. Petersburg, 1914, 354 pp. and 100 illust. 5,000 copies is-sued. (KL Oct. 25, 1914 #27132.)
35. *Slavny rytsar Don Kikhot Lamanchski*, roman v dvukh tomakh. Novy polny perevod S. M. s portretom

Servantesa i 36 kartinami Gustava Doré, s primechaniami i statyeyu L. Viardo, "Zhizn i proizvedenia
Servantesa" (novel in two vols. New complete translation by S. M. with Cervantes' portrait and 36 illustrations by Doré, notes and Viardot's article "The Life
and Works of Cervantes"), Moscow, 1895. Bookseller
is A. K. Kolchugin. Vol. I has 421 pp. and vol. II has
460. Library of Congress has a copy of this edition.

36. *Slavny rytsar Don Kikhot Lamanchski*, roman v
dvukh tomakh. Novy polny perevod S. M. s portretom
Servantesa i 75 kartinami Gustava Doré, s primechaniami i statyeyu L. Viardo, "Zhizn i proizvedenia Servantesa. Moscow, 1910, vol. I has 334 and iv pp., vol. II
has 373 and xxxviii pp., 3,000 copies issued. (KL May
8, 1910 #10365.)

37. *Don Kikhot Lamanchski*, Servantesa, Odessa, 1899
(OPB #1137).

38. Miguel Cervantes. *Don Kikhot Lamanchski*, roman v
dvukh chastyakh i risunkami Gustava Doré, perevod
s ispanskago L. A. Murakhinoi (novel in two parts with
illustrations by Gustave Doré, translated from the
Spanish by L. A. Murakhina), part I, Moscow, 1899
(FL p. 83).

39. Miguelya Servantesa. *Don Kikhot Lamanchski*, Moscow, 1899. SF, the source of this information, describes
it as follows: "Dos tomos en un volúmen. T. I: 352 págs.
que comprenden: Portada en cuyo verso hay el pie de
imprenta, portadilla, al verso de la cual está el retrato
de Cervantes. Sigue luego una breve noticia del mismo,
prólogo de la primera parte y texto de los 52 capítulos
que la componen. T. II: 375 págs. conteniendo: portada. prólogo y el texto de los 74 capítulos de la segunda parte. Edición adornada con láminas y dibujos
bastante borrosos, de Gustavo Doré." Neither translation has been examined, but it is possible that both #36
and #37 are the same. (SF #1205.)

40. Servantes—*Don Kikhot*, sokraschenny perevod dlya
yunoshestva s kratkim ocherkom o zhizni Servantesa,
yego portretom i 43 risunkami v tekste, izdanie vtoroye,
ispravlennoye, izdanie knizhnago magazina P. V. Lukovnikova (abbreviated translation for young people
with a short biography of Cervantes, his portrait and

43 illust. in the text, second edition, revised, publications of the book store of P. V. Lukovnikov), St. Petersburg, passed the censorship July 3, 1903, viii and 193 pp. There are 28 chapters based on both parts of the *Quixote*. The illustrations are by Bertall and Forest. (RR #647, SF #1208.)

No information has been available about the first, third and fourth editions. #62 may be the fourth edition.

41. Servantes—*Don Kikhot*. Sokraschenny perevod dlya yunoshestva s kratkim ocherkom zhizni Servantesa, yego portretom i 43 risunkami, izdanie pyatoye P. Lukovnikova (Lukovnikov's fifth edition), St. Petersburg, 1915, 216 pp., 43 illust., and 1 portrait, 8,200 copies issued. (KL Dec. 31, 1915 #25828.)

42. *Bezpodobny rytsar Don Kikhot Lamanchski*, sochinenie Miguelya Servantesa Saavedry, perevod s ispanskago s predisloviem, biografiei avtora i primechaniami sdelal Mark Basanin, izdanie A. S. Suvorina (translated from the Spanish with a preface, biography of the author, and notes done by Mark Basanin, published by A. S. Suvorin), St. Petersburg, 1903. Vols. i and ii devoted to part i of the *Quixote* and vols. iii and iv to part ii. Vol. i: pp. iii-vi translator's note, vii-x a short biography of Cervantes, xi-xvi all the material from Tasa through Dedicatoria, xvii-xxvi prologue, 1-310 text. Vol. ii: pp. 3-338 text. Vol. iii: pp. iii-v dedication to the Conde de Lemos, vii-xiv prologue, 1-327 text. Vol. iv: pp. 3-369 text. Chapter 35 of part i is broken into two—chapter 35 tells of Don Quixote's incident with the wine bags, and 36 terminates the "Curioso impertinente." (OPB #4826, FL p. 83.) Both the Library of Congress and the British Museum have copies of this book.

43. Servantes Saavedra, M. *Rytsar Don Kikhot iz Lamanchi*, sokraschenny i obrabotanny perevod M. Basanina (abbreviated and revised translation of M. Basanin), Leningrad, 1925, 198 pp. with illust., 5,000 copies issued. (EG p. 379.)

44. *Don Kikhot Lamanchski*, v dvukh chastyakh, polny perevod s ispanskago, s risunkami Gustava Doré, izdanie t-va I. D. Sytina, pod redaktsiei N. V. Tulu-

pova (in two parts, complete translation from the Spanish, with illustrations of Gustave Doré, published by Sytin, under the editorship of N. V. Tulupov), Moscow, 1904, vols. ı and ıı have xix and 825 pp. The Library of Congress has a copy of this translation. (FL p. 83, RR #648, SB #898.)

45. Servantes, *Don Kikhot Lamanchski*, izdanie M. Konradi (edited by M. Konradi), Moscow, 1907, 190 pp. (KL 1907 #6948.)

46. *Istoria udivitelnago rytsarya Don Kikhota Lamanchskago*, po Servantesu, izdanie t-va I. D. Sytina (published by Sytin), Moscow, 1907, 20 pp. and 3 illust. No author mentioned, cf. #46. (KL 1907 #7689.)

47. *Don Kikhot, Istoria udivitelnago rytsarya*, dlya detei srednyago vozrasta, izdanie I. D. Sytina, Pyatnitskaya (for older children, published by Sytin, Pyatnitskaya), Moscow, 1910, 20 pp. and illust., 10,000 copies issued. (KL Dec. 31, 1910 #28565.)

48. *Don Kikhot, Istoria udivitelnago rytsarya*, dlya detei srednyago vozrasta, izdanie I. D. Sytina, Pyatnitskaya, Moscow, 1912, 20 pp. and illust., 10,000 copies issued. (KL Oct. 6, 1912, #24858.)

49. *Don Kikhot, Istoria udivitelnago rytsarya*, dlya detei srednyago vozrasta, izdanie I. D. Sytina, Pyatnitskaya, Moscow, 1914, 20 pp. and 6 illust., 10,000 copies issued. (KL May 3, 1914 #10247.)

50. *Don Kikhot, Istoria udivitelnago rytsarya*, dlya detei srednyago vozrasta, izdanie I. D. Sytina, Pyatnitskaya, Moscow, 1915, 20 pp. and illust., 10,000 copies issued. (KL Nov. 7, 1915 #23012.)

51. *Don Kikhot, Istoria udivitelnago rytsarya*, dlya detei srednyago vozrasta, izdanie I. D. Sytina, Pyatnitskaya, Moscow, 1916, 20 pp. and illust., 10,000 copies issued. (KL April 2, 1916 #5671.)

52. *Don Kikhot, Istoria udivitelnago rytsarya*, dlya detei srednyago vozrasta, izdanie I. D. Sytina, Pyatnitskaya, Moscow, 1918, 20 pp. and illust., 10,000 copies issued. (KL Jan. 1918 #43.)

53. *Ostroumno-izobretatelny idalgo Don Kikhot Lamanchski*, sochinenie Migelya de Servantesa Saavedra, polny perevod s ispanskago M. V. Vatson, s primechaniami, biograficheskim ocherkom i portretom Ser-

vantesa, risunki dona Rikardo Balaka, izdanie F. Pavlenkova, tipografia I. N. Skorokhodova (Nadezhdinskaya, 43) (complete translation from Spanish by M. V. Vatson, with notes, biographical sketch and portrait of Cervantes, illustrations by Ricardo Balaca, publication by F. Pavlenkov, press of I. N. Skorokhodov, Nadezdinski St. 43) St. Petersburg (SF gives the place of publ. as Warsaw, but the address of the press is St. Petersburg), 1907, 2 vols. Vol. i: translator's foreword pp. iii-iv, biography of Cervantes pp. vii-xxviii, documents of the publ. of the *editio princeps* pp. xxx-xxxi, dedication to the Duque de Béjar p. xxxii, prologue, poems and text pp. 1-422, table of contents pp. 423-425. Vol. ii: documents relating to the publ. of editio princeps pp. iii-vii, dedication to the Duque de Lemos p. viii, prologue and text pp. 1-471, table of contents pp. 473-475. It has colored plates and illustrations. The title pages of both vols. bear the seal of the edition of 1605. The cover of the unbound edition has a picture of Don Quixote in his library. This is the best and the most complete Russian translation of *Don Quixote*, with the exception of the one published later by the Soviet Academia. There is a copy of this edition in the British Museum. N. Gabinski (*Novaya Zarya*, San Francisco, Dec. 6, 1947) says that the first edition of this translation was published by Marks in 1897. We have no other information concerning this early edition. (FL p. 83, RR #650, SF #1211 and #1212.)

54. *Ostroumno-izobretatelny idalgo Don Kikhot Lamanchski*, sochinenie Migelya de Servantesa Saavedra, polny perevod s ispanskago M. V. Vatson, s primechaniami, biograficheskim ocherkom, izdanie t-va A. F. Marks (complete translation from the Spanish by M. V. Vatson, with notes and biographical sketch, published by A. F. Marks), Petrograd, supplement to the magazine "Niva" for 1917. Vol. i: translator's foreword pp. ii-v, Cervantes' biography pp. vi-xxvii, documents of the publ. of *editio princeps* pp. xxviii-xxix, dedication to the Duque de Béjar p. xxxi, prologue, poems, and complete text of part i pp. 1-505, table of contents pp. i-iii. Vol. ii: documents relating to the publ. of the *editio princeps* and dedication to the

Duque de Lemos pp. 3-9, prologue and text of part II pp. 14-549, table of contents pp. 550-552. This is a reprint of the edition of 1907, but without illustrations and on very poor paper. Copies of this edition are in the British Museum and New York Public Library. (KL May 13, 1917, #4724, FL p. 83, SF #1214.)

55. *Don Quixote de la Mancha,* translated by M. V. Vatson, "Krasnaya Nov," A. Lunacharski, 1924. A copy of this edition is in C. T. Keller's private collection in Boston, Mass. (FL p. 83.) This may be the translation mentioned in our text, p. 193.

56. *Ostroumno-izobretatelny idalgo Don Kikhot Lamanchski,* sochinenie Migelya de Servantesa Saavedra, perevod M. V. Vatson, predislovie P. S. Kogana, biograficheski ocherk Ya. I. Shura, illyustratsii Gustava Doré, izd-vo "Molodaya Gvardia," Yunosheskaya Biblioteka Klassikov Russkoi i Inostrannoi Literatury (M. V. Vatson's trans. introduction by P. S. Kogan, biographical sketch by Y. I. Shur, G. Doré's illust., publications of "Mol. Gvardia," in Yun. bibl. kl. rus. i inostrannoi lit.), Moscow-Leningrad, 1929, xvi and 515 pp., 10,000 copies issued. (EG Knigi v 1929 g. p. 608.)

57. *Ostroumno-izobretatelny idalgo Don Kikhot Lamanchski,* sochinenie Migelya de Servantesa, perevod M. V. Vatson, predislovie P. S. Kogana, biograficheski ocherk Ya. I. Shura, illyustratsii Gustava Doré, izd-vo "Molodaya Gvardia," Yunosheskaya biblioteka klassikov russkoi i inostrannoi literatury, Moscow-Leningrad, 1930, x and 545 pp. with illustrations and portrait, 10,000 copies issued. (KL Oct. 1930 #26291, SF #1215.)

58. *Priklyuchenia Don Kikhota Lamanchskago, rytsarya pechalnago obraza* po Servantesu, izd. i tip. torg. doma E. Knovalova i Ko., B. Andronyevskaya (published by E. Knovalova & Co., B. Andronyevskaya), Moscow, 1910, 24 pp. with illustrations, 6,300 copies issued. No information available about the second edition. (KL Jul. 17, 1910, #14763.)

59. *Priklyuchenia Don Kikhota Lamanchskago, rytsarya pechalnago obraza* po Servantesu, izd. i tip. Knigoizdania Konovalovoi i Ko., B. Andronyevskaya, Moscow,

1912, third edition, 24 pp. with illustrations, 6,300 copies issued. (KL Oct. 27, 1912 #27632.)

60. *Priklyuchenia Don Kikhota Lamanchskago, rytsarya pechalnago obraza* po Servantesu, izdanie chetvertoye tip. E. Konovalovoi i Ko. (Fourth edition of Konovalova & Co.), B. Andronyevskaya, Moscow, 1914, 24 pp. with illustrations, 10,000 copies issued. (KL Sept. 20, 1914 #3859.)

61. *Don Kikhot Lamanchski*, v obschedostupnom izlozhenii I. A. Lyubicha-Koshurova, s risunkami khudozhnika Doré (in a simplified version by I. A. Lyubich-Koshurov, with Doré's illustrations), Moscow, 1910, 63 pp., 5,000 copies issued. (KL May 1, 1910 #9726.)

62. *Don Kikhot*, sokraschenny perevod s ispanskago M. Vatson [an abbreviated translation from the Spanish by M. Vatson], izdanie Vyatskago Knigoizdatelstva "Narodnykh Bibliotek," 358 pages, 1 portrait, St. Petersburg, 1911, 5,100 copies issued. (KL Jan. 29, 1911, #2591.)

63. Servantes Saavedra, M., *Don Kikhot Lamanchski*, sokraschenny perevod dlya yunoshestva I. Vvodenskago, izdanie A. Askarkhanova (shortened version for young people by I. Vvodensky, publ. by A. Askarkhanov), St. Petersburg, 1911, 136 pp. with illustrations, 2,200 copies issued. (KL May 28, 1911 #12144.)

64. Servantes, *Don Kikhot*, sokraschenny perevod dlya yunoshestva, izdanie chetvertoye Tip. Russkaya Skoropechatnya (abbreviated version for young people, fourth edition, the press is Rus. Skoropechatnya), St. Petersburg, 1911, 214 pp. and illustrations. 7,000 copies issued. (KL Jan. 7, 1912, #567.) This is all the information given, but it may be the unaccounted-for fourth edition of P. Lukovnikov, cf. #40 and #41.

65. *Don Quixote de la Mancha*, Moscow, 1912, 2 vols. A copy of this edition is in C. T. Keller's private collection in Boston, Mass. (FL p. 83.)

66. *Don Quixote de la Mancha*, abbreviated edition by E. A. Sinkevich. F. A. Toganson, 1912. A copy of this edition is in C. T. Keller's private collection in Boston, Mass. (FL p. 83.)

67. Servantes Saavedra, Miguel de, *Don Kikhot Lamanchski*, roman v obrabotke dlya shkol i naroda. "Biblioteka

dlya shkol i naroda," pod redaktsiei F. P. Borisova i
N. I. Lavrova (in a version for the schools and the
people. "Library for the Schools and the People,"under
the editorship of F. P. Borisov and N. I. Lavrov), Moscow, 1915, 160 pp. with illust. 4,000 copies issued. (KL
Apr. 18, 1915 #9694.)

68. *Ispanskaya literatura* xvi-xvii *vekov, "Don Kikhot"*
M. Servantesa i "Lazarilio iz Tormes" (Spanish literature of xvi-xvii centuries, Cervantes' *Don Quixote* and
Lazarillo de Tormes) pod red. Prof. V. M. Friche, sos-
tavili V. V. Golubkov, N. P. Gornostayev, B. E. Lukyanovski i V. I. Sakharov (done by Golubkov, Gornostayev, Lukyanovski, and Sakharov under the editorship of Prof. Friche), Moscow-Leningrad, 1926, 140
pp., 10,000 copies issued. (KL Jan. 7, 1927 #119.)

69. Servantes Saavedra, Migel, *Don Kikhot Lamanchski*,
sokraschennoye izlozhenie N. Sher (abbreviated version
of N. Sher), 228 pp. with illust. by Gustave Doré, Leningrad, publishing house "Priboi," 1927. (KL Feb. 17,
1928 #2562, EG Kniga v. 1928 g. p. 531.)

70. Servantes Saavedra, Migel, *Don Kikhot Lamanchski*,
peredelan dlya detei pod redaktsiei M. Leontyevoi s
illyustr. G. Doré, Biblioteka dlya detei i yunoshestva
(revised for children under the editorship of M. Leon-
tieva, with Doré's illustrations, Library for Children
and Youth), Odessa, 320 pp. (EG Kniga v 1928 g. p.
564.)

71. Servantes Saavedra, Migel, *Don Kikhot*, izbrannye
stranitsy v sokraschennom perevode pod red. Ál.
Deicha (selected pages in an abbreviated translation
under the editorship of A. Deich), Moscow, 1928, 47
pp., cover by V. Korinski. (KL Jul. 13, 1928, #12110,
EG Kniga v 1928 p. 531.)

72. Servantes Saavedra, Migel, *Khitroumny idalgo Don
Kikhot Lamanchski*, perevod pod redaktsiei i vstup.
statyami B. A. Krzhevskogo i A. A. Smirnova, vvdenie
P. I. Novitskogo, 67 illyustratsii (translation under the
editorship and the introductory articles by Krzhevski
and Smirnov, preface by Novitski, 67 Illustrations),
Moscow-Leningrad, 1929, publ. of Academia. The
poems were done by M. A. Kuzmin and M. L. Lozinski,
the title page is printed in red and black, cloth binding

with gold ornaments. The ornamentation of the book by S. M. Pozharski. Vol. ɪ: Portrait of Cervantes by Juan Xauregui, Novitski's "'Don Kikhot' Servantesa" pp. v-xxxvii, Krzhevski's "'Don Kikhot' na fone ispanskoi literatury xvɪ-xvɪɪ st." pp. xxxix-lxxix, Smirnov's "O perevodakh Don Kikhota" pp. lxxxi-xci, title page xcii, dedication to the Duque de Béjar p. xciv, prologues, poems and text of part ɪ pp. 3-811, notes done by Smirnov pp. 815-840, table of contents pp. 841-845. Vol. ɪɪ: Dedication to the Conde de Lemos pp. 7-8, prologue and text of part ɪɪ pp. 11-862, notes by Krzhevski pp. 865-902, table of contents pp. 905-910. It is the best Russian translation of the *Quixote* and is very handsomely printed. 10,000 copies issued. (KL Oct. 15, 1929 #19206, EG Kniga v 1929 p. 608.)

73. Servantes Saavedra, Migel, *Khitroumny idalgo Don Kikhot Lamanchski*, perevod pod redaktsiei i vstup. statyami B. A. Krzhevskogo i A. A. Smirnova, vvedenie P. I. Novitskogo, 67 illyustratsii, Moscow-Leningrad, Academia, 1932, 2 vols. exactly the same as #70. There is a copy of this edition in the New York Public Library. (SF #1216.)

74. Servantes Saavedra, Migel, *Khitroumny idalgo Don Kikhot Lamanchski*, perevod pod redaktsiei i vstup. statyami B. A. Krzhevskogo i A. A. Smirnova, vvedenie P. I. Novitskogo, 67 illyustratsii, Moscow-Leningrad, publ. of the Academia, vol. ɪ of the present writer's copy bears the date 1935 and vol. ɪɪ bears the date 1934. It is exactly the same as #73 (SF #1217).

75. Another edition of this translation, 1936, is cited by N. Gabinski (*Novaya Zarya*, San Francisco, Dec. 6, 1947). 62,000 copies.

76. Same source cites another edition of same work in 1941. 50,000 copies.

NOVELAS EJEMPLARES

77. *Vygadlivy idalgo Don Kikhot z Lamancha* z ispanskoi pereklav i sokrativ M. O. Ivanov (translated from the Spanish and abbreviated by M. O. Ivanov), Kharkov, 1927, illustrated, xi, and 365 pp. A copy of this edition is in the New York Public Library. N. Gabinski (*Novaya Zarya*, Dec. 6, 1947) says that this translation had

three editions. He also states that translations have been made into the following languages of the USSR: Armenian, Azerbaijan (two editions), Georgian, Tartar (two editions), Turkmen, the White Russian dialect (two editions) and Yiddish (two editions).

78. Servantes, *Dve lyubovnitsy*, gishpanskaya povest Mikhaila Tservantesa Saavedry, avtora Don Kikhota, perevedena s frantsuzskago (*Las dos doncellas*, Spanish nouvelle by Cervantes, the author of the *Quixote*, translated from the French), Moscow, 1763, 78 pp. (MK #124.)

79. Dve lyubovnitsy, gishpanskaya povest, sochinenie Mikhaila Servantesa Saavedry, perevedena s frantsuzskago (*Dos doncellas*, Spanish nouvelle by Cervantes, translated from the French), Moscow 1769 (SO II #3104).

80. *Tsyganka (prekrasnaya) Neotsena*, ispanskaya povest, soch. M. Servanta, perev. s frantsuzskago (*La Gitanilla*, translated from the French), Smolensk, 1795, a rare provincial edition. (SO v #12546.) N. Gabinski (*Novaya Zarya*, Dec. 6, 1947) gives 1789 as the date for this translation, and says that it was made from the Spanish. He may be in error.

81. *Povesti Mikhaila Servantesa*; perev. s frants. F. Kabrit (*Novelas ejemplares* of Cervantes; trans. from the French by F. Kabrit), 3 parts, Moscow, 1805 (SO IV #8359).

82. *Sila krovi* (*La fuerza de la sangre*) in "Otechestvennie Zapiski," 1839 (EFR).

83. *Khitana* (*La Gitanilla*) in "Syn Otechestva," 1842 (EFR).

84. *Siniora Kornelia* (*La señora Cornelia*) in "Russki Vestnik," 1872, no. 8 and no. 9, pp. 235-269, translated by A. Kirpichnikov. (EFR, Sto.)

85. *Rinkonet i Kortadilio* (*Rinconete y Cortadillo*), St. Petersburg, 1892.

86. *Revnivets iz Estremadury* (*El celoso extremeño*) in "Vestnik Inostrannoi Literatury," 1892, no. 10, pp. 163-198 (EFR), translated by Glivenko.

87. *Lisensiat Steklyanny* (*El Licenciado Vidriera*) in the Homage volume to N. I. Storozhenko, Moscow, 1902, translated by L. Y. Shepelevich.

88. *Rinkonete i Kortadilio* (*Rinconete y Cortadillo*) *i Lisensiat Steklyanny* (*El Licenciado Vidriera*) povesti Servantesa, perevod L. B. Khavkinoi (translated by L. B. Khavkina), Moscow, 1913, 93 pp. in "Universalnaya Biblioteka," no. 901.

89. *Rinkonete i Kortadilio. Lisensiat Steklyanny*, povesti Servantesa, perevod L. B. Khavkinoi, Moscow, 1916, izdanie vtoroye (second edition) "Universalnaya Biblioteka," 94 pp., 5,000 copies issued. (KL Sept. 10, 1916 #13401.)

90. *Velikodushny vlyublenny* (*El amante liberal*), in "Severnia Zapiski," 1916, nos. 4-5, pp. 40-88, translated by M. Vatson.

91. *Revnivy estremadurets* (*El celoso extremeño*), in "Sovremenny Mir," 1916, no. 4, pp. 91-121, translated by M. Vatson.

92. *Proslavlennaya sudomoyka* (*La ilustre fregona*) in "Vestnik Yevropy," 1916, vol. IV, pp. 129-183, translated by M. Vatson.

93. *Plutovskaya novella "Rinconete y Cortadillo"* (the picaresque novel "Rin. y Cort.") perevod i obrabotka Al. Deicha (translated by A. Deich), Moscow, 1927, 15,000 copies issued, 51 pp. (KL Oct. 14, 1927 #16393, EG Kniga v 1927, p. 508.)

94. *Steklyanny student "El Licenciado Vidriera,"* novella, Moscow, 1929, "Biblioteka vsemirnogo yumora," no. 7, 31 pp. 65,000 copies issued, supplement to the journal "Chudak." (KL Jul. 16, 1929, #14111, EG Kniga v 1929 p. 608.)

95. *Nazidatelnya novelly* (*Novelas ejemplares*), Migel de Servantes Saavedra, perevod i primechania B. A. Krzhevskogo, vstupitelnaya statya F. V. Kelyina, gravyury na dereve G. D. Epifanova, stikhi perevedeny M. Lozinskim, (Translation and notes by B. A. Krzhevski, introductory article by F. V. Kelyin, gravures on wood by G. D. Epifanov, poems translated by M. Lozinski), Academia, Moscow-Leningrad, 1934, 2 vols. Vol. I: Title page printed in orange and black, a portrait of Cervantes from a French edition of 1768 on the frontispiece, Kelyin's article on Cervantes' *Novelas ejemplares* pp. 7-47, Cervantes' prologue, dedication, and poems pp. 51-60, "*Tsiganochka*" (*La Gitanilla*) pp. 61-

150, *Velikodoushny poklonik* (*El amante liberal*) pp. 151-214, *Rinkonete i Kortadilio* pp. 215-266, *Angliiskaya ispanka* (*La española inglesa*) pp. 267-322, *Litsensiat Vidriera* pp. 323-359, *Sila krovi* (*La fuerza de la sangre*) pp. 361-386, notes pp. 389-412, list of illustrations (one portrait and five gravures in colors), table of contents. Vol. ɪɪ: *Revnivy estremadurets* (*El celoso extremeño*) pp. 9-58, *Vysokorodnaya sudomoika* (*La ilustre fregona*) pp. 59-184, *Seniora Kornelia* pp. 185-237, *Obmanaya svadba* (*El casamiento engañoso*) pp. 239-258, *Novella o besede* (*El coloquio de los perros*) pp. 259-348. Supplement, *Posdstavnaya tetka* (*La tía fingida*) pp. 349-373, notes pp. 377-401, list of illustrations (three gravures), table of contents. The volumes are well printed and attractive, with orange bindings with gold lettering and designs. It is the best Russian translation of the *Novelas*. All but *El casamiento engañoso* and *Coloquio de los perros* were done from the text of R. Schevill and A. Bonilla, Madrid, 1923, supplemented by that of F. Rodríguez Marín, Madrid, 1917. The *Casamiento* and the *Coloquio* were done from the *edición crítica* of Amezúa y Mayo, Madrid, 1912, supplemented by the above-mentioned editions of Schevill-Bonilla and Rodríguez Marín. This translation had four editions in two years totaling 31,200 copies.

ENTREMESES

96. *Salamanskaya peschera* (*La cueva de Salamanca*), translation completed by A. N. Ostrovski on Feb. 12, 1879. It was first published in "Izyaschnaya literatura," May, 1885, pp. 1-22. (TPD p. 373.)
97. *Teatr chudes* (*El retablo de las maravillas*), translation completed by A. N. Ostrovski on Feb. 20, 1879. It was first published in "Izyaschnaya literatura," July, 1884, pp. 1-20. (TPD p. 373.)
98. *Dva boltuna* (*Los habladores*), translation completed by A. N. Ostrovski, March 8, 1879 (TPD p. 373). This Interlude has often been attributed to Cervantes, but without sure foundation.
99. *Revnivy starik* (*El viejo celoso*), translated by A. N. Ostrovski, March 14, 1879. (TPD p. 374.)

100. *Sudya po brakorazvodnym delam* (*El juez de los divorcios*), translation completed by A. N. Ostrovski, March 21, 1879, first published in "Izyaschnaya literatura," Dec. 1883, pp. 230-243. (TPD p. 374.)

101. *Biskaets-Samozvanets* (*El vizcaíno fingido*), translation completed by A. N. Ostrovski, March 31, 1879. (TPD p. 374.)

102. *Izbranie alkaldov* (*La elección de los alcaldes de Daganzo*), translation completed by A. N. Ostrovski, April 12, 1879. (TPD p. 374.)

103. *Bditelny strazh* (*La guarda cuidadosa*), translation completed by A. N. Ostrovski, April 19, 1879, first published in "Izyaschnaya literatura," Jan. 1884, pp. 260-282. (TPD p. 374.)

104. *Vdovy moshennik* (*El rufián viudo*), translation completed by A. N. Ostrovski, April 27, 1879. (TPD p. 374.)

105. *Intermedii Miguelya Servantesa Saavedra v perevode s ispanskago, s portretom A. N. Ostrovskago, grav. na stali, Izdanie Martynova,* (*Cervantes' Interludes*, translated from Spanish, with a portrait of A. N. Ostrovski, gravures, published by Martynov), St. Petersburg, 1886. Apparently all but *El rufián viudo* were included in this edition. 100 copies issued. (TPD p. 233 and MG #11945.)

106. *Dva boltuna* (*Los habladores*), intermedia, perevod s ispanskago A. N. Ostrovskago. (Inostranny Teatr, no. VIII) Izdanie Teatr. Otd. Narodnago Komissar. po Prosvesch. (Interlude, translated from the Spanish by A. N. Ostrovski [Inostranny Teatr, no. VIII], publications of Teatr. Otd. Nar. Kom. po Prosvesch.), St. Petersburg, 1919, 16 pages. 5,000 copies issued. (KL no. 13, March 17, 1919, #2707.)

107. *Revnivy starik* (*El viejo celoso*), intermedia, perevod s ispanskago A. N. Ostrovskago (Inostranny Teatr, no. IX) Izdanie Teatr. Otd. Narod. Komissar. po Prosvesch. Interlude, translated from Spanish by A. N. Ostrovski (Inostranny Teatr, no. IX), publ. by Teatr. Otd. Nar. Kom. po Pros. St. Petersburg, 1919, 20 pages, 5,000 copies issued. (KL no. 19-20, May 28, 1919 #3733.)

108. *Salamanskaya peschera* (*La cueva de Salamanca*),

intermedia, perevod s ispanskago A. N. Ostrovskago (Inostranny Teatr, no. xi) Izdanie Teatr. Otd. Narod. Komissar. po Prosvesch. Interlude, translated from Spanish by A. N. Ostrovski (Inostranny Teatr, no. xi), publ. of Teatr. Otd. Nar. Kom. po Pros. St. Petersburg, 1919, 21 pages, 3,000 copies issued. (KL no. 25, June 30, 1919, #4380.)

109. *El rufián viudo* translated by B. A. Krzhevski in 1923. (Cited by K. Derzhavin in BAH xciv, 1929, p. 216.)

110. *Vdovy moshennik* (*El rufián viudo*) translated by A. N. Ostrovski, was printed in "Sbornik Petrogradskogo Ob-va A. N. Ostrovskogo," Petrograd, 1923.

111. *Intermedii,* perevod s ispanskogo A. N. Ostrovskogo, Moscow-Leningrad, 1939. Publishing house "Iskusstvo." 10,000 copies.

LA GALATEA

112. Galatea, pastusheskaya povest perevel s frantsuzskago Aleksei Pechenegov (pastoral novel translated from the French by Aleksei Pechenegov), Moscow, 1790. (SO v, #12405.)

113. *Galatea,* pastusheskaya povest, s prilozheniem opisania zhizni Servanta, sochinitelya Gishpanshkoi Galatei, Don Kishota, i drugikh; perevel A. Khanenko (pastoral novel with a supplement of the description of the life of Cervantes, the author of the Spanish *Galatea, Don Quixote,* and others; translated by A. Khanenko), St. Petersburg, 1799. (SO v, #12404.)

EL CERCO DE NUMANCIA

114. *Numansia,* translated by V. Pyast, publisher is "Iskusstvo" (cited by N. Gabinski, *Novaya Zarya,* Dec. 6, 1947).

INDEX OF NAMES

251